SHADOW PUPPETS, SONGS, AND SACRED FEASTS

The Other Voice in Early Modern Europe: The Toronto Series, 110

FOUNDING EDITORS

Margaret L. King

Albert Rabil Jr.

SENIOR EDITOR

Margaret L. King

SERIES EDITORS

Vanda Anastácio

Julie D. Campbell

Jaime Goodrich

Elizabeth H. Hageman

Sarah E. Owens

Deanna Shemek

Colette H. Winn

EDITORIAL BOARD

Margaret Ezell

Anne Larsen

Leah Middlebrook

Elissa Weaver

Shadow Puppets, Songs, and Sacred Feasts

Celebrations of the Indo-Portuguese Nuns in the
Eighteenth-Century Real Convento de Santa Mónica, Goa, India

A BILINGUAL EDITION

∼

Edited with a critical introduction by

DANIEL MICHON

Translated by

DANIEL MICHON *and* D. A. SMITH

Iter Press
NEW YORK | TORONTO

2025

© 2025 Daniel Michon and D. A. Smith

The copyright owners grant Iter Press an exclusive license for publication and distribution. For information and permissions, contact Iter Press: 347 Fifth Avenue, Suite 1402-332, New York, NY 10016, USA; IterPress.org.

978-1-64959-125-8 (paper)
978-1-64959-126-5 (pdf)
978-1-64959-127-2 (epub)

Library of Congress Cataloging-in-Publication Data

Names: Michon, Daniel, editor, writer of introduction, translator. | Smith, David Addison, translator.

Title: Shadow puppets, songs, and sacred feasts : celebrations of the Indo-Portuguese nuns in the eighteenth-century Real Convento de Santa Mónica, Goa, India / edited with a critical introduction by Daniel Michon ; translated by Daniel Michon and D.A. Smith.

Other titles: Entrada de bonifrate para festa dos reis.

Description: A bilingual edition. | New York : Iter Press, 2025. | Series: The other voice in early modern Europe. The Toronto series ; 110 | Contains the transcription and translation of two unpublished manuscripts (Entrada de bonifrates para Festa dos Reis, a puppet show performed January 6, 1741, and Cartepaço da muzica, songs performed June 24, 1766) prepared by the nuns at the Augustinian Real Convento de Santa Mónica in Goa (1606-1835) held at the Arquivo da Cúria Patriarcal de Goa, located in the archbishop's palace in Altinho, ten kilometers from the convent. | Includes bibliographical references and index. | English and Portuguese. | Summary: "Bilingual edition and translation (from Portuguese) of two unique dramatic works--a puppet show and a choral program--composed and performed in the eighteenth century by the nuns of the Indo-Portuguese Royal Convent of Santa Monica (1606-1835) in Goa, India, displaying the complex cultural interactions between European and South Asian literary and religious traditions"-- Provided by publisher.

Identifiers: LCCN 2024039460 (print) | LCCN 2024039461 (ebook) | ISBN 9781649591258 (paper) | ISBN 9781649591265 (pdf) | ISBN 9781649591272 (epub)

Subjects: LCSH: Puppet plays, Portuguese--18th century. | Portuguese drama--18th century. | Music--India--Velha Goa. | Manuscripts, Portuguese. | Manuscripts--India--Velha Goa. | Real Convento de Santa Mónica (Velha Goa, India)--History. | Augustinian nuns--India--Velha Goa--History--18th century. | Arquivo da Cúria Patriarcal de Goa.

Classification: LCC PN1978.I4 S53 2025 (print) | LCC PN1978.I4 (ebook) | DDC 869.2/2--dc23/eng/20241107

LC record available at https://lccn.loc.gov/2024039460

LC ebook record available at https://lccn.loc.gov/2024039461

Cover Illustration

A shadow puppet created by artist and puppeteer Lynn Jeffries, based on a 16th-century illustration from the *Códice Casanatense* 1889 (photo by Lynn Jeffries).

Cover Design

Maureen Morin, Library Communications, University of Toronto Libraries.

Contents

Acknowledgments	ix
Abbreviations and Shortened Titles	xi
Illustrations	xiii
Introduction	1
The Other Voice	1
Historical Background and Analysis of the Texts	3
The Real Convento de Santa Mónica and the Mónicas	3
Entrada de Bonifrate para Festa dos Reis	12
Cartepaço da Muzica	39
A Note on the Translations	49
Translations	
Entrada de Bonifrate para Festa dos Reis	57
Cartepaço da Muzica	127
Appendices	
1. Nuns Commemorated in *Entrada de Bonifrate para Festa dos Reis*	179
2. Nuns Commemorated in *Cartepaço da Muzica*	184
Bibliography	191
Index	199

Acknowledgments

This book is the second collaboration with David Smith, and I thank him for all his camaraderie and hard work. I am especially indebted to Dr. Lilia d'Souza, the archivist at the Arquivo da Cúria Patriarcal de Goa in Panjim for granting me access to these manuscripts and to director Blossom Medeira and archivist Balaji Shenoy at the Historical Archives of Goa. Thanks to those who read and commented on drafts, including Timothy Joel Coates, Jamel Velji, Lynn Jeffries, and so many others who listened to me over dinners and drinks. Thanks also go to the Museum of Christian Art, Goa, particularly Clive Figuerido, Natasha Fernandes, and Sister Edwige Maria Antony; the Gabinete de Estudos Arqueológicos da Engenharia Militar (GEAEM); and Cambridge University Press for allowing to use their images in the book. I would like to also thank the editors of this series, and in particular Margaret L. King, William R. Bowen, Margaret English-Haskin, and the anonymous reviewers who read the manuscript so carefully and offered many good suggestions for improvement. Finally, thanks and love go to my wife, Lina Patel, and daughter, Robin Patel-Michon, who have supported me throughout this endeavor.

Special thanks go to artist and puppeteer Lynn Jeffries, who created the shadow puppet depicted on the cover. Her puppet is based on a sixteenth-century Portuguese illustration from the *Códice Casanatense* 1889. The original image depicts a Malabari Christian of Kerala, India, and is found in the rare manuscript *Album di disegni, illustranti usi e costumi dei popoli d'Asia e d'Africa con brevi dichiarazioni in lingua portoghese* housed at the Biblioteca Casanatense in Rome. Jeffries's interpretation transforms this historical figure into a delicate shadow puppet, visualizing the scene found in verses 65–66 of the *Entrada de Bonifrate para a Festa dos Reis*. In this scene, the audience is presented with magic balls of fire that hover in the air but do not burn the cloth screen upon which the show takes place. Both the Mestre and the Malabari puppets express wonder at this spectacle and invite the nuns to come closer and observe. This photograph, capturing the puppet illuminated by flame, brings to life the interplay between light and shadow suggested in these lines.

DANIEL MICHON
Claremont, CA
October 2024

Abbreviations and Shortened Titles

Book of Elections	*Livro das Eleiçoens.* Apud: Fr. Manual da Ave Maria, *Da Congregação da India Oriental dos Eremitas de N. P. S. Agostino*, chapter 9. Reprinted in *Documentação para a História das Missões do Padroado Português do Oriente*, ed. Antónia da Silva Rego (Lisboa: Agência Geral do Ultramar, 1954), 11:128–41.
Book of Professions	*Livro das Profissões do Mosteiro de Santa Mónica de Goa*. Apud: António Francisco Moniz Júnior, *Relação completa das religiosas do Mosteiro de Sta. Monica de Goa*. In *O Oriente Português*, 15:177–98, 16:284–94, 16:354–63, 17:92–102, 17: 188–97; second series, 2–3:111–19.
Cunha Rivara, *APO*	Cunha Rivara, J. H. da. *Archivo Portuguez-Oriental, Fasciculo 6, Supplementos Primeiro & Segundo* (New Delhi: Asian Educational Services, 1992).
Diccionario da Lingua Portugueza	Rafael Bluteau and Antônio de Morais. *Diccionario da Lingua Portugueza composto pelo Padre D. Rafael Bluteau, reformado, e accrescentado por Antonio de Moraes Silva natural do Rio de Janeiro*, 2 vols. (Lisboa: Joseph Antonio da Sylva, Impressor da Academia Real, 1789).
Glossário Luso-Asiático	Sebastião Rodolfo Dalgado. *Glossário Luso-Asiático*. 2 vols. (Coimbra: Imprensa da Universidade, 1921).
Relação	*Relação Sumaria e Verdadeira dos Proçidimentos que o Arçebispo de Goa Dom Ignaçio de Santa Thereza Teve com as Religiozas do Convento de Santa Mónica da Mesma Çidade no Anno de 1731 1732 e 1733*, 1734, Archivum Romanum Societatis Iesu, Fondo Gesuitico 1433/9, no. 52 (Busta no. 74B).
Supplemento ao Vocabulario Portuguez	Rafael Bluteau. *Suplemento ao Vocabulario Portuguez e Latino*, 2 vols. (Lisboa: Officina de Pascoal da Sylva, Impressor de Sua Magestade, 1727–1728).
Vocabulario Portuguez	Rafael Bluteau. *Vocabulario Portuguez e Latino*, 10 vols. (Lisboa: Officina de Pascoal da Sylva, Impressor de Sua Magestade, 1712–1721).

Illustrations

Cover.	A shadow puppet created by artist and puppeteer Lynn Jeffries, based on a 16th-century illustration from the *Códice Casanatense* 1889 (photo by Lynn Jeffries).	
Map 1.	*Projecto para a nova Cidade de Gôa: por Joze de Moraes d'Antes Machado, Sargento mor de Infantaria com exercisio de engenheiro* (Plan for a new City of Goa: by Joze de Moraes d'Antes Machado, Sargeant Major of Infantry, trained as an engineer), ca. 1776 (Cota Antiga: A4; G3; P3: no. 44-4 [v2627], Cota moderna: 1241-2A-24A-111), showing both the Convento de Santo Agostinho (C) and the Real Convento de Santa Mónica (K). Image credit: Gabinete de Estudos Arqueológicos da Engenharia Militar/Direção de Infraestruturas do Exército, Portugal.	xiv
Map 2.	"The Portuguese in Asia." K. N. Chaudhuri, *Trade and Civilization in the Indian Ocean* (Cambridge: Cambridge University Press, 1985), 70. Reprinted with permission.	xvi
Figure 1.	Holy Water Font and Sprinkler. Provenance: Donation of Mr R. Roy, Mumbai. Image Credits: Antonio Cunha under the commission of the Calouste Gulbenkian Foundation. ©Museum of Christian Art, Goa.	52
Figure 2.	Incense Boat. Provenance: Old Goa, Basilica of Bom Jesus. Image Credits: Antonio Cunha under the commission of the Calouste Gulbenkian Foundation. ©Museum of Christian Art, Goa.	52
Figure 3.	Angel Gabriel. Provenance: Old Goa, Convent of Santa Monica. Image Credits: Antonio Cunha under the commission of the Calouste Gulbenkian Foundation. ©Museum of Christian Art, Goa.	53
Figure 4.	Statue of St. John the Baptist. Provenance: Old Goa, Church of Santa Monica. Image Credit: Clive Figueiredo. ©Museum of Christian Art, Goa.	54
Figure 5.	Chalice and Paten. Provenance: Old Goa, Basilica of Bom Jesus. Image Credits: Antonio Cunha under the commission of the Calouste Gulbenkian Foundation. ©Museum of Christian Art, Goa.	55

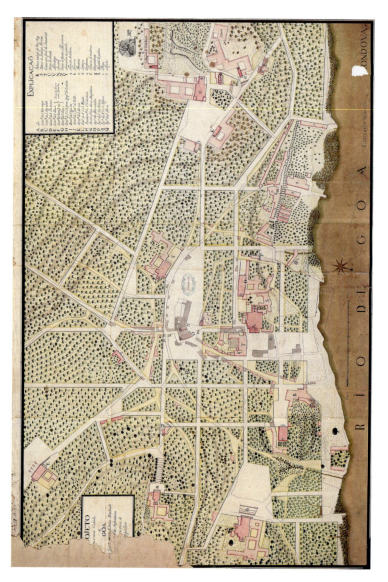

Map 1. *Projecto para a nova Cidade de Gôa* (Plan for a new City of Goa), ca. 1776, showing both the Convento de Santo Agostinho (C) and the Real Convento de Santa Mónica (K). Image credit: Gabinete de Estudos Arqueológicos da Engenharia Militar/Direção de Infraestruturas do Exército, Portugal.

Explicação (Legend)

A	Se [The See Cathedral]	R	Palacio antigo do Vice-Rey [Old Palace of the Vice-Roy]
B	Convento de S. Domingo	S	Palacio do Arcebispo Primas [Archbishop's Palace]
C	Convento de S. Agostinho	T	Cazas que forão da Inquisição [Offices of the Inquisition]
D	Convento de S. Francisco	U	Cazas do Senado [Offices of the Senate]
E	Convento de S. Paulo	V	Alfandega [Custom House]*
F	Convento do Bom Jesus	X	Arcenal [Arsenal]*
G	Convento do S. Roque	Z	Cazas do Junta e Tezourarias [Houses of Council and Treasuries]
H	Convento de N. S. do Carmo, Congressão do Oratorio [Oratory Congregation of Goa]	Y	Armarens de petrechos [Armory equipment]
I	Convento de S. Caetano	a	Trem da Artelharia [Artillery equipment]
J	Convento de S. João de DEOS	b	Ferraria [Blacksmith]*
K	Convento de S. Monica	c	Latoaria [Tinsmith]*
L	Collegio de N. S. do Populo	d	Cordoaria [Rope factory]
M	Recolhimento [Shelter] de N. S. da Serra	f	Telheiros de madeiras [Wood sheds]
N	Recolhimento [Shelter] de S. Maria Magdalena	g	Carpintaria [Carpenters Workshop]
O	Igreja da Misericordia [Church of the House of Mercy]	h	Hospital dos pobres [Hospital for the poor]
P	Igreja [Church] de S. Caeterina	i	Tronco [Stocks]
Q	Igreja [Church] de N. S. do Rosario	I	Aljube [Jail]
Q	Igreja [Church] de S. Aleixo		

*These sites are not indicated on the map.

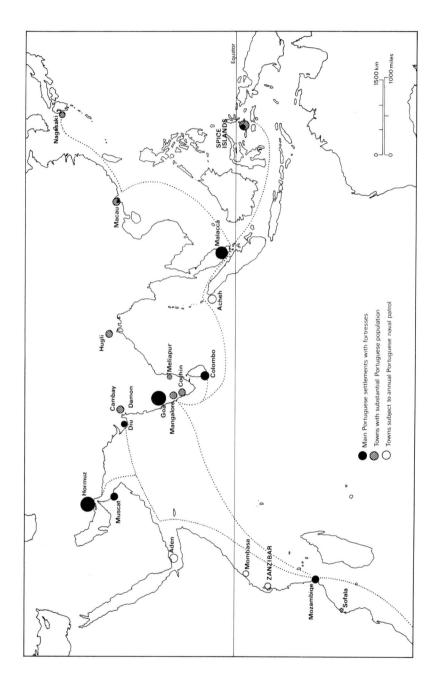

Map 2. "The Portuguese in Asia." K. N. Chaudhuri, *Trade and Civilization in the Indian Ocean* (1985), 70. Reprinted with permission.

Introduction

The Other Voice

In Europe between 1300 CE and 1700 CE, women emerged as learned figures, overcoming the constraints of a male-dominated society to assert their intellectual autonomy. The majority of these women were members of the "nobility and urban elites, and their works were often in genres that permitted little direct personal expression."[1] One location for such learned production was the female convent, where, without the demands of childbearing and domestic life, women could pursue an intellectual life. In the mid-sixteenth century, however, the Council of Trent (1545–1563) imposed new restrictions on women religious. The policy of strict enclosure, which Tridentine canons and decrees elevated to an unavoidable requirement for female religious life, serves as the most visible symbol of this increasing patriarchal control over women. And just as nuns were no longer permitted to leave the confines of the convent, restrictions were put in place to prevent them from fully participating in public intellectual life. There are examples of nuns who publicly challenged these Tridentine norms,[2] but the vast majority of literary, religious, and philosophical writing was subject to strict church censorship. Despite such restrictions, nuns persisted in translating their conventual lives into devotional treatises, letters, poetry, and autobiographies intended for public consumption. They also produced works that were not to be read by those outside the convent walls and, therefore, were less inhibited. Fortunately for us, such works found their way into archives and remained unpublished until, often centuries later, scholars brought them to light.[3]

This volume includes an introduction to and translations of two such unpublished works written by and for the nuns living in the Indo-Portuguese Real Convento de Santa Mónica (1606–1835) in Goa, India. The first, the *Entrada de Bonifrates para Festa dos Reis*, is a carnivalesque shadow-puppet show composed in 1740 and performed at the convent on January 6, 1741. The second, the

---

1. Marguerite d'Auge, Renée Burlamacchi, and Jeanne du Laurens, *Sin and Salvation in Early Modern France: Three Women's Stories*, ed. Colette H. Winn, trans. Nicholas Van Handel and Colette H. Winn (Toronto and Tempe: Iter Press and Arizona Center for Medieval and Renaissance Studies, 2017), 1.

2. For an example from The Other Voice in Early Modern Europe series, see the works of the seventeenth-century Benedictine nun Arcangela Tarabotti published as *Paternal Tyranny*, ed. and trans. Letizia Panizza (Chicago: University of Chicago Press, 2004), and *Convent Paradise*, ed. and trans. Meredith K. Ray and Lynn Lara Westwater (Toronto and Tempe: Iter Press and Arizona Center for Medieval and Renaissance Studies, 2020).

3. María del Carmen Alarcón Román, "Convent Theater," in *The Routledge Research Companion to Early Modern Spanish Women Writers*, ed. Nieves Baranda and Anne J. Cruz (London: Routledge, 2017), 103.

Cartepaço da Muzica, is a notebook (*cartepaço*, or perhaps better, a songbook) that records a series of songs intended to commemorate the birth of St. John the Baptist. These songs were performed for the first time on June 24, 1766 (St. John's Day), in honor of the prioress of the convent, Francisca do Sacramento. None of the songs in the *Entrada* or the *Cartepaço* were intended to be read or heard outside the convent. After the dissolution of the religious orders by Queen Maria II of Portugal in 1834, these two manuscripts and a large portion of the convent library were dispersed. In the subsequent two hundred years, much of the library has been lost, but some of its contents have found their way into archives. The *Entrada* and the *Cartepaço* ended up in the Arquivo da Cúria Patriarcal de Goa, which is located in the archbishop's palace in Altinho, ten kilometers from the Real Convento de Santa Mónica.[4]

These works represent the "other voice" of the early modern period, in contradistinction to the "first voice" belonging to the educated men of western Europe,[5] in two significant ways. First, because the intended audience was the Mónicas themselves, and not the larger public outside the convent, we can discern moments of unguarded candor as they address each other free from the expectations, judgment, and censorship of patriarchal authority. Although it is probable that two Augustinian friars attended the 1741 performance, as they are mentioned in several quatrains of the *Entrada*, the historical introduction will demonstrate that these friars were not sitting in judgment of the nuns but rather were complicit in the very project of rebelling against the archbishop of Goa, Dom Ignácio de Santa Teresa.[6] Indeed, the *Entrada* can be understood as an act of celebratory

---

4. There is evidence that other convent manuscripts of this type existed, but they have since disappeared after being destroyed, lost, or forgotten in private collections. For example, Alberto Osório de Castro, in his early twentieth-century collection of poems *A Cinza dos Myrtos: Poemas* (Nova Goa: Imprensa Nacional, 1906), mentions that he saw a few such manuscripts. In one poem, "As Monjas," he imagines some young nuns yearning for a love that they would never experience. They huddle together in the convent garden, the *Valle dos Lyrios*, secretly reading aloud "the little verses of 'Venus and Flora'" (110) from a songbook. The songbook is not fictitious; Osório de Castro consulted the original and noted that it contained

> beautiful love verses, probably from the XVIII century, which are part of a songbook manuscript from the Nuns of St. Monica, from the end of the XVIII century, beginning of the XIX, and today belonging to my friend Mr. Francisco Mourão Garcez Palha. [The song to Venus and Flora] comes among *Romances, Loas, Falas para Madre Prioresa hir ao Deposito, Falas das vesperas de S. João, Baile em aplauso da Mt.º Rev.ª Madre Prioresa Soror Catherina do Sacramento*, etc. (Osório de Castro, *A Cinza dos Myrtos: Poemas*, 215)

5. See Margaret L. King and Albert Rabil Jr., "The Other Voice in Early Modern Europe: Introduction to the Series," reprinted in many of the early volumes of this series and available on the Iter Press website: https://iterpress.org/the-other-voice-in-early-modern-europe-series/.

6. Note that while the Biblioteca Nacional de Portugal catalogues the archbishop of Goa's name as "Inácio de Santa Teresa," we have chosen to adhere to the spelling in almost all eighteenth-century documents, "Ignácio de Santa Teresa."

defiance against the oppressive religious authority from which the nuns had just been liberated. As with the *Entrada*, the *Cartepaço* was intended for the convent only, and its songs served to affirm the dignity and worth of every member of the community, from the prioress to the lay nuns to the youngest postulant. Even in the more transgressive songs to Cupid and secular Love, the intention is not to shock but rather to affirm and celebrate their decision to join the convent. Second, these women were the geographic "other"; they were colonial Indo-Portuguese women residing in Goa, India, far from the European centers of culture. By the turn of the eighteenth century in Europe, hundreds of convents housed tens of thousands of women religious, and convents and convent life were deeply woven into the century's social and cultural fabric. Female convent life was exported to Spain's New World colonies with great zeal, and by the early seventeenth century, thirty-six female convents had been established in New Spain, fifteen of which were in Mexico City alone. In colonial Asia, however, this was not the case. From as far east as China and Japan, across southeast Asia, the many islands in the Pacific, and the Indian subcontinent, all the way to Persia and the east coast of Africa, European colonial powers established only three female convents. Manila's Franciscan Clarist Monasterio de Santa Clara (1621) was the sole convent established by the Spanish across all their Asian possessions. The Portuguese established only two in the Estado da Índia:[7] the Augustinian Real Convento de Santa Mónica in Goa (1606) and the much smaller Franciscan Clarist Mosteiro de Santa Clara in Macau (1632). At its height, the Real Convento de Santa Mónica was the most prestigious of the three, housing approximately one hundred nuns and their hundreds of servants and slaves. Located on a hill overlooking Goa—the administrative, ecclesiastical, and economic heart of the Portuguese Estado da Índia—the Real Convento became a symbol of the righteous Catholic Portuguese presence in the hostile, pagan lands of Asia.

Historical Background and Analysis of the Texts

The Real Convento de Santa Mónica and the Mónicas

The Augustinian Convento de Santa Mónica was one of three institutions for women founded by the archbishop of Goa, Dom Aleixo de Meneses, at the turn of the seventeenth century.[8] All three were intended to safeguard the virtue of

---

7. "Estado da Índia" was the name given to the extensive network of Portuguese territories and trading posts established along the coasts of Africa, the Arabian Peninsula, and Asia from the end of the fifteenth century to the middle of the twentieth century.

8. The Augustinian friar Dom Aleixo de Meneses was archbishop of Goa from 1595 to 1612, and he also served as governor of the State of India from 1607 to 1609; see Carlos Alonso, *Alejo de Meneses, O.S.A. (1559–1617), Arzobispo de Goa (1595–1612): Estudio Biográfico* (Valladolid: Estudio

Portuguese noble women in a distant, dangerous, and pagan land. Indeed, by the late sixteenth century, the Estado da Índia was notorious for its violence, and the widespread mistreatment of women drew particular fascination and condemnation. According to a well-known late-sixteenth-century account, one repeated by many subsequent chroniclers of Portuguese Asia, over the course of two years, fifty-two noble women in Goa alone had been put to the sword by their husbands for adultery.[9] The need for the protection of women was clear. The first of these three institutions, the Recolhimento de Nossa Senhora de Serra (est. ca. 1600), was intended to provide a safe haven for Portuguese women, especially girls and young women (*donçellas*), who lacked appropriate familial support and protection. Many of the inhabitants of this house were orphans, but some were also women left temporarily alone while their husbands and fathers went to war or sailed afar on business. A second institution, the Recolhimento de Santa Maria Madalena (est. 1608), housed "fallen" women seeking refuge and redemption under the protection of the church.[10] This study focuses on the third institution, the Convento de Santa Mónica, one of only two Portuguese nunneries in all of Asia. The convent accepted professions from many prominent and wealthy families in Asia, and it quickly became the crown jewel of the Portuguese Empire.

The establishment of the two Recolhimentos was met with little opposition, but this was not so for our Augustinian convent.[11] The Franciscans, the first order to enter the Estado da Índia, had already petitioned King Felipe II[12] to establish a Clarissan convent in Goa. But Dom Aleixo de Meneses allied himself with a local wealthy widow, Donna Philippa Ferreira,[13] and leveraged both his

---

Agustiniano, 1992). For a general introduction to the Mónicas and their convent, see Rozely Menezes Vigas Oliveira, *Nas Clausuras de Goa: A Comunidade das Mónicas no Monte Santo e Sua Economia Espiritual (1606–1721)* (Porto: Editora Cravo, 2023).

9. Frei Agostinho de Santa Maria, *História da Fundaçaõ do Real Convento de Santa Monica da Cidade de Goa, Corte do Estado da Índia, e do Império Lusitano do Oriente* (Lisboa: António Pedrozo Galram, 1699), 65.

10. In a 1609 letter to the Augustinian Provincial in Portugal, Dom Aleixo de Meneses put it this way: "Many women who were *caught in the snare of this land* are being received into [the Recolhimento de Santa Maria Madalena]," (italics mine), cited in Alonso, *Alejo de Meneses, O.S.A., Estudio Biográfico*, 212.

11. While all the details need not detain us here, Francisco Bethencourt provides a full accounting and detailed analysis of these conflicts in his "Os Conventos Femininos no Império Português: O Caso do Convento de Santa Monica em Goa," in *O Rosto Feminino Da Expansão Portuguesa Actas*, ed. Francisco Bethencourt (Lisboa: Comissão para a Igualdade e para os Direitos das Mulheres, 1995), 631–52.

12. From 1580 to 1640, the Crowns of Castile and Aragon and the Kingdom of Portugal were united in the Iberian Union. The Spanish King Felipe III was known as King Felipe II in Portugal.

13. Donna Philippa was born in the Portuguese colony of Ormuz, Persia, to Dom Belchior Cerniche and Elena Mendes. She married Dom Gaspar de Louzade de Sá in 1580. They lived together in Taná, a small Portuguese trading post in the Northern Provinces near the island of Bombay, where their

power as archbishop and his prior relationship with King Felipe II to persuade the monarch to endorse an Augustinian nunnery instead.[14] On September 6, 1606, Mother Philippa de Trindade, Donna Philippa's professed name, and twenty other women, including her daughter, Maria de Sá, professed to the newly established convent. Mother Philippa de Trindade would become the convent's first prioress and soon after came to be considered its spiritual founder. Immediately after its establishment, the convent met with more opposition due to its rapid growth and accumulation of wealth. By 1613, the convent housed forty-seven professed nuns of the black veil and at least fifty nuns of the white veil (lay sisters, novices, and postulants), in addition to the nuns' servants and other staff.[15] In the following decade, its population would encompass eighty nuns of the black veil, numerous nuns of the white veil, and countless others required to maintain the convent.[16] The convent received a substantial dowry with each woman who joined, and each vow of celibacy meant one less noblewoman available for marriage. Therefore, while the convent was a financial and recruitment success, many argued that it diverted vital resources away from the Estado da Índia, which, after a century of prosperity, had begun to experience a decline in its fortunes. This success caused resentment in the struggling colony, and the local Goan City Council (*Câmara de Goa*), individual merchants and nobles, and the other religious orders protested

---

daughter, Maria de Sá, was born in 1589. Dom Gaspar de Sá died in 1595, leaving Donna Philippa widowed. Donna Philippa did not want to marry again, so she professed tertiary Augustinian vows at the hands of a local Portuguese Augustinian, Fr. Antonio de Gouva, and began to live as a "bride of Christ" as best she could without a full monastic community around her. She approached Archbishop Dom Aleixo de Meneses during his 1597 ecclesiastic visitation to Taná and asked him to found a convent for women where both she and her daughter could profess to the black veil and live properly as choir nuns. It was her conviction that convinced Dom Aleixo de Meneses to petition the king for permission to found the convent. The story of the pious Donna Phillipa and her daughter spread quickly, and reports of her noble blood and noble soul brought status and legitimacy to the project. Full details of her story are found in Santa Maria, *História da Fundaçaõ do Real Convento de Santa Mónica*, 74–86 and 486–547, and Miguel Vicente de Abreu, *Real Mosteiro de Santa Monica de Goa: Memoria Historica* (Nova-Goa: Imprensa-Nacional, 1882), vi–xv; see also Margareth de Almeida Gonçalves, *Império da Fé: Andarilhas da Alma na Época Barroca* (Rio de Janeiro: Rocco, 2005), 57–92.

14. Bethencourt, "Os Conventos Femininos no Império Português," 632. For an analysis of the activities of the Augustinians in the Estado da Índia in the second half of the sixteenth century and the first decades of the seventeenth century, see Margareth de Almeida Gonçalves, "A Edificação da Cristandade no Oriente Português: Questões em Torno da Ordem dos Eremitas de Santo Agostinho no Limiar do Século XVII," *Revista de História (São Paulo)* 170 (2014): 107–41.

15. Lay sisters, novices, and postulants were all considered nuns of the white veil; see Ben James, "Convents in Lisbon: Practices against Seclusion," in *Gendering the Portuguese-Speaking World*, ed. Francisco Bethencourt (Leiden: Brill, 2021), 117.

16. Bethencourt, "Os Conventos Femininos no Império Português," 634.

against its growing power in an effort to reduce its size and reclaim some of its wealth for themselves.[17]

Diogo de Santa Anna, the Augustinian friar appointed by Dom Aleixo de Meneses to oversee and care for the convent, responded to these threats in a series of sermons and published treatises.[18] Indeed, Fr. Diogo de Santa Anna emerged as a dedicated champion and defender of the convent during its turbulent first three decades. Midway through the 1630s, the conflicts began to subside after Fr. Diogo de Santa Anna outwitted his opponents with two clever moves. First, he successfully petitioned the Crown to put the convent under royal patronage. As Francisco Bethencourt argues, this change in the convent's official status was "a masterstroke, as the convent would come under royal patronage, thus removing arguments [concerning the convent's accumulation of wealth] from the City Council and placing it outside their political pressure."[19] Henceforth, the convent would be known as the Real (Royal) Convento de Santa Mónica. Second, Fr. Diogo de Santa Anna was instrumental in confirming and publicizing a miracle that occurred in the church of the convent.[20] On February 8, 1636, a group of nuns and their servants were praying in the choir when an image of the crucified Christ opened its eyes and gazed down at the women. In the weeks that followed, the Christ image began communicating with the community regularly: it opened its eyes and looked with compassion on the women, turned its head from side to side, mouthed words, dripped blood from its crown of thorns, and shook violently. Fr. Diogo de Santa Anna interpreted all of this as Christ's desire to "refute the slander that the monastery had suffered."[21] Thus, not only was the convent transformed

---

17. Bethencourt, "Os Conventos Femininos no Império Português," 636.

18. Margareth de Almeida Gonçalves has written a series of articles exploring the early-seventeenth-century sermons and treatises of Fr. Diogo de Santa Anna; see her "Doutrina Cristã, Práticas Corporais e Freiras na Índia Portuguesa: O Mosteiro de Santa Mônica de Goa na alta Idade Moderna," in *Corpo: Sujeito e Objeto*, ed. Marta Mega de Andrade, Lise Fernanda Sedrez, and William de Souza Martins (Río de Janeiro: Pinteio, 2012), 115–38; "'Gloria de Deus, Ao Serviço Do Rei e Ao Bem Desta Republica': Freiras de Santa Mônica de Goa e a Cristandade no Oriente pela Escrita do Agostinho Frei Diogo de Santa Anna na Década de 1630," *História (São Paulo)* 32, no. 1 (2013): 251–80; and "'Despozorios Divinos' de Mulheres em Goa na Época Moderna: Eloquência e Exemplaridade no Púlpito do Mosteiro de Santa Mônica (Frei Diogo de Santa Anna, 1627)," *Locus: Revista de História* 21, no. 2 (2015): 365–95.

19. Bethencourt, "Os Conventos Femininos no Império Português," 645.

20. Diogo de Santa Anna, *Relaçam verdadeira do milagroso portento, & portentoso milagre, q[ue] aconteceo na India no Santo Crucifixo, q[ue] està no coro do observantissimo mosteiro das Freiras de S. Monica da cidade de Goa, em oito de Fevereiro de [1]636. & continuou por muitos dias, tirada de outra, que fez o Reverendo P. M. Fr. Diogo de S. Anna*, ed. Manuel da Silva (Lisboa: Manoel da Sylva, 1640).

21. Diogo de Santa Anna, "Resposta por parte do insigne mosteiro de freira de Sancta Monica de Goa," 1636, Arquivo National de Torre de Tombo, Manuscritos da Livraria, no. 816, fls. 275r–276v, cited in Bethencourt, "Os Conventos Femininos no Império Português," 646.

into a royal institution, but it also became a site of miracles, demonstrating that it had gained Christ's favor.

Now under the protection of Christ and Crown, the convent enjoyed a period of peace and prosperity for the remainder of the seventeenth century. Archbishops and viceroys, procurators and prioresses, and numerous nuns came and went, all while the convent's wealth increased. In 1699, the publication of Frei Agostinho de Santa Maria's eight-hundred-page *Historia da Fundaçaõ do Real Convento de Santa Monica da Cidade de Goa* brought the convent fame throughout the Lusophone world. The *Historia* not only chronicled the origins of the convent but also provided biographies of the first thirty-six nuns who professed to and entered the order. Frei Agostinho de Santa Maria portrayed the convent as a beacon of virtue in a pagan land and a powerful and wealthy institution that brought honor to the Portuguese in Asia. If for the previous seventy-five years the convent had flown under the radar, now the entire kingdom was certainly aware of its prestige, power, and wealth. This newfound visibility, however, also brought problems. In 1703, shortly after the publication of the *Historia*, King Pedro II received a series of reports from his royal agent Domingos Dourado de Oliveira on the state of the Estado da Índia. Oliveira's reports criticized the condition of the clergy in the Estado and lamented the lost opportunities for the Portuguese Crown to gain converts and increase its wealth.[22] In the same year, the king also received a report from the Goan City Council describing the difficulty they had in providing the significant financial support the convent received from the State.[23] With these two reports on his desk, one detailing the failing finances of the Estado and the other indicating a flourishing convent that received State support, King Pedro II demanded a financial audit of the convent. The 1704 audit is astounding: not only did the convent receive annual support from the State and continue to accumulate dowries with each profession, but its land holdings in Goa and its adjacent territories, from which it earned profits, were vast.[24] But before King

---

22. Domingos Dourado de Oliveira, "Parecer do Desembargador Domingos Dourado de Oliveira," January 18, 1703, Historical Archives of Goa, Livro das Monções do Reino, no. 68 (codex 77); reprinted in Cunha Rivara, *APO*: 161–72.

23. The archives do not contain the Goan city council's original report, but in a letter to the viceroy, King Pedro II wrote,

> The officials of the Goan City Council have forwarded to me a copy of the document that details the support that the Convento de Santa Mónica receives from this State, given to the nuns of the Convent of Santa Mónica in accordance with the contract they made at the time of its foundation ... and therefore I request that you order the superior to provide me with information regarding the income of the convent. (King Pedro II, "Carta de Rei Pedro II a Câmara de Goa," March 3, 1703, Historical Archives of Goa, Livro das Monções do Reino, no. 67 [codex 76], fl. 63r.)

24. "Lista das Fazendas que pessui O Convento de Santa Monica nesta Ilha de Goa, e nas Ilhas adjacentes," December 22, 1703, Historical Archivers of Goa, Livro das Monções do Reino, no. 67 (codex

Pedro II could take any action regarding the convent, he fell ill and died, leaving the kingdom in the hands of his eighteen-year-old son, João.

In the 1710s, King João V addressed the issue of the convent's wealth and privilege as part of his plan to curtail the orders' considerable power by removing its members from positions of leadership and replacing them with secular clergy. For the Real Convento de Santa Mónica, this meant that the convent's Augustinian procurators and confessors, friars who lived right next to the convent in the Convento de Nossa Senhora da Graça, were replaced with secular priests deemed more loyal to the Crown. The Mónicas immediately objected to this and sent a series of protest letters signed by all the nuns in the convent. As a result, King João V relented and allowed the Augustinian friars to continue in their administration of the convent. However, a greater conflict would emerge when King João V appointed the reform-minded Dom Ignácio de Santa Teresa to the position of archbishop of Goa in 1721. Dom Ignácio de Santa Teresa professed to the Canons Regular of Saint Augustine in 1687,[25] and he was educated in Coimbra, where he became part of an elite reform group called the *Jacobeia*. This movement emphasized frequent confession to properly trained priests, a return to daily "mental prayer," and total obedience to the church in an effort to rid the clergy of what it perceived to be their sloppiness and growing incompetence.[26] Dom Ignácio de Santa Teresa's attempts to put these ideas into practice in Goa would spark disputes—not only with the Augustinians and the Real Convento de Santa Mónica but also with the Franciscans, Dominicans, and Jesuits—from the moment of his arrival in Goa in 1721 to his departure in 1741.

The conflict between the Mónicas and the archbishop over who controlled its administration and thus its land holdings and finances simmered for the first ten years of his leadership. He made periodic visits to the convent, where he reviewed the nuns' conduct and administered punishments in an attempt to gain control over the convent and its wealth.[27] During this period, the nuns divided into two factions: the obedient nuns, also called the partisans (*parçiaes*), who supported the archbishop and followed his orders, and the disobedient nuns, who bitterly

---

76), fls. 67r.–70v. and 79r. The convent owned palm plantations as far away as the Northern Provinces, which included the region surrounding Bombay.

25. The Canons Regular of St. Augustine differ from Augustinian friars in that they do not take a vow of corporate poverty and are not considered one of the mendicant orders.

26. Elisa Maria Lopes da Costa, "A Jacobeia: Achegas para a História de um Movimento de Reforma Espiritual no Portugal Setecentista," *Arquipélago História*, 2ª Série, XIV–XV, 2010–2011, 31–48.

27. For a full history of the conflict, see Daniel Michon and D. A. Smith, *To Serve God in Holy Freedom: The Brief Rebellion of the Nuns of the Royal Convent of Santa Mónica, Goa, India, 1731–1734* (London: Routledge, 2020); Leopoldo da Rocha, "Uma Página Inédita do Real Mosteiro de Santa Mónica de Goa (1730–1734)," *Mare Liberum* 17 (1999): 240–66; and Rozely Menezes Vigas Oliveira, "Em busca do 'Bem Comum do Convento': O Conflito entre o Convento de Santa Mônica de Goa e o Poder Episcopal na Primeira Metade do Século XVIII," *Revista Feminismos* 9, no. 1 (2021): 27–47.

protested the archbishop's meddling.²⁸ The partisans were a smaller group—never more than ten adhering to their cause—made up of nuns from less prestigious and less wealthy families,²⁹ whereas the disobedient faction was a much larger group of sixty-three nuns who were the daughters of the best families in the Estado. The archbishop's attacks on the convent became harsher and more frequent, and in a report from 1731, he accused some nuns (no doubt these nuns were part of the disobedient faction) of "reprehensible and scandalous communication (by letters, public gestures, clandestine meetings, and joint encounters) with some religious of their Order [the Augustinian friars]."³⁰ The conflict reached a breaking point after Viceroy João de Saldanha da Gama resigned and a three-member interim governing council consisting of two Portuguese noblemen, D. Cristóvão de Mello and Tomé Gomes Moreira, and Archbishop Ignácio de Santa Teresa himself was appointed in his absence. Archbishop Ignácio de Santa Teresa used his newfound authority to exert even more pressure on the convent. The nature of his interference is best described by Mother Magdalena de Santo Agostinho:

> For at least the last two years, the Archbishop has entered the cloister two or three times a week for an hour and a half after midday during the time of silence when the nuns withdraw to their cells to rest. This caused a notable uproar in the community, as in reality there was no necessity for it, nor did he provide any reasons to explain his motives. As for those who wanted to feast their eyes on him and obtain his personal favors, he paused with them to converse and even say the Ave Maria . . . and these intrusions upon our silence at different times of the day were continued and repeated, primarily during those two years before we ended our obedience to him.³¹

---

28. In the report of the archbishop's actions from 1733, Mother Magdalena de Santo Agostinho blames the archbishop for these divisions: "The Archbishop formed and fomented divisions and factions between the sisters, from which have followed the pernicious effects of discord, disunity, and disorder, which we have experienced, [and has resulted in] the total ruin of the peace and charity which Christ commands us to observe," translated in Michon and Smith, *To Serve God in Holy Freedom*, 28–29. These protests were often in the form of letters, see Rozely Menezes Vigas Oliveira, "Cartas de Freiras: Os Dois Lados de uma Crise Conventual na Goa Setecentista," *Prajñā: Revista de Culturas Orientais* 1, no. 1 (2020): 149–76.

29. Michon and Smith, *To Serve God in Holy Freedom*, 5.

30. Ignácio de Santa Teresa, "Nomeação do Conservador, Mónicas," 1731, Arquivo Nacional de Torre de Tombo, Conselho Geral do Santa Oficio, Liv. 284, folios not numbered; cited in Ana Maria Mendes Ruas Alves, "O Reyno de Deos e a Sua Justiça: Dom Frei Inácio de Santa Teresa (1682–1751)" (PhD thesis, Universidade de Coimbra, 2012), 179.

31. "Relação Sumaria e Verdadeira dos Procidimentos que o Arçebispo de Goa Dom Ignaçio de Santa Thereza Teve com as Religiozas do Convento de Santa Mónica da Mesma Çidade no Anno de 1731 1732 e 1733," 1734, Archivum Romanum Societatis Iesu, Fondo Gesuitico 1433/9, no. 52 (Busta no.

Unwilling to tolerate his incursions any longer, in late May 1732, the disobedient faction of nuns broke cloister, abandoning the convent and leaving the obedient nuns behind, and took up residence in a dilapidated fortress across town.³² They stayed in the fortress for six months, aided by Augustinians and Jesuits, agreeing to reenter the convent only after they were assured their grievances would be remedied immediately upon the arrival of the new viceroy, Dom Pedro de Mascarenhas, the Count of Sandomil.

Once the new viceroy arrived in Goa in October 1732, the disobedient nuns returned to the convent full of hope, but the conflict did not end. Rather, the archbishop continued to try and bend the wills of the disobedient nuns to his rule, and in turn, the disobedient nuns continued to protest against the archbishop and his partisans. The conflict continued for another three years, and both sides sent letters and reports to the governmental and ecclesiastical authorities in Goa, Rome, and Lisbon complaining about the situation. With all of this correspondence circulating both within Goa and across the oceans, the conflict became widely known. The entire affair was considered scandalous, a stain on the once revered convent, and a poor reflection of those involved. Viceroy Pedro de Mascarenhas, who was undoubtedly aware of such opinions, repeatedly expressed his exasperation with the situation to King João V. Finally, in 1736, King João V decisively intervened to put an end to the chaos: he ordered the aggrieved parties to cease all correspondence and demanded "perpetual silence to be kept about everything concerning the Nuns of Santa Mónica."³³ Simultaneously, the Estado's focus shifted to a more urgent matter, the Maratha threat to Portuguese rule in the Northern Provinces. With the king's demand for silence and the war in the Northern Provinces underway, the conflict began to wind down.

The definitive end to the conflict can be marked by the election of Mother Catharina do Sacramento as prioress in 1738. For the previous six years, Mother Brites do Sacramento, the leader of the obedient faction, governed the convent as prioress. Mother Brites was elected by a mere eight sisters in 1732 because the disobedient nuns, residing in the fortress outside the cloister, were unable

---

74B). For a transcription, translation, and historical introduction to this manuscript, see Michon and Smith, *To Serve God in Holy Freedom*.

32. Thirty-five choir nuns, twenty-two lay nuns, five novices, six postulants, and many of their servants left the convent to live in the fortress. There were nineteen choir nuns and ten lay nuns among the obedient nuns who stayed in the convent. See Michon and Smith, *To Serve God in Holy Freedom*, 5–10, for a description of these events.

33. King João V, "Se perpetuo silencio en tudo do que dizem respeito as Freiras da Santa Monica," April 5, 1736, Historical Archives of Goa, Livro das Monções do Reino, no. 105 (codex 127), f. 40r. See also Menezes Vigas Oliveira, "Cartas de Freiras: Os Dois Lados de uma Crise Conventual na Goa Setecentista," 168.

to cast votes.³⁴ Even after their return to the convent, the disobedient nuns, led by Mother Magdalena de Agostinho, considered her illegitimate and insisted on artfully referring to her as the "Intruder Prioress" in all their communications. Finally, in 1738 a new election was held, and Mother Catharina do Sacramento, a member of the disobedient faction, won. Surprisingly, Archbishop Ignácio de Santa Teresa did not object. Perhaps this was because he could clearly see the end to his time in India, as earlier he had petitioned King João V to relieve him of his duties. Sure enough, on February 13, 1740, he was appointed as the Bishop of Algarve.³⁵ The notice of this appointment would reach Goa in September 1740, and Dom Ignácio de Santa Teresa would board the next ship bound for Lisbon in February 1741.³⁶ But before he disembarked for the metropole and his new position, he left his mark on the convent: the last profession Archbishop Ignácio de Santa Teresa oversaw was for a nun who took the name Mother Juana de Santa Thereza.³⁷ With this act, the name "Santa Thereza" would remain on the lips of the Mónicas for years to come, a subtle but clever jab at the disobedient nuns.

But the Mónicas got in the one last jab at the archbishop as well. On January 6, 1741, just before the archbishop would board a ship to Portugal, the Mónicas staged an elaborate shadow puppet show, the *Entrada de Bonifrate para Festa dos Reis*. During the show, every woman religious in the convent was celebrated, by name, with music and song. There were only two guests invited from outside the convent, and Archbishop Ignácio de Santa Teresa was not one of them. Rather, the guests of honor were the confessor and conservator of the convent, both Augustinian friars, the very friars that the archbishop had tried to remove from those positions years earlier. And so, thanks to our good luck that these documents found their way to the archive, we can now travel back almost three centuries to Goa, India, and take a peek at what kind of entertainment the nuns provided for themselves and their honored guests on January 6, 1741, the Feast of the Kings.

---

34. See Michon and Smith, *To Serve God in Holy Freedom*, 57.

35. José Maria Mendes, "Inácio de Santa Teresa: Construindo a Biografia de um Arçebispo" (PhD thesis, Universidade de Lisboa, 2012), 59.

36. He would arrive back in Portugal in fall 1741, and on November 29, 1741, Ignácio de Santa Teresa entered Faró as the Bishop of Algarve to great fanfare; see Alves, "O Reyno de Deos e a Sua Justiça," 251–53.

37. The date recorded for Sister Juana de Santa Thereza's ceremony in the *Book of Professions* is April 9, 1741. It is not clear whether the archbishop was actually present for this profession or if he arranged to be the presiding ecclesiast *in absentia*. It is most likely the latter, as April would be quite late for a ship to leave for Portugal. Most ships tried to set sail before the end of February to avoid the southern autumn/winter weather as they rounded the Cape of Good Hope. For a good overview of the timing of the overseas voyages, see Filipe Vieira de Castro, *The Pepper Wreck: A Portuguese Indiaman at the Mouth of the Tagus River* (College Station: Texas A & M University Press, 2005), 21–22.

Entrada de Bonifrate para Festa dos Reis

Vignette #1: January 6, 1741 (The Feast of the Kings), early evening, Goa, India
    A refreshing ocean breeze blows off the Mandovi River, up the slopes of a hill, the so-called Holy Mount, and enters through the open windows of the Real Convento de Santa Mónica. The convent, a massive three-story structure, sits on the eastern edge of the Indo-Portuguese city of Goa, and perched on its hilltop, it holds a commanding presence as it looks down on the docks, markets, homes, and many churches that make up the capital of the Portuguese maritime empire. The cool breeze reaches the inner garden of the convent, a large rectangular area divided into separate cultivated plots, causing the myriad of blooming flowers to sway and spread their fragrance throughout the space. On the southern cloister veranda, which overlooks the inner garden, a few women gather behind a large white cloth that will serve as the screen for this evening's performance. They light a row of oil lamps that sit on a wooden crossbar about a foot behind the screen, projecting their light onto the back of it. The stars of the show are the *bonifrates*, the puppets, whose figures were cut from leather and then perforated in intricate ways to allow the play of light and dark to create shadows. But just as important are the human performers: the nun-puppeteers hidden from the audience behind the screen and the nun-musicians standing off to the side, tuning their guitars, trumpets, and drums. As the puppeteers and musicians prepare themselves, the audience begins to file into the garden, two by two. Chairs have been arranged in and around the flower beds, and those closest to the screen are taken by more than three dozen women with black habits. These women, the Mothers of Santa Mónica, are fully professed Augustinian nuns who have spent the better part of their lives within the convent walls. Behind them sit the nuns of the white veil, the lay nuns who also live their lives as brides of Christ but have not taken full vows. A few of the black-veiled mothers sit closer to the back so that they can keep an eye on their charges: the novices and postulants, young girls who aspire to join the ranks of the professed but are still in training. Once the nuns are seated, the inner garden fills up with more than a hundred other women. These are the servants and slaves that keep the convent running on a day-to-day basis. These women are markedly darker in complexion: some come from the rural areas surrounding Goa, some from the south of the subcontinent, and others' ancestors come from Africa. All the women chat excitedly as they wait; the convent has not seen such a performance in many years, as the archbishop of Goa's heavy hand

kept them in fear of punishment for untoward behavior. Suddenly, a hush overcomes the crowd and all eyes look to the left, where from the main gatehouse enter two Augustinian friars, the Father Confessor and the Father Procurator. These men take their places of honor in a specially constructed "theater box," which separates them from the women in the courtyard. The sun dips below the horizon, and the oil lamps flicker. All eyes focus on the cloth screen.

Four shadow puppets appear on the screen, illuminated by the oil lamps from behind. The Master (Master of Ceremonies) puppet moves to the center of the "stage." The Master gestures to the prioress of the convent, Mother Catherina do Sacramento, and in a rhyming quatrain, welcomes her and wishes her much joy in the evening's entertainment. Next, the Malavar (representing an inhabitant of the Malabar Coast) puppet takes center stage, and he welcomes the whole Holy Community, making sure to recognize the noble blood that runs through the veins of many in the audience. Then the Canarim (a pejorative term the Portuguese used to identify the native, non-Portuguese inhabitants of India) puppet chimes in and tells the ladies in the audience that he and his colleagues have come to perform a puppet show in order to please them—the audience laughs at the idea that this puppet does not realize that he is a puppet, but rather believes he is a human about to perform a puppet show! The Master again steps forward, perhaps with a flourish, pushing the silly, ignorant Canarim to the back. The Master thanks the Mother Prioress for the invitation and gestures toward the Father Confessor in the theater box; he says that the puppet troupe is here to entertain His Reverence. The Malavar then moves forward to deliver his next quatrain, but the Canarim quickly moves in front of him, pushing him aside, and hastily recites two quatrains to aggrandize himself: *I* am here to serve His Lord Reverence. *I* intend to give him pleasure. *I* will dance and sing and play instruments for him. In fact, the Father Confessor asked specifically for *me*! At this point, the fourth puppet, the Cafre (a slave from Africa), has had enough of the Canarim's ridiculous attempts at flattery. He sings, "O dishonest Canarim, herewith stop with such lies. You have come to this festival only to cause trouble!" The audience erupts with laughter and delight: the Cafre is smarter and more aware than the Canarim! The two puppets confront each other on the stage, staring each other down. Perhaps they will fight; perhaps the puppeteer manipulates the movable arms so that their fists are raised, ready to engage in fisticuffs. The Master has to step in and say, "Now, now, my friends, stop this bickering already. Take up your instruments and cry out the revelries!" The

Malavar, Canarim, and Cafre move about the stage in agitation, and the Master addresses them, "Now, settle down, settle down, beautiful jokesters; I will sing with you all night long!" All four take center stage, face the audience, and sing, "All through this joyful night, join with us, and we will sign together!" And the show begins.

Over the next two to three hours, the four shadow puppets will perform magic tricks, comedic skits, and dances; they will recite recipes, tell jokes, and sing ditties. In addition to the four main shadow puppets, we will be introduced to paper representations of the two Augustinian friars and twelve of the most important Mónicas. The various scenes are often set off by interludes in which a wide range of other shadow puppets take the stage: old men and old women; fidalgos and donas; priests and nuns; bailiffs and judges; merchants and musicians; thieves, African slaves, and dogs. All of these acts and interludes serve to frame the main event of the evening: the singing of praises to the two Augustinian friars (the father confessor and father procurator) as well as to each and every female Augustinian religious (professed, lay, novice, postulant) living in the convent. The evening winds down with odes sung to various everyday Goan objects—a tower, a cobra, a cup, a peacock, a cross, a stake—and a series of short skits, including some local folk songs that elicit a call-and-response from the audience. Finally, the Master stands alone on the stage. Darkness has fallen over the convent as the hour grows late, and the Master looks out at the audience, his silhouette lit from behind by only a single oil lamp. The effect of this single lamp gives the impression that the Master holds a ball of fire in his hand. The Master softly, even mournfully, sings: "With God, my Mothers, is where I want to dwell, After [I leave] don't say that I did not bid you all farewell," and he dramatically plunges the "ball of fire" into a bowl of water, extinguishing it. His shadow disappears. Applause. The show is over; it has been a remarkable evening.

The *Entrada de Bonifrate para Festa dos Reis*, perhaps best described as a puppet variety show, was composed sometime in the year 1740.[38] Due to the text's

---

38. The approximate date of composition of the *Entrada* can be determined by cross-referencing the list of nuns contained in verses 89–115, the "Community Hymns," with the convent's *Book of Professions* and *Book of Elections*. In the *Entrada*'s "Community Hymns," each nun—professed, lay, novice, and postulant—has a single verse written in her honor, providing a record of all the nuns living in the convent at the time of composition. This list can be compared to the list in the *Book of Professions*, which contains the profession and death date for each nun from 1607 to 1834. The *Book of Professions* records Sister Anna de Jesus Maria's death on October 21, 1739, and there is no commemorative verse dedicated to her in the "Community Hymns." Therefore, Madre Ana de Jesus Maria must have died prior to the *Entrada*'s composition, making her death the *terminus post quem* of the text. To determine

intimate knowledge of the nuns' lives and personalities, it is reasonable to assume that it was written by a member of the convent community, likely a nun or a committee of nuns. It was performed on January 6, 1741, the day of Epiphany, or the *Festa dos Reis* of the title.[39] The *Entrada* mirrors the traditions of early modern conventual theater,[40] but the convent's location in Portuguese India, far from the centers of European culture, frees it from some of those norms and allows it to mix with the specificity of Indian life. It is a puppet show and, as such, does not involve live actors, although it is accompanied by live music performed by the nuns themselves. Further, it is not a "play" in any conventional sense, and rather than a coherent narrative running through the text, it is a series of eclectic skits that frame the central part of the performance, the celebration of each individual nun in the community. It also imitates, but does not quite conform to, the conventions of Portuguese puppet opera, an immensely popular eighteenth-century performance genre that centered on classical themes and narratives.[41] It also draws upon Indian shadow puppetry in its staging and European baroque literary conventions in its language.[42] But it does not strictly adhere to any of these traditions. The *Entrada* is best understood, then, as a product of the unique history and conditions of Indo-Portuguese nuns in eighteenth-century Goa.

As a puppet show, the *Entrada* combines elements from the puppetry traditions in both India and Portugal. On the one hand, there is little doubt that at least

---

the *terminus ante quem* of its composition, the convent's *Book of Elections*, which records the prioresses' names and dates of governance, can be consulted. The prioress at the time of composition had to be Mother Catharina do Sacramento. Mother Catharina do Sacramento and Mother Anna de Jesus were the only living nuns not mentioned by name in the *Entrada*, and thus they must be the nuns referred to by their titles, prioress and subprioress, respectively. Mother Catherina do Sacramento's governance of the convent ended on January 18, 1741, providing a *terminus ante quem* for the text. Therefore, the text was written between October 21, 1739 and January 18, 1741.

39. The second text translated in this volume, the *Cartepaço da Muzica*, was also performed to mark the end of Prioress Francisca do Sacramento's three-year term in office.

40. Elissa B. Weaver's *Convent Theatre in Early Modern Italy: Spiritual Fun and Learning for Women* (Cambridge: Cambridge University Press, 2002) has inspired much scholarship on convent theater in the last two decades, and since its publication conventual theater has become a field of study in its own right. For a succinct summary of the functions, purposes, and challenges surrounding the writing and performance of convent plays in early modern Europe, see Román, "Convent Theater," 103–14.

41. The performance of theatrical opera in Portuguese culture, complete with "trumpets, *timbali*, and music," on Epiphany was introduced in 1713, quite early in King João V's reign; see Giuseppina Raggi, "Rethinking the Artistic Policy of King John V of Portugal and Queen Maria Anna of Habsburg: Architecture and Opera Theatre," in *Politics and the Arts in Lisbon and Rome: The Roman Dream of John V of Portugal*, ed. Pilar Diez del Corral Corredoira (Liverpool: Liverpool University Press, 2019), 198 and n50.

42. The other manuscript transliterated and translated in this volume, the *Cartepaço da Muzica*, serves as a better example of baroque literary style and language. Therefore, we will discuss the influence of the baroque in more detail in that section.

some convent residents—the nuns and the countless servants and staff members who came from all over India, but especially from southern India—were familiar with the tradition of Indian puppetry and shared their knowledge with the community. On the other hand, the convent was also linked with the cultural milieu of eighteenth-century Lisbon, and the increased interest in puppet opera in the metropole certainly found its way to the colony.

Although India has numerous traditional forms of puppetry, the *Entrada*'s internal evidence strongly suggests that the puppets are in fact shadow puppets. Eighteenth-century Indian shadow puppetry[43] relied on fire as the light source that cast shadows on a cloth screen.

Throughout the *Entrada*, the audience's attention is intentionally drawn to the qualities of an enchanted (*emcantado*) fire. An early stage direction states that a fire has broken out in the *purçula*, the "theater-box."[44] The puppets attempt to extinguish the fire by immersing it in water, but it continues to burn. The puppets are astonished by this, and the women in the audience are invited to approach, to "Come and see, Senhoras, come close!" (v. 32) to bear witness that "the fire is in water without being quenched" (v. 31). A bit later, a firebird is produced, but the bird, although "scorched by flames, does not die" (v. 41). In another brief scene, a miraculous fire appears, this time in the form of fireballs that do not burn the cloth they touch. The cloth indicated here is probably the very screen upon which the shadows are cast. The balls of fire float in the air, hovering for all to see (vv. 65–70). The conclusion of the performance, which is marked by the extinguishing of the fire, is most revealing. The Master puppet, the Master of Ceremonies, enters alone and sings,

---

43. The tradition of shadow puppets was also present in Portugal as early as the sixteenth century. See Esther Fernández, "Rebellious Silhouettes: Arabic Shadows to Optical Illusions in Iberia," n.d. (I would like to thank Esther Fernandez for providing me an advanced copy of this article), and this could have also been a source of inspiration for the Mónicas. The term "bonifrate" is one of the terms used to describe puppets in Portugal. Other terms include *fantoches*, *marionettes*, and *bonecos*. *Bonifrates* and *bonecos*, the only two terms for puppets found in the nuns' *Entrada* (see the stage directions after v. 85, where a *buneca* enters from above), were the most popular terms used in Lisbon; see Hélder Julio Ferreira Montero, *Os Bonifrates no Teatro Português do Século XVIII* (Salamanco: Luso-Española, 2009), 70–75.

44. Such boxes were common in eighteenth-century Portuguese theater architecture. Often, they were meant for members of the clergy so that they could attend these secular entertainments without being seen by the audience. According to testimony from an attendee to a puppet opera in Lisbon, "in the so-called 'friars boxes' (*camarotes dos frades*), through the thick latticework that concealed them, one could see the venerable heads of the most serious, distinguished, and reverend fathers of all the religious orders, not excepting the inquisitors, who always attended the first representations in great numbers and filled the room reserved for them"; see José María Asensio, *Un Cervantista Português del Siglo XVII Quemado por El Santo Oficio de la Inquisición: Apuntes Biográficos* (Sevilla: E. Rasco, 1885), 1–2. Perhaps the action left the stage and took place in such a theater box, or, more likely, all this played out in shadows on the cloth screen.

269	A deos minha Madres	Goodbye, my Mothers,
	que eu me quero hir	for I want to go,
	depois não digais	after I leave, don't say
	que de vos não despedi	that I did not bid you all farewell.

Or perhaps more poetically, it can be translated as,

> With God, my Mothers,
> is where I want to dwell,
> After I leave don't say
> that I did not bid you all farewell!

As the Master puppet sings this farewell, he "puts the fireball in a bowl [of water], and with this [action] it goes out" (v. 263). We can also read this last line as, "and with this, [the show] ends." That is, once the light source is extinguished, the puppet no longer casts his shadow and "leaves" the convent, ending the show. In these ways, the *Entrada* draws attention to its own medium, shadow puppetry, and cleverly integrates its light source into the show.

Shadow puppetry (Malayalam: *olapavakuttu*; Tamil: *tolpavakuttu—ola/tola/thola*, palm-leaf or leather; *pāva*, doll or puppet; *kūttu*, drama; thus "palm-leaf puppet drama" or "leather puppet drama") has a long history in the southern Indian states of Andhra Pradesh, Tamil Nadu, Kerala, and Karnataka. In the late nineteenth and early twentieth centuries, Sanskrit scholars identified a few references to shadow puppets in ancient Indian texts, but it was generally thought that shadow puppetry disappeared from the subcontinent as it spread to Indonesia and other Southeast Asian cultures, where it flourished as an important medium for retelling the *Rāmāyaṇa*.[45] Whatever survived of this tradition was overshadowed by other performative arts, in particular forms of theater that relied on human performers of dance and song. However, the tradition of shadow puppetry did not disappear in India. Rather, in the sixteenth century, we have evidence that shadow puppetry moved from the region of Maharashtra (which included Goa on its southernmost borders) to south India as Shivaji sought allies in his fight against the Mughals.[46] In the 1930s, Otto Spies's research brought attention back to the shadow-puppet tradition in Mysore, Karnataka, and renewed scholarly interest in Indian forms of shadow puppetry in general.

45. See Friedrich Seltmann, "Schattenspiel in Kêrala," *Bijdragen Tot de Taal-, Land- En Volkenkunde* 128, no. 4 (1972): 458–90. The shadow puppet shows that continue in India today also focus on retelling the *Rāmāyaṇa*.

46. Friedrich Seltmann argues that the shadow puppet performers served as spies for the Maratha rulers as they extended their influence southward. He notes that many of the performers in Tamil Nadu speak Marathi among themselves and use Tamil only for their shadow plays; see Friedrich Seltmann, "Schattenspiel in Süd Tamiḷ-Nāḍu," *Bijdragen Tot de Taal-, Land- En Volkenkunde* 135, no. 4 (1979): 457–58.

The puppets in the Indian shadow puppet tradition are made from either palm leaves or leather (Malayalam: ola; Tamil: tōl). There are two different techniques for creating these figures. In the first technique—more common in Andhra Pradesh, Tamil Nadu, and Karnataka—the artist draws a broad outline of the figure, which is then cut out and filled with colored foil, rendering them "transparent and shimmering with bright colors."[47] The other technique, which is most common on the Malabar Coast (Kerala) and was most likely the one employed by the Mónicas, uses multiple perforations within the cutout figure to create a contrast between light and dark on the screen. Friedrich Seltmann describes the process: "The outlines and designs of the figure to be made are drawn on the leather. This patterning is done in such a way that the subsequent cuts and perforations produce the best possible effects, so that the shadow combinations on the canvas clearly reveal the outlines of bodies, faces, robes, jewelry, weapons, and the like."[48] The puppets are then outfitted with a sheath attached to their backs, into which a bamboo rod is inserted. A series of oil lamps are placed on a long crossbar, which in turn is placed about a foot behind the screen and serves as the light source. The puppeteers sit behind the screen, hidden from the audience, and insert the figures between the screen and the oil lamps, casting the shadows seen by the audience.[49] The figures can have moving body parts, and each figure is controlled by a single puppeteer. During the performance, the puppeteers are joined by musicians and singers who sit to the side of the screen. These musicians play drums and cymbals, and there is also a special whistle-like instrument that is blown to indicate scene changes and other breaks in the show.[50] All of this accords well with the internal evidence from the *Entrada*.

But the nuns' interest in puppetry also derived from the Portuguese character of the convent. Portuguese inhabitants in India marked themselves as superior to the local populace by embracing their Portuguese heritage, and thus "performing" Portugueseness was taken very seriously. Despite the long distance between Lisbon and Goa, there is no doubt that cultural norms from the metropole were readily adopted in the colony. In his study *The Theme of India in Portuguese Theater*, Duarte Ivo Cruz argues that "on the caravels, among missionaries, sailors, noblemen and merchants, soldiers, heroes, saints, and bandits, follows a first generation of playwrights who, on board or already in the lands of India, open new perspectives to the Portuguese culture of Expansion."[51] In eighteenth-century

---

47. Otto Spies, "Das Indische Schattentheater," *Theater Der Welt* 2, no. 1 (1938): 1.

48. Seltmann, "Schattenspiel in Kêrala," 464.

49. For a good description of this set-up from Malabar, see K. B. Iyer, "Shadow Play in Malabar," *Marg: A Magazine of the Arts* 31, no. 3 (1968): 24; and Seltmann, "Schattenspiel in Kêrala," 471.

50. Seltmann, "Schattenspiel in Süd Tamil-Nāḍu," 470–71.

51. Duarte Ivo Cruz, *O Essencial Sobre o Tema da Índia no Teatro Português* (Lisboa: Imprensa Nacional-Casa da Moeda, 2011), 28. Cruz primarily details how India traveled to Portugal, but the opposite

Portugal, an interest in the arts was spurred by the rule of Dom João V. Crowned on January 1, 1707, at age eighteen, Dom João V's youthful exuberance injected a new cultural vibrancy into Lisbon. One year later, in 1708, he married the twenty-five-year-old princess Maria Anna of Austria, daughter of the Hapsburg Emperor Leopold I, who further encouraged a broader vision of Portuguese court culture that looked beyond the long-influential Spanish models to wider European influences.[52] This renewed cultural vigor and these cosmopolitan influences went beyond the court and touched every level of Portuguese society.

Dom João V's cultural interests ranged from history and architecture to music and theater. He established the Royal Academy of History in 1720 to memorialize Portugal's major achievements and spent thirty-three years building the great palace at Mafra. But most importantly for our nuns in Goa, he supported Italian opera both at court as well as in numerous public theaters throughout Lisbon. Indeed, during his fifty-year reign, he encouraged a "collective enthusiasm for . . . [the] convergence of theatrical forms that combined the musical traditions of Italy, Spain, and the 'manner of Portugal.'"[53] With all these new influences combining with traditional forms, Lisbon's music and theater scene in the first half of the eighteenth century was quite dynamic, and Lisbon supported a variety of performance genres. Comedies, operas, and puppet operas all vied for the

---

was also just as true: Portugal traveled to India. See also Mário Martins, SJ, *Teatro Quinhentista nas Naus da Índia* (Lisboa: Brotéria, 1973).

52. King João V welcomed such a cosmopolitan outlook. He was obsessed with all things Roman, and thus Italian by extension, but also absorbed ideas from France, England, and other European communities. This is not to dismiss the Spanish cultural influence in King João V's Portugal. According to Hélder Julio Ferreira Montero, Portugal's transition away from its Iberian neighbor took time in the first half of the eighteenth century:

> [Portuguese] nationalism, as well as attempts to get away from everything that represented or reminded one of the "Spanish," and the search for one's own identity, are carried out slowly and gradually. In this way, Spain continues to be (although less ostensibly than in previous eras) at the base of a cultural influence that is slowly being replaced by Italian and then French culture.
> (Montero, *Os Bonifrates no Teatro Português*, 52)

53. These are the words of the Viennese representative to the Portuguese court, Giuseppe Zignoni, written in 1711, see Raggi, "Rethinking the Artistic Policy of King John V of Portugal and Queen Maria Anna of Habsburg: Architecture and Opera Theatre," 198. See also Giuseppina Raggi, "Trasformare la Cultura di Corte: La Regina Maria Anna d'Asburgo e l'Introduzione dell'Opera Italiana in Portogallo," *Revista Portuguesa de Musicologia* 5, no. 1 (2018): 18–38. More evidence of this Italian-Spanish-Portuguese nexus comes from the works of the most famous eighteenth-century Portuguese creators of puppet opera, the librettist António José da Silva and composer Antonio Texeira. As Juliet Perkins argues, "he [da Silva] and Texeira were less concerned with the parody of Italian opera *per se*, than with Italianising the Spanish musical theatre with which they were obviously familiar, whilst stressing the Portuguese context," *A Critical Study and Translation of António José Da Silva's Cretan Labyrinth: A Puppet Opera*, Mellen Studies in Puppetry, v. 5 (Lewiston, NY: Edwin Mellen Press, 2004), 74.

patronage of the Hospital Real de Todos os Santos (All Saints' Royal Hospital), the institution from which all such performances needed to gain approval.[54]

Particularly popular were the puppet operas of António José da Silva (1705–1739), also known as "O Judeo," as he was a member of the New Christian community of Jewish converts.[55] In collaboration with the composer António Teixeira (1707–1770), da Silva produced eight puppet operas that were performed in Lisbon between 1733 and 1739.[56] As a New Christian, da Silva ran into problems with the Inquisition. He was first arrested in 1726, and it was only after his release that he began to write his puppet operas.[57] However, this popularity did not make him immune to further harassment by the Inquisition, and he was arrested again in 1734 along with his mother, Lourença Coutinho, and his wife, Leonor Maria de Carvalho (a fellow New Christian whom he married in 1734). All three were in prison for two years, where they were interrogated and tortured.[58] These details of da Silva and his family's fate are important to understanding the relationship the nuns had with the Portuguese metropole. In the *Entrada*, an ode to a stake suggests knowledge of these grim events:

54. Other than a brief period in the late 1720s when, under pressure from more conservative factions within Portugal, the hospital temporarily shut down many of Lisbon's public theater venues, musical theater thrived among the general populace during the reign of King João V. For a succinct history of the Hospital Real de Todos os Santos' control of Lisbon theater, see Perkins, *A Critical Study and Translation of António José Da Silva's Cretan Labyrinth*, 57–68.

55. New Christians were "descendants of Portuguese Jews forcibly converted in the late fifteenth century and were differentiated from Old Christians, who had no trace of Jewish or Moorish blood"; see Perkins, *A Critical Study and Translation of António José Da Silva's Cretan Labyrinth*, 10.

56. Two excellent studies of António da Silva's puppet operas are José Oliveira Barata, *História do Teatro Em Portugal (Séc. XVIII): António José da Silva (o Judeu) no Palco Joanino* (Algés: DIFEL, 1998) and Juliet Perkins' "Introduction" to her *A Critical Study and Translation of António José Da Silva's Cretan Labyrinth*, 1–128. Juliet Perkins, in another article, laments, "unfortunately, there is no record of any of these productions, no eyewitness accounts of how the puppets were manipulated, or where the singers and musicians were positioned"; see Juliet Perkins, "Translating António Da Silva's *O Judeu*," in *Theoretical Issues and Practical Cases in Portuguese English Translations*, ed. Malcom Coulthard and Patricia Anne Odber de Baubeta (Lewiston, NY: Edwin Mellen Press, 1996), 97.

57. To what degree António da Silva's puppet operas contributed to his arrest continues to be a subject of debate. Nathan Wachtel argues that a "set of reasonable arguments strongly supports the thesis that António José was condemned because of the subversive ideas spread by his theater to the public"; see Nathan Wachtel, *The Faith of Remembrance: Marrano Labyrinths* (Philadelphia: University of Pennsylvania Press, 2013), 313. See also Roger Chartier, "Le Don Quichotte d'António José Da Silva, Les Marionnettes Du Bairro Alto et Les Prisons de l'Inquisition," in *Jewish Culture in Early Modern Europe: Essays in Honor of David B. Ruderman*, ed. Richard I. Cohen et al. (Pittsburgh: University of Pittsburgh Press, 2014), 216–26.

58. For details of this story, see Barata, *História do Teatro Em Portugal (Séc. XVIII): António José da Silva (o Judeu) no Palco Joanino*, 39–40, n1 and n2; Perkins, *A Critical Study and Translation of António José Da Silva's Cretan Labyrinth*, 15; for primary sources (translated into French), see Claude-Henri Fréches, *António José da Silva et l'Inquisition* (Paris: Fundacao Calouste Gulbenkian, 1983), 56–67.

244	espeito	stake
	Lianor vem sem respeito	Leonor remains defiant
	para os pes the quemar	until the flames reach her feet;
	lorença mais devagar	Lorença holds out longer,
	porem ambos com espeito	but both are burned at the stake.

While conveying an intimate knowledge of events in Portugal, the story told in this short quatrain mixes up its facts: Leonor and Lourença were not burned at the stake but were "reconciled" to the church and released. However, António da Silva was not so lucky; after two long years of interrogations, he was garroted and burned in 1739. It seems that when the puppet opera craze that gripped Lisbon crossed the oceans, the story that accompanied it did as well.

The Mónicas mixed together elements from both the Indian tradition of shadow puppetry and the Iberian dramatic tradition throughout the *Entrada*. The Indian influence on the structure of the *Entrada* is readily apparent in the opening scene (vv. 1–10, reimagined as part of vignette #1), in which the four main puppets engage in witty banter and humorous disagreements. These verses emulate the openings to both Sanskrit drama and Indian shadow puppetry. Sanskrit dramas often open with a humorous dialogue between a jester-like character (the *vidūṣaka*) and the director and stage-manager of the play (the *sūtradhāra*).[59] These scenes make the audience laugh, and only when the *sūtradhāra* asks for a prayer to the gods does the tomfoolery end and the play begin in earnest. Similarly, in Keralan shadow puppetry, a humorous scene introduces the show, and this farce ends when the jester character reminds the audience to remain calm and to pay attention to the play.[60]

In the *Entrada*, there are four puppets that drive the show: the Master, Malavar, Canarim, and Cafre. The Master takes on the director/stage manager role (*sūtradhāra*), and the jester role (Skt. *vidūṣaka*) is shared among the other three puppets. The humor derived from these three characters is linked to the social status that their names indicate. Surely, the authors of the *Entrada* meant for the audience to understand the name "Malavar" in its double meaning: a "Malavari" is a native Indian from the Malabar Coast, and the term derived from it, "malabarista," is used in Iberian performance for the juggler/jester character.[61] The Canarim represents the social position of "Canarim," which by the eighteenth century was a derogatory word used for native inhabitants of Goa itself. As Charles Boxer argued:

59. L. S. Rajagopalan and Rustom Bharucha, "Sutradhara and Vidushaka," in *The Oxford Encyclopedia of Theatre & Performance*, ed. Dennis Kennedy (Oxford: Oxford University Press, 2003).
60. Seltmann, "Schattenspiel in Kêrala," 477–78.
61. According to Dalgado, "It is a neologism related to juggling games, used as a synonym for 'sleight of hand or pantomime,'" (*Glossário Luso-Asiático*, 2:14).

As Yule and Dalgado have pointed out in their respective glossaries, the term *Canarim* should apply, strictly speaking, to the inhabitants of Canara, the old Carnatic region of the Deccan. But the Portuguese, from their pioneer days, mistakenly applied the term to the people of Goa, who, geographically are Konkani-Marathi, ethnically Indo-Aryan, and glottologically are Indo-European. The term *Canarins* was sometimes used to designate those who became Christian, sometimes those who remained Hindu, and sometimes for both categories indiscriminately. During the eighteenth century and perhaps earlier, the word *Canarim* acquired an offensive connotation, presumably because the Portuguese were apt to be so contemptuous of the native inhabitants of Goa.[62]

Fittingly, the Canarim is presented in the *Entrada* as an obsequious idiot. Finally, the Cafre represents the Black African slave population of Goa. Both male and female slaves were in abundance in eighteenth-century Goa, brought to the imperial Asian capital from the Portuguese African colonies, both from the east African ports of Mombasa and Sofala and the Atlantic port of Luanda, Angola.[63] In these first ten verses of the *Entrada*, these three puppets engage in humorous dialogue, and we can assume that their movements are equally humorous. The crux of the scene revolves around the idea that the Canarim (representative of the local Goan) is less intelligent than the Cafre (representative of the slave population). After this humorous introduction, much like the conventions of both Sanskrit drama and Keralan shadow puppetry, the tomfoolery ends with the Master calling for its cessation and for the audience to pay attention to the play.

---

62. C. R. Boxer, *Race Relations in the Portuguese Colonial Empire, 1415–1825* (Oxford: Clarendon Press, 1963), 84–85. See also *Glossário Luso-Asiático*, 1:197–98.

63. Ann M. Pescatello, "The African Presence in Portuguese India," *Journal of Asian History* 11, no. 1 (1977): 26–48, details the ubiquity of slaves in Goa with particular reference to the convent:

> Records on the famous Convent of Santa Monica reveal the nuns' complaints that the 120 slaves allotted them was insufficient and pointed out that even European, Eurasian, or mulatto artisans could have "15 or 20 female slaves," or "26 women and girls," while a *juiz ordinaria* (judge) or a *desembargador* (lawyer) held "85 female slaves . . . and ladies had over 300" [Santa Maria, *História da Fundaçaõ do Real Convento de Santa Mónica*, 263]. These documents indicate vast numbers of slaves in Goa and also are supportive of the Portuguese colonial ideal that maintenance of large slave households lends social status and personal prestige to a person. (43)

See also Ana Paula Sena Gomide, "Mestizajes y Las Mediaciones Culturales en los Espacios de la India Portuguesa (Siglos XVI y XVII)," in *Tratas, Esclavitudes y Mestizajes: Una Historia Conectada, Siglos XV–XVIII*, ed. Rafael M. Pérez García, Manuel F. Fernández Chaves, and Eduardo França Paiva (Sevilla: Editorial Universidad de Sevilla, 2020), 369–82; and Herbert S. Klein, "The Portuguese Slave Trade from Angola in the Eighteenth Century," *Journal of Economic History* 32, no. 4 (1972): 894–918.

Further influence from Portuguese theater reveals itself in the short interludes that separate the longer scenes in the *Entrada*. That is, the longer scenes that feature the singing of quatrains by the four main shadow puppets are separated by what seems to be an approximation of the Spanish *entremés*, a theatrical form that found its way into Portuguese theater.[64] The entremés, a comic interlude between acts of the main stage production, entered the Iberian peninsula in the early fifteenth century[65] and fully developed during the golden age of Spanish comedia in the sixteenth and seventeenth centuries. The traditional entremés lasts only a few minutes while the stage crew changes the props and the actors change costumes, and it serves as a form of social commentary, poking fun at contemporary norms. The characters in the entremés are not the same as those who are the main characters of the play, and the short skits are often accompanied by music and dances. The entremés became a genre in itself, and various Spanish playwrights became famous for their biting and hilarious entremeses, including perhaps the most famous author in early modern Spain, Miguel de Cervantes Saavedra.

The short descriptions that occur periodically between the main scenes of the *Entrada*, when taken as a whole, form a single narrative that exhibits the characteristics of the entremés. These interludes were not written out in full, perhaps because of their transgressive nature (the *Entrada* was written and performed by nuns in a convent, after all), but it is clear that they serve as prompts for a full scene. The basic narrative is of a *cafrinha*, a little slave girl of African descent, who seeks refuge in the convent to escape her Portuguese master. The interludes, extracted and placed in sequence, that outline this story are as follows:

First interlude
A whistle blows; a tambourine player and a trumpeter enter; a whistle blows; a *cafre* enters singing a song of woe; a whistle blows; a *malim* (a gardener?) enters singing a song that begins, "Mother Felipa..."

Second interlude
Donna Aldonça enters singing "[Oh] little girl..."

Third interlude
A whistle blows; a Senhor and a *negrinha*, "little black girl," enter; the Senhor sings, "Why did you run away from me?"; a whistle blows; a Senhora enters.

---

64. Emilio Cotarelo y Mori argues that by the sixteenth century, Portugal was familiar with the entremés; see *Colección de Entremeses, Loas, Bailes, Jácaras y Mojigangas desde Fines del Siglo XVI á Mediados del XVIII* (Madrid: Casa Editorial Bailly-Bailliére, 1911), lvi.

65. Cotarelo y Mori, *Colección de Entremeses*, liv.

Fourth interlude
A whistle blows; two Canarins (local Goans) enter; a whistle blows; two judges enter; an unidentified character enters and sings a song.[66]

Fifth interlude
A whistle blows; two *cafres* from Angola enter singing a *maraquita*;[67] a whistle blows and a gentleman called Langara Samgoma enters.

Sixth interlude
A whistle blows; two mestizos enter singing; a dog comes on stage;[68] a whistle blows; a *cafrinha*, "little slave girl," enters once again and sings "The Song of the *Cafrinha*."

"Song of the Cafrinha"
This is not an interlude; rather, the song is written out in full and is to be performed by the *cafrinha* herself and not by one of the four members of the puppet troupe.

Seventh interlude
A whistle blows; enter a merchant, a dog, and a bailiff dragging a slave with a noose around her neck; they all exit.

On its own, each interlude is certainly puzzling. For example, in the first interlude, we are not given any more information on who the *cafre* or *malim* are, nor are the lyrics to the songs supplied. Why a song of woe? What is the *cafre* lamenting? And why a song to "Mother Felipa," the founder of the convent? While extracting them and putting them together in a single narrative helps, we are still left with only an outline, and many questions remain. With these limitations in mind and acknowledging that we are speculating here, we can try to understand the story as a whole.

The protagonist is a little slave girl (the *cafre*, *menina*, *negrinha*, and *cafrinha* all seem to be the same character). She arrives at the convent and sings her song of woe. Perhaps this song details her mistreatment at the hands of her master and her request to the Mónicas to let her into the convent, where she will be protected from him. The song is heard by a local gardener (*malim*), and he approaches the Mónicas on the *cafrinha*'s behalf, singing a song about the founder of the convent,

---

66. The text is almost completely illegible here; the only words that seem to make sense are *en**** (entra?) and *canta*.

67. A *maraquita* is a love song, see Caroline Sheridan Norton, *Maraquita: A Portuguese Love Song* (London: Chappell & Co.: 1840).

68. The text here is illegible, and it is unclear what role the dog plays in the scene.

Mother Felipa, to remind the nuns of her extraordinary compassion. The "woes" of the *cafrinha* are then substantiated by a pillar of the community, a Portuguese noblewoman, Donna Aldonça,[69] in her song "Oh little girl." But the Senhor, the master of the little slave girl, has tracked her down. He arrives at the convent, asking her, "Why did you run away from me?" She is his property, after all, and he can do with her as he wishes. The Senhora who enters after his song could be his wife.

Let us take a moment here and imagine the scene in front of the convent: the little slave girl is begging to be rescued from her overbearing master; the gardener and Donna Aldonça have taken up her cause; and now the master and his wife have arrived and demand that she come back with them. In the next interlude, the townsfolk begin to gather around to witness the fraught scene. Two Canarins (local Goans) and two judges enter. We are not told what these characters do, but

---

69. The appearance of Donna Aldonça is further evidence that the authors relied on the Spanish entremés as a model for the *Entrada*'s own interludes. Donna Aldonça seems to be the Portuguese form of Doña Aldonza, who is a character that appears in a number of entremés from early modern Spain. She first appears in a 1615 entremés by Miguel de Cervantes Saavedra, *Entremés del Juez de los Divorcios* (reprinted in Cotarelo y Mori, *Colección de Entremeses*, 1–5). In this entremés, Doña Aldonza comes before a judge as her husband, "The Surgeon," seeks to divorce her, accusing her of not being devoted to him. After her husband gives four reasons for the divorce (mostly that she is "devilish" and does not respect him), Doña Aldonza gives a hilarious retort in which she offers to recount not four but four hundred reasons for why she, too, wants a divorce. She begins by engaging with each of her husband's complaints, turning them on their heads, skewering her husband, and most importantly, revealing that he is not a surgeon at all and thus she was wed under false pretenses! The judge has to interrupt her before she can continue with the other 396 reasons for wanting to be rid of her husband. She next appears in the 1661 entremés attributed to Don Diego de Figueroa y Córdoba. The entremés was originally titled *La Presumida* (*The Presumptuous Woman*), but at some point, the title was changed to *Doña Rodríguez*. Cotarelo finds this name change strange, and he suggests it should be called "*Doña Aldonza*" as she is the protagonist (Cotarelo, p. cxxxii). Thus, Doña Aldonza further takes on the identity of the presumptuous woman who is vain and exhibits a false devotion to her husband. She also appears in an entremés by Julio de la Torre titled *Entremés Famoso del Alcalde de Burguillos* (reprinted in Cotarelo y Mori, *Colección de Entremeses*, 218–20), in which she gives a speech about the dangers of women acting on their desires (218). This entremés repeats a well-worn theme of a gallant trying to see his beloved, who is guarded by her older husband, invariably a lawyer or a doctor (see Cotarelo y Mori, *Colección de Entremeses*, cxlvi).

Another possibility is that Donna Aldonça is the Mónicas' adaptation of Cervantes's Aldonza from *Don Quixote*. In Cervantes's novel, Aldonza, a peasant woman, is transformed by the knight into his imaginary beloved, Dulcinea. While the novel's part 1 was published in Spanish in 1605, it was not translated into Portuguese until 1794 (see Marta Pérez Rodríguez, "Tras un Siglo de Recepción Cervantina en Brasil: Estudios Críticos sobre el *Quijote* (1900–2000)," MA thesis, Universidade de São Paolo, 2007: 4). But perhaps the Mónicas encountered Aldonza through their second-hand knowledge of António da Silva's puppet plays. In 1733, António da Silva staged a puppet play in Lisbon titled *Vida do Grande Dom Quixote de la Mancha e do Gordo Sancho Pança*, and therefore Cervantes's novel must have been on the minds of the Portuguese (see J. Mendes dos Remédios. *Vida Do Grande D. Quixote de La Mancha e Do Gordo Sancho Pança: Opera Jocosa*. Coimbra: França Amado, 1905). Many thanks to the anonymous reviewer who suggested this connection.

perhaps the judges call for witnesses to ascertain the status of the little slave girl, as in the fifth interlude, two Angolan slaves arrive along with a "man of distinction," one Langara Jangoma. In the sixth interlude, two mestizos enter and sing a song. A dog also enters. Then the little slave girl takes center stage again, and she tells her story in the "Song of the *Cafrinha*." This song, unlike her first song and the songs of the *malim*, Donna Aldonça, and the Senhor, is written out in full. Unfortunately, the song is very difficult to understand, due both to the ruined state of the text and the lack of context, and it leaves us with more questions than answers. What we can discern from the text is that the *cafrinha* is walking down a road when she meets a priest praying with a group of mourners at a funeral pyre (is this a critique of the local indigenous priests, as it would not be proper for a priest to be at a Hindu cremation ritual?). The *cafrinha* joins the group, and she, or someone in the group (it is unclear), offers her food and drink. The *cafrinha*, or someone in the group, is then instructed to praise God and bring more firewood for the cremation fire. The rest of the song is even more perplexing, but it could be read to say that a bailiff (*mirinho*) is called. The song ends here, but the story is not quite over. In the seventh interlude, a merchant (the Senhor?), a dog (the Senhor's dog?), a thief, and a bailiff (the very bailiff called for in the *cafrinha*'s song?) leading a slave with a noose around her neck (the *cafrinha* herself?) all enter. Then they all exit. Did the judges decide that the *cafrinha* should remain with her master? Did they call the bailiff to come and take the *cafrinha*, led by a noose around her neck, back to the Senhor's house? The interpretation presented here of these interludes is quite speculative, but it is clear that these seven interludes are connected in a single narrative.

However intriguing these interludes are, they do not constitute the bulk of the text. Rather, the majority of the *Entrada* consists of a series of songs for the puppets to sing. Each song is clearly marked off, and while some of them have titles, others do not, and we have included titles in square brackets for sections that lack them.

Song 1, 1–10: [*Introduction to the Evening*]
The puppet troupe—Master, Malavar, Canarim, and Cafre—enters. They perform a humorous introduction as they welcome the Prioress and the Father Confessor (see vignette #1).

Song 2, 11–14: *The Dance of the Ring*
The Master requests that the musicians play their instruments so that a copper ring will dance on a table. He invites the nuns, whom he refers to as "princesses," to "come and see" this magical ring dance on its own.

Song 3, 15–28: [*Quatrains in Honor of Seven Prominent Members of the Community, Part I*]

This next section is preceded by the stage directions instructing the nuns to "set out seven painted paper figures." The painted paper figures[70] must be representations of the seven prominent members of the community commemorated in this section: the father confessor, father procurator, prioress [Sister Catharina do Sacramento], subprioress [Sister Ana de Jesus], Mother Mareçiana [Sister Emerençiana de Santa Maria], Mother Bitona [Sister Brites do Sacramento], and Mother Izabel de Madre de Dios. Each person is honored with the singing of two commemorative quatrains. In the first quatrain, the Master presents the subject of the quatrain with a gift that fits their status and personality, and in the second quatrain, one of the other three puppet troupe members (Malavar, Canarim, and Cafre) elaborates on the gift's significance.

15–16: The Father Confessor receives a royal eagle with a crown as his sentiments (his longing for God, or perhaps his general character) soar, like an eagle, to the heavens.

17–18: The Father Procurator is awarded a "planet," the sun, because he shines just as brilliantly. However, we are then informed that he shines brighter than the sun, and the sun loses its worth in his presence.[71]

19–20: The Mother Prioressa receives a palm crown, or martyr's crown, that perfectly fits her.[72] Her virtues (in this case, the virtue of suffering is connected to the suffering of Jesus's Passion) will be preached far and wide.

21–22: The Mother Subprioressa is rewarded for her singing with three pink nacreous pearls. As with the gift to the Father Procurator discussed previously, we are informed that these pearls are worthless in comparison to her.

23–24: Mother Mareçiana receives a crown of thorns, and she is instructed to keep it in her heart as if it were her husband. The crown of thorns is therefore Jesus himself, as he is her husband.

---

70. These painted paper figures do not seem to be shadow puppets but some other form of likeness. We will see these figures again in four other sections of the show.

71. Perhaps this is a subtle way of expressing the nuns' disapproval of the Archbishop Ignácio de Santa Teresa. The verse elevates the Augustinian friar above the disfavored archbishop.

72. Perhaps this is a reference to the afterlife, as at death nuns would "be crowned and united with Jesus"; see Joelle Mellon, *The Virgin Mary in the Perceptions of Women: Mother, Protector and Queen Since the Middle Ages* (Jefferson: McFarland, 2008), 120.

25–26: Mother Bitona receives an açusena flower, which signifies her purity and sincerity. She is told she is certainly worthy of it.

27–28: Mother Izabel de Madre de Dios: this section of the manuscript is badly worm-eaten and barely legible. However, it appears that her beauty and grace are compared to those of Venus. The second quatrain reveals that Mother Izabel is "mad" about Jesus,[73] and that she promises to devote her entire life to serving him.

Song 4, 29–32: *Fire in the Theater Box*

This section discusses the enchanted qualities of fire, a recurring theme throughout the show. The Master describes fire and water as opposites but states that in this instance, they will become one. The Malavar links their unity to the festival itself. The Canarim observes that the fire is now burning in the water without being quenched, and he is astonished. At this point, we can imagine that the audience's interest is piqued and that the sisters are straining in their seats to see what is going on in front. And so, in the final quatrain, the Cafre invites the sisters to "come and see . . . come close" and witness it for themselves.

Song 5, 33–39: [*Quatrains in Honor of Seven Prominent Members of the Community, Part II*]

Stage directions indicate that the seven painted paper figures of those honored in vv. 15–28 are to be brought out again. The four troupe members address them once more, but this time only one quatrain is sung by each puppet. Each quatrain expands on the previous gift.

33: The Master exchanges the Father Confessor's eagle (which we learn is engraved on a mitre) for a golden sun.

34: The Malavar calls the Father Procurator's golden sun "St. Augustine's cipher" but leaves any exchange of gifts up to the Father.

35: The Canarim tells the Mother Prioressa that he gave great consideration to her gift of the crown made of palms. The rest of this verse is illegible except for a reference to seeking out Jesus.

---

73. This interpretation might very well be wrong. In the companion quatrain (v. 39), the Cafre suggests that Mother Izabel should be wary of Cupid, Venus's child. This idea that Cupid makes lovers mad is seen again in the 1766 *Cartepaço da Muzica*, vv. 103–10, *Cantiga de Cupido*.

36: The Cafre tells the Subprioress that the pearls he gave her represent the sheep that go to meet the good Shepherd. That is, the pearls are the sisters in the Convent, and the good Shepherd is the Lord.

37: The Master tells Mother Emerençiana that she looks so beautiful wearing the martyr's crown, but in reality, she should keep it in her heart.

38: The Malavar tells Mother Brites do Sacramento that she should trust in her spouse (Jesus). A "fortunate/lucky figure" (*papel ditoso*) is taken out, and the Malavar exclaims, "Behold the Divine Man."

39: The Cafre once again tells Mother Izabel de Madre de Dios that Venus sought her out and that her son, Cupid, will come in disguise and bring "Divine Love." This seems to be a warning to Mother Izabel not to confuse Divine Love with Human Love.

Song 6, 40–43: *The Fire-Bird*

The Master introduces a bird that sings and dances in fire. The Malavar is astonished, as the bird, although scorched by flames, does not die. The Canarim is also astonished and suggests that the bird is enchanted. Finally, the Cafre indicates that this "art" (*arte*) is the work of the magician Brites (*brites caninha*).[74] Mother Brites do Sacramento was the very "Intruder Prioress" who led the obedient nuns against the disobedient nuns in the conflict that dominated the convent in the previous decade, and perhaps this is a subtle jab at her complicity with the Archbishop Ignácio de Santa Teresa. Mother Brites was one of the choir nuns not from Goa itself, but rather her birthplace is recorded as Couronya, which must have been a very small village as it is not listed as a place-name in any contemporary sources or modern databases.[75]

---

74. *caninha*: The entry in *Glossário Luso-Asiático* (1:205) reads:
    CANIANE: canoniane (malaiala *kaṇiyān*). Astrólogo, feiticeiro no Malabar. V. *canaiate*.
    1606 — «Manda o sagrado Concilio que nemhuma pessoa se cure com *Curumbim* o Canoniane, ainde que sejão christãos». — Quinto Concilio de Goa in *Archivo*, iv, p. 265.
Translation of *Glossário Luso-Asiático* entry above:
    CANIANE: canoniane (in Malayalam *kaṇiyān*). Astrologer, magician from Malabar. V. *canaiate*.
    1606 — "The Sacred Council mandates that no person should cure themselves with a Curumbim or Canoniane, even if they are Christians," Fifth Council of Goa in *Archivo*, iv, p. 265.
Curumbim is the agricultural or śūdra caste (lowest socio-economic status in the Indian hierarchy) from the Goa-Malabar region, see *Glossário Luso-Asiático*, 1:338.

75. Mother Beatris do Sacramento is listed as nun #263 in the *Book of Professions*, 16:363. She professed on May 14, 1690, and she died on December 30, 1757. Her parents were Luis Prestrello de Souza and Donna Maria de Figueredo, from Couronya.

Song 7, 44–57: *Becoming Christian* [*Quatrains to Seven Sisters, Part I*]

Stage directions indicate that "seven painted paper figures" are brought out. These are likenesses of the next seven longest professed nuns that were not praised in the previous quatrains. The title of this section is "Faz Christandade," and while "Becoming Christian" is not an exact translation (a more literal translation might be something like "Make Christendom" or "Let's Make Christendom!"), it conveys the idea that these verses are meant to describe the circumstances of each nun's decision to abandon the secular world and dedicate her life to the church. Running through all seven commemorations is the idea that they were tempted to enter the secular world. For women in early modern Goa, this meant marriage. All the nuns are described as beautiful and worthy of marriage, but they reject secular love and turn to the Church instead.

44–45: In the first quatrain, Cupid shoots an arrow at Mother Antoca (Mother Antonia de Encarnação) but misses. The arrow is lost, and the bow is rendered useless. The next quatrain completes the story: Cupid's attempt to capture the love of Mother Antonia de Encarnação—that is, Cupid has a human match intended for Mother Antonia—is punishable by death. A decree has been declared (by whom we are not told), and the death-sentence is pronounced. The gallows upon which Cupid is to be hung are readied.[76]

46–47: In the first quatrain, the Master offers Mother Ignaçia de Anunçiação a surangam flower, which was commonly worn in women's hair to enhance their beauty. The manuscript is severely damaged here, and the second quatrain is very hard to read, but it seems that this gift accentuates her beauty.

48–49: The Master praises the beautiful body of Mother Paula de Espírito Santo as she gets ready to bathe. Her body is said to be unique (*singular*) in its beauty. The Cafre then brings scented water for her to add to her bath (this scented water will be used at the end of this section). This is one of the more sensuous poems in the whole manuscript.

50–51: Mother Aninha (Anna da Virgem Maria) is compared to a flower encased in amber. The flower in the amber gives it a gold hue, connoting nobility. In fact, the Master says that amber and nobility, both gold and permanent, confer such beauty and grace.

---

76. The theme of Cupid's love-matching being problematic runs throughout both the *Entrada* and the *Cartepaço*.

Introduction 31

52–53: These two quatrains are very difficult to read, but it seems that Mother Micaella (Mother Michaella da Conçeição) is given a carnation that is fixed in her heart. Mother Michaella must have had a beautiful voice and been the choir master, as the Canarim alludes to her beautiful voice and her ability to teach others.

54–55: The Master points to a painting, which must be a scene of the "carnation of Arrochel," and tells Mother Antonia do Sacramento that her heart is like these flowers in their great affection. The Malavar alludes to the idea that Mother Antonia finds consolation in the choir singing the Divine Office.

56–57: The first quatrain to Mother Antonia de Santa Roza compares her to an orange blossom, a flower that, when crushed, emits a delightful fragrance. Thus, the orange blossom maintains this fragrance. This may indicate that Mother Antonia de Santa Roza was reticent and reserved and that her "fragrance" must be sought out in order to be experienced. The second quatrain is entirely unintelligible.

This section ends with the following stage directions: "Mistress Roza" (*Mestre Roza*) sets a piece of cloth on fire and douses it with the scented water that was brought out in verse 49. Here we have the fire of secular love quenched by the fragrance of the convent life dedicated to their Lord and husband, Jesus Christ.

Song 8, 58–64: [*Becoming Christian: Quatrains to Seven Sisters, Part II*]
Again, stage directions instruct the "seven painted figures" to be brought out, and each sister is once more addressed with a quatrain. This section elaborates on the previous section's theme, further explaining how each nun came to their profession. Some of the themes and metaphors are quite obscure, but the nuns must have been familiar with them.

58: The quatrain to Mother Antoca picks up the Cupid story in quatrains 44–45. This time, we are told that Cupid was successful in shooting Mother Antoca with his arrow of love. But rather than secular love (the arrow that Cupid shot missed her), this arrow created a love for Jesus, and it changed the girl she was into the Sister she is now. Her name, "of the incarnation," thus alludes to this love for the human Jesus.

59: Mother Ignaçia's suranga flower indicates the Holy Trinity's love for her.

60: The manuscript is damaged here, but it seems Mother Paula de Espírito Santo is given a rose, and there is an allusion to the "starry Heavens" (*Ceos estralhado*), which connects her name with the ethereal "Holy Spirit" aspect of the Trinity.

61: Mother Aninha, the nickname for Mother Anna da Virgem Maria, is said to have been transformed by Jesus into a beautiful, and of course virginal, wife.

62: The manuscript is slightly damaged here, so the meaning of the quatrain is not clear. But there seems to be a connection between Mother Michaella da Conçeição and the veneration of the Assumption of Mary. The first line, "*cravos de teu espouzo*," can be taken as either "the nails of your husband"—a reference to his crucifixion—or "the carnations of your husband." In the following verses, *cravos* seems to be carnations, but here, the nails from his crucifixion might make more sense.

63: Mother Antonia gave her heart to Jesus as she contemplated the Passion. During the Passion, Mary cried tears, which turned into carnations.

64: For Mother Antica, the orange blossom is linked to the crucified Christ.

Song 9, 65–66: *Ball in a Cloth*

This short song describes how a ball of fire hovers over a cloth (most likely a reference to the cloth screen upon which the show is cast). The fire does not burn the cloth, nor is the ball consumed by fire. The sisters are once again encouraged to come and see.

Song 10, 67–70: *Balls of Fire*

Now there are multiple balls on fire. They float through the air and pass over a table without touching it.[77]

Song 11, 71–76: [*A Song to Langara Jamgoma and a Recipe*]

A gentleman named Langara Jamgoma enters and performs a lively dance. It is unclear who Langara Jamgoma is, but he is referred to as a "man of distinction," a "friend," and a "guest of the Mother Subprioress." Or, he is the convent

---

77. M. Carmen d'Assa Castel-Branco, "The Presence of Portuguese Baroque in the Poetic Works of the Sisters of Santa Monica in Goa," in *Goa and Portugal: History and Development*, ed. Charles J. Borges, Óscar G. Pereira, and Hannes Stubbe, trans. Charles J. Borges (New Delhi: Xavier Centre of Historical Research, 2000), 254, suggests these balls are covered in animal skin, but it seems more likely that the balls are made of wool (*laia*).

baker, as in the next few verses Langara Samgoma instructs the nuns to bring out the wheat, make the *rulão* cake,[78] fry the eggs, and bring out wine "from the head of Malabar" (*cabeiça de Malavar*). The sisters implore him to hurry and make the "jaggery and coconut" cake so they can have it for supper.

Song 12, 77–81: *The Little Slave Girl's Song*

This song is the culmination of the little slave girl's narrative that has played out in the interludes scattered throughout the first half of the manuscript. As has been seen (pp. 23–26), the *cafrinha* is walking down a road when she meets a priest praying with a group of mourners at a funeral pyre. The *cafrinha* joins the group, and she, or someone in the group (it is unclear), brings out food and drink: a small platter of fried fish coins and a mug of warm *cura*. Perhaps because she is hungry, or perhaps because she realizes that this priest is her way to escape her master, her heart races with joy (it goes *chaçu chaçu*). The *cafrinha*, or someone in the group, is then instructed to praise God and bring more firewood for the cremation fire. A bailiff arrives.

Song 13, 82–85: *Dance of the Kite*

This song provides an etymological explanation as to why the word *mioto*, which means "raptor," also means "thief." Castel-Branco aptly summarizes the scene's opening by stating, "attentive kites hover, hiding their treacherous intentions to capture little chicks under the beauty of their flight."[79] The narrative continues as follows: the song's narrator owns a chicken that hatches fifteen chicks. The kite carries away ten of them, leaving only five behind. The narrator carefully raises the five remaining chicks, but because she is sinful, God sends another kite to steal them. The entire community recites the final line in unison: "the kite thief, my egg, the kite thief" (*milhano miouto, minha ovo, milhano miouto*). Thus, *miouto/mioto* is both a raptor and a colloquial word for thief.

Song 14, 86–165: [*The Community Hymns*]

This section is the centerpiece of the evening celebration. Immediately before it, the narrative of the woeful *cafrinha* comes to its conclusion as the bailiff drags the *cafrinha*, a noose around her neck, offstage, followed by the merchant, thief, and dog. After they all leave, Donna Aldonça enters and declares, "Give me a paper for each!" A paper effigy of each member of the community is brought out, accompanied by two Malavars who sing a "courteous" song. Perhaps the paper effigies are processed to the stage with great pomp. We can imagine this

---

78. A *bolo de rulão*, also called *baath* or *batica*, is a coconut and semolina cake that is traditionally prepared for Christmas in Goa.

79. Castel-Branco, "The Presence of Portuguese Baroque in the Poetic Works of the Sisters of Santa Monica in Goa," 255.

procession in two ways: it could have been a solemn moment meant to honor the members of the community. Or, and we think this is more likely as it fits the spirit of the church traditions of "sacred folly," it could have been a comedic moment meant to parody the daily routines that served to codify the hierarchies within the convent.[80] That is, rather than the actual nuns processing two by two, as they were required to do as they attended the various daily ritual gatherings, the paper effigies would take their place. We can imagine the nuns straining to find their own effigy as it passed through the middle of the garden. The incongruity of it all, the solemn procession for a bunch of paper effigies, would have been captivating.

Once the paper effigies find their way to the front of the garden, the Master held up a heavy iron cup. He announces that he is astonished by its weight. Again, perhaps a comedic moment and a reference to the intensely ritualized lives of the nuns? Nonetheless, this action is followed by the singing of seventy-nine quatrains dedicated to the Father Confessor, the Father Procurator, and every female religious in the convent. Each quatrain, accompanied by the paper effigy of its subject, serves as a small portrait of the individual, capturing the essence of their character, their personality traits, daily habits, or notable achievements. The collective result is a tapestry of the community, and each quatrain is a thread that contributes to the overall composition. This section also served as a light-hearted form of entertainment, even as it held a mirror to the community, thereby strengthening the community's sense of identity and unity. It should be noted that the focus was not on the quality of the poetry itself, and while there are a few quatrains that strike the reader as clever or beautiful, most are pedestrian at best.

Many of the quatrains refer to the constancy, excellence, good behavior, and grace of the nuns. Other commemorations focus on the nun's elegance (*bizarria*) and beauty (*fermoza*). The quatrain to Mother Francisca do Sacramento is a good example here:

121	Francisca do Sacramento	Francisca of the Sacrament
	cuia gala e bizarria	whose refinement and elegance
	ha de vir a ser aumento	will come to enhance
	desta nossa companhia	this company of ours.

---

80. See Max Harris, *Sacred Folly: A New History of the Feast of Fools* (Ithaca: Cornell University Press, 2011) for a thorough reevaluation of the "Feast of Fools." Harris demonstrates that what scholars have understood as the radical tradition of the "Feast of Fools," a Christmastime tradition (often falling on Epiphany itself) of debaucherous excess and misrule that the church adamantly opposed, is rather more aptly considered a day of "sacred folly." This kind of activity—role reversal, absurd performances, and rowdy feasting—certainly occurred, but not in opposition to ecclesiastical authority but rather under its supervision. He also connects this sacred folly to "a broader explosion of amateur dramatic activity" in the early modern period (243).

The nuns are often compared to a flowers: roses, jasmine, lilies, daisies. Still others play upon the nuns' professed name. The quatrain to Mother Clara de Jesus reads:

102	Na Clara se consiste	In Clara resides
	toda lux e claridade	all light and clarity;
	que com Jesus estais sempre	may you always be accompanied
	de luzas acompanhada	by the light of Jesus.

Some nuns chose as their professed name the name of a saint. This is a way to connect with the saint's virtues and strive to emulate their qualities. Mother Maria de São Joachim takes her name so that he will defend her in the same way that St. Joachim, the mother of Mary, defended his own family. Or, in a more suggestive example, Mother Francisca de São José (1715–1776) is commemorated as follows:

111	Francisca hunico estremo	Francisca, one of a kind,
	de São Joseph quis chamar	wanted to be called "of Saint Joseph";
	para com o mesmo nome	she wanted to be known by this very name
	o que he significar	and what it signifies.

Saint Joseph, the foster father of Jesus Christ, is revered in the Christian tradition for his righteousness and obedience. His commitment to work exemplifies the dignity of labor and dedication to one's responsibilities. Alternatively, it may be as straightforward as his example of sexual restraint: St. Joseph is honored by those who take a vow of chastity.

However, a few quatrains give us insight into the nuns beyond describing their constancy, beauty, or good qualities. One sister, Mother Maria dos Gerarguias, is celebrated for her musical ability:

119	Alegreçe todos prezente	Everyone here is pleased
	com muzica e armonia	with music and harmony
	que assiste aqui com nosco	because attending [this festival] with us
	Maria de Gerarguia	is Maria of Gerarguia.

Another, Mother Lionarda de Trindade, is known for her wit:

114	Lionarda de Trindade	Lionarda of the Trinity
	engraçada contento	witty, delightful;
	bem pode repetir ia	we would do well to have another marvel
	venha cá esta protento	such as she come here again.

There are two verses that are biting in their portrayals. Mother Senhorinha de Jesus is parodied for being so fat that she *always* appears to be pregnant:

108	A Jesus troxe Maria	Mary carried Jesus in her womb
	nova mezes em seu ventre	for nine months;
	mais grossa sinhorinha	Senhorinha, who is fatter,
	he de Jesus para sempre	is always "with Jesus."

And Mother Brites de Santa Anna must have been so willing to please that her constant response of "*sim sim* (yes, yes)" was like the annoying, incessant buzz of a mosquito:

126	Brites de Santa Anna	Brites de Santa Anna,
	bem ornado jasmin	well adorned jasmine,
	tão bem simples mosqueta	just like a simple mosquito
	repita todos sim sim	you repeat all the time, yes yes.

Song 15, 166–245: [*Odes to Everyday Objects*]

The stage directions indicate that another batch of paper images is to be brought out, but this time they are not effigies of our priests and nuns but rather representations of Goan objects and other items. These items are presented in no particular order, but they can be categorized in various ways: the maritime world: ship, anchor, fish hook, current; animals: monkey, tiger, mouse, pelican; people and angels: drunkard, Cupid, seraphim and cherubim; religious objects: aspergillum, rosary, cross; abstract principles: *saudade* (longing), *amor e auzençia* (love and loss); religious imagery: heart with roses, weeping heart, burning heart; and many everyday objects: spyglass, sack, spinning wheel, wicker basket, flask, and so on. This section contains exactly the same number of quatrains as the previous one, and due to this symmetry, it is tempting to interpret the quatrains in each section as pairs, but there is no discernible pattern connecting the two sections.[81]

---

81. Although the manuscript does not specify the relationship between these two sections, there are numerous possible explanations for how this portion of the performance unfolded. For example, as I described the *Entrada* to a friend of mine, Lynn Jeffries, a professional puppeteer and a founding member of the innovative theater group Cornerstone, she immediately offered an explanation: "Oh yes, this is something our theater company has done!" What you do is put every paper representation of an object in a big bowl and mix it up, then you bring each member of the community, one at a time, up to the front. You read out their poem aloud before randomly selecting an object from the bowl and reading that poem aloud as well. The juxtapositions created are sometimes fitting and sometimes not, sometimes hilarious and sometimes poignant. The spectacle relies on the evident and obscure connections between the individuals and the objects, which generate juxtapositions that are at times appropriate, amusing, and emotionally resonant. The amusement or sincerity results from the community's close relationship with every individual and object. Audience members are, of course, free to forge their own associations; doing so is a way to both honor the community and inject some humor into it.

However, it is possible that there are hidden connections that we cannot readily discern. Anna Weerasinghe found a possible connection between Sister Mariana de Jesus (v. 117) and the ode to the spyglass (v. 175).

| 117 | You are Manona a pretty Cherubim; you are called "of Jesus," you are a Serafim. | 175 | If you wish to see up close that which vision cannot reach, you can with great confidence rely upon this instrument. |

The connection is not evident in the text, but Weerasinghe uncovered a historical clue from a decade prior:

> According the [1731] visitation records of the then-Archbishop of Goa, Ignácio de Santa Theresa,[82] Sister Mariana had been using the spyglass to "watch from a distance" the comings and goings of one Friar Manuel de Nossa Senhora, an Augustinian monk at the neighboring Monastery of Nossa Senhora da Graça. Under pressure, Sister Mariana confessed that she and Friar Manuel had been exchanging notes and small gifts for the past year; even more damning, one of the notes was recovered rolled up inside an *appam* (a type of fermented pancake, often made with rice flour). The contents of the note were deemed too scandalous to include in the record, but the implication was clear: Sister Mariana, a pristine and virginal bride of Christ, was lusting after a very mortal man.[83]

Sister Mariana de Jesus was punished by the archbishop with "six months of penitent silence and fasting in her cell . . . [and] spyglasses were banned from the convent."[84] Was this connection recognized by the audience? We have no real way of knowing the answer to this, but Weerasinghe's argument is certainly suggestive. Further, the inclusion of the spyglass, which had been banned by the archbishop a

---

Is this what the nuns were up to? We cannot say for certain. However, we do know that there are eighty quatrains in the laudatory section (one introductory quatrain, one quatrain for each of the seventy-seven women, and two quatrains for the Augustinian friars in attendance) and there are eighty objects; paper representations of each nun and each object were present; and this section was the centerpiece of the evening.

82. Ignácio de Santa Teresa, "Sentenças dadas contra algu[m]as Relig[ios]as na vizita de 1731," Archivio Apostolico Vaticano 367, Relationes Dioecesium Goan, fol. 79v–81r. I would like to thank Anna Weerasinghe for these insights and for generously sharing her transcription of this report with me.

83. Anna Weerasinghe, "Sister Mariana's Spyglass: The Unreliable Ghost of Female Desire in a Convent Archive," in https://nursingclio.org/2021/04/06/sister-marianas-spyglass-the-unreliable-ghost-of-female-desire-in-a-convent-archive/, original post April 6, 2021. This post by Weerasinghe connects this incident to larger issues including the deliberate erasure of women's desires from early modern archives and the monitoring of women's sexuality in both the early modern and contemporary worlds.

84. Weerasinghe, "Sister Mariana's Spyglass."

decade earlier, is further evidence that the nuns had effectively overcome his oppressive power and reclaimed the convent as their own.

Song 16, 246–53: [*Hymn to the Beloved*]
    This is a song about the nuns' longing to be with the *escarramão*, or the beloved.[85] Images of love, absence, marriage, and devotion run throughout.

Song 17, 254–58: [*The Two Monkeys*]
    The two monkeys of this song represent the wild, animal nature of secular love. The first quatrain is the voice of the Mónicas, and they declare that God loves us (the Mónicas) and not you (secular love). Secular love, like a monkey, does not want to stay firm but rather continues to jump around. The second quatrain is in the voice of the monkeys, and they describe their wild nature. This verse ends with the refrain that God loves the Mónicas and not the monkeys. The last three quatrains describe how secular love causes one to act in monkey-like foolishness: lovers make silly faces, chatter nonsensically, and are fickle ("run hot and cold"); lovers half-close their eyes as they engage in "ridiculous gestures / revealing [their] vigor," perhaps a reference to the sexual act; lovers arise in the dawn, still hungry, their love unsatisfied. The implication here is that satisfying love comes only from God.

Song 18, 259–63: *The Old Woman's Song*
    This seems to be a well-known local folk song. Each quatrain describes how an honorable old man buys a fancy item of clothing (a hood, a shirt, a jacket, shorts, and shoes), which makes his old wife happily dance and ring a bell (the sound of the bell is voiced as *dadão*). The first three lines are sung by one of the puppets in the troupe, and perhaps the last line is sung in unison by the community as a whole, ending on the resounding *dadão*!

---

85. The choice of the term *escarramão* to refer to Christ as the "Beloved" might seem a bit odd here, as this term usually refers to the seventeenth-century Spanish character Escarramán, who appears in many plays and poems of this era (see Armando Cotarelo y Valledor, *El Teatro de Cervantes: Estudio Crítico*, Madrid: Tip. de la "Revista de Archivos, Bibliotecas, y Museos: 1951: 600–616). Escarramán was a ruffian from Seville, and he is often presented in a romanticized way with an emphasis on his beauty and charisma. How does referring to Christ as *escarramão*, a ruffian or rogue (albeit a beautiful one), fit with the theme of this poem? In Portugal, the stories of Escarramán were converted into a sacred, religious version titled *Romance de Escarramão Convertido al Divino* (*Escarramão Converted to the Divine*), in which Escarramão appears as a defender of the Immaculate Conception (see Teófilo Braga. *Cancioneiro e Romanceiro Geral Portuguez*, vol. 1, Porto: Typografia Lusitana, 1867: 207). Perhaps the Mónicas knew only the adapted, religious version and did not associate *escarramão* with his roguish background.

    There is another, simpler possibility. *Escarramão* can also mean "admirável," "atrativo," or "cativante," all terms denoting a person with a captivating, beautiful character (we would like to thank the anonymous reviewers of the manuscript for this information).

Song 19, 264: *Cantiga*

All but the first line of this song has been crossed out in the manuscript. It seems to be some kind of hybrid or creolized Konkani. It is unclear exactly what the song is about, but most likely it is a song about the harvest (*supa* could refer to a woven basket made of bamboo used to separate wheat from the chaff) or an offering of flowering marigolds (*gonde fulali*).[86] A *chipeti* could refer to a box or gift; perhaps this contains flowers that are set out for the show. While its inclusion is quite suggestive of a local tradition of presenting flowers, its full meaning remains opaque.[87]

Song 20, 265–68: *The Flaming Sword*

This is a song about a magical flaming sword that is designed to kill enemies but does not burn the hand that holds it.

Song 21, 269: [*Farewell*]

After Donna Aldonça makes one last appearance (we are not told what she does), the Master of Ceremonies ends the show with his farewell.

Cartepaço da Muzica

Vignette #2: June 24, 1766 (The Feast of St. John), early evening, Goa, India

The late afternoon sun sinks in the sky over the Real Convento de Santa Mónica. More than sixty nuns, the eponymous Mónicas, sit quietly in the choir, having just finished their prayers. Despite the silence, one can feel the anticipation running through the community; they have been eagerly waiting for this day to come. The hot, dry days of May, with their relentless sun and blistering temperatures, have been replaced by blustery June days as the blue-black rainclouds of the southwesterly monsoon blow in. The monsoon rains arrived a week or two earlier, and since their arrival, the Mónicas have worked diligently in the garden. Their work has been rewarded with a riotous blooming of flowers whose fragrance reaches every corner of the convent, blanketing the community in natural perfumes. A nun moves to the front of the choir, looks at her fellow Mónicas, and sings the refrain of a rondo in the key of G: "Let's go out to the

---

86. *fula* is the Portuguese equivalent of the Indian *phul*, flower. For example, see Osório de Castro's 1906 glossary of Indian words in *A Cinza dos Myrtos: Poemas*, 179.

87. We would like to thank all the suggestions we received from the online "Indo-Portuguese History" group regarding these lines. We culled through the many hints and clues to our inquiry from Radharao Gracias, Ananya Kabir, Sayaji Solokhe, Selma Carvalho, D. Fernandes, Pramod Kolambkar, Richard Afonso, and Luis Francisco Dias.

garden with great zeal, for it is important to celebrate the Festival of St. John!" In unison, the community repeats back the refrain in dulcet tones, "Let's go out to the garden with great zeal, for it is important to celebrate the Festival of St. John!" The nuns now stand, line up, and get ready to descend the staircase, which leads them into the convent garden. Another nun sings forth, "Come without delay, most exquisite flowers, to reverently celebrate the birth of St. John!" Her quatrain is met with the community refrain, "Let's go out to the garden with great zeal, for it is important to celebrate the Festival of St. John!" Another nun sings about the joyous day and how the nuns will sing and dance, united as one community. The refrain rings out. The nuns begin to process to the garden. At the back of the procession are four nuns: the Prioress Mother Francisca do Sacramento, the Subprioress Mother Joanna de Santa Roza, the first Prelate Mother Izabel de Aprezentação, and the second Prelate Mother Britis de Trindade. These four wait in the wings as the rest of the community arranges itself in the garden. Prioress Francisca enters, and a nun welcomes her, singing, "The Rose, just like a Queen, radiates her beauty just like our beloved Prioress in all her beauty strolls." The refrain rings out. She is followed by the entrance of Subprioress Joanna de Santa Rosa, and a nun sings, "The honest Lily delights all in its display, just like our Subprioress who walks with such composure." The refrain rings out. Finally, Mother Izabel de Aprezentação and Mother Britis de Trindade enter. Mother Izabel, we learn, is like a sulena flower, and Mother Britis is like a light that illumines all. With all the black-veiled professed nuns and the white-veiled lay nuns gathered in the garden, they then sing an invitation and are joined by the novices, the postulants, and two Augustinian friars, all of whom are compared to various flowers. The introductory song ends, and the garden is tranquil.

The oil lamps flicker, some sisters light a few small bonfires, and we hear a distant rumble of thunder as the wind picks up. Then Prioress Mother Francisca do Sacramento positions herself in front of all the professed nuns, lay sisters, novices, and postulants (and, of course, the ever-present but invisible God). She looks around at all four cloister verandas, opens her arms, and sings in the key of D, "Everyone, without exception, I want to invite you all today to come and celebrate Saint John's Day!" As the rest of the convent's inhabitants—cooks, servants, and slaves—emerge from their basement quarters and move toward the garden, all the Mónicas join together in a song of invitation: all should come and celebrate with great passion; all should enjoy the bonfires; all should revel in the birth of St.

John the Baptist. Finally, with everyone present, the nuns sing, "All, with not one left out, come to the garden now! For here I want to have a special day."

The evening revelry continues with songs to St. John, to the celestial bodies above, to the prioress, to the subprioress, and to the mothers of the various offices. The nuns sing beautifully; they are obviously well trained. The songs take different forms: some are rondos with the verses in quatrain, others in sextain; others contain seven or eight verses; most are in Portuguese, but four are in Spanish; they are sung in the keys of G, C, and D. Later in the evening, the tone of the songs takes a subtle and unexpected turn. A nun begins to sing the praises of the Augustinian friars who live right next door in the Convento de Nossa Senhora de Graça. This song begins like the previous ones, praising the "Graçianos" for their perfections. But then we hear, "You are called lively, I don't think I am saying anything untoward, because your vigor and perfection should be brought forth. / Passionate lovers, and so discreet, artfully and subtly you know how to steal the heart [of a sister] / You leave us vulnerable, captive without liberty, [so much so] that on the altar of your desire [we are] a willing sacrifice." This causes a stir among the nuns and staff. The song itself artfully does not disclose too much, but everyone understands the subtext: at times, the Augustinian nuns and friars get too close. The next song takes up the theme of love sickness, with Cupid as the protagonist. The wily and mischievous Cupid is responsible for these breaches of virtue: he makes lovers crazy, and they lose all judgment, not being able to tell three from four. He drives lovers to madness. But he pays for his "pagan sins" by being bound and whipped, made to crawl through the streets, and then sentenced to hang. Later in the evening, in another song to Cupid, we learn that he escapes death: the stay is given, and he limps away, a wing broken, his pride in tatters.

These songs all serve to frame the main event of the night: the singing of praises of each and every Augustinian religious woman or girl—professed, lay, novice, postulant—living in the convent. Each woman or girl (postulants could be as young as five years old) steps forward to receive her praise. Most of these verses are simple: they compare the subject to a flower, use clever wordplay to explain their taken religious name, or sometimes comment on an aspect of the subject's personality. The evening ends with a few more songs and a short five-verse farewell. The oil lamps are extinguished, the bonfires are smothered, and everyone heads off to bed to get a few hours of sleep. After all, while this evening's Vespers and Compline have been canceled due to the festival, tomorrow is a new day, and Matins is but a few hours away.

As the title indicates, *Este Cartepaço he da muzica do terceiro ano da Madre Francisca do Sacramento Prioreza do Ano de 176* was written during the third year of Mother Francisca do Sacramento's tenure as prioress, a position she held between 1764 and 1767. As it contains songs to be performed during the feast of the Nativity of St. John the Baptist celebrated on June 24, they must have been composed by Mother Francisca do Sacramento in the first half of 1766. In her analysis of both the *Cartepaço* and the *Entrada*, M. Carmen d'Assa Castel-Branco argues that the Mónicas were influenced by the literary style of seventeenth-century baroque poetry, "which was in vogue in Europe, [and] in Portugal through the influence of the Spanish Baroque, [and] through the models of its conceptualists, Luis de Gongora [*sic*], Quivedo [*sic*], et. al."[88] Indeed, while it is true that the influence of the baroque was fading in most of Europe by the late seventeenth century, this was not so in Portugal. As Jorge Ruedas de las Serna argues, "Portugal was the European country in which Góngora's [baroque] influence was most prolonged and pronounced."[89] Castel-Branco provides a list of baroque "stylistic resources" that the Indo-Portuguese nuns employed, including metaphor, hyperbole, antithesis, paradox, repetition, and elegy, followed by examples of each from both manuscripts. Further, many, but not all, of the songs in the *Cartepaço* are modified rondos, a popular musical form that emerged during the Baroque era and became increasingly popular in the late eighteenth century.[90] Additional influence from the Iberian baroque is seen in the language of the text: four of the twenty-two songs are written in Spanish.

The vast majority of the songs detail the lives, personalities, and occupations of the women religious living in the convent. In addition, there is one song that is specifically dedicated to the Augustinian friars, two songs that investigate the nature of Cupid (the angel of secular love), and one song that assesses the nature of Love itself. Like the *Entrada*, the songs frame a long section in which each nun in the convent is honored with a quatrain. Also like the *Entrada*, the *Cartepaço*'s performance is meant to produce a lively, almost raucous at times, atmosphere. The songs are to be performed in the manner of the *fólia* (*fulia*), a musical and dance

---

88. Castel-Branco, "The Presence of Portuguese Baroque in the Poetic Works of the Sisters of Santa Monica in Goa," 249.

89. Jorge A. Ruedas de la Serna, "Góngora in Spanish American Poetry, Góngora in Luso-Brazilian Poetry: Critical Parallels," in *Baroque New Worlds: Representation, Transculturation, Counterconquest*, trans. Patrick Blaine (Durham, NC: Duke University Press, 2010), 344.

90. Malcolm S. Cole, "Rondo," in *The New Grove Dictionary of Music and Musicians*, ed. Stanley Sadie and John Tyrrell, 2nd ed. (New York: Grove, 2001).

form that originated in Portugal.[91] The *fólia* is a short, formulaic verse of four lines with eight syllables each,[92] and it is accompanied by a "a particular boisterous (*de mucho ruido*) Portuguese dance, resulting from many participants dancing (*de ir muchas figuras á pie*) with rattles and other instruments."[93] Further, the images of the nuns as flowers are scattered throughout the *Cartepaço*, and the blooming of these flowers due to the monsoon rains is compared to the explosion of fireworks, both producing riotous colors and sweet fragrances to entertain the community.[94]

Song 1, 1–15: *Cantiga para hir a horta*

The first song, a rondo, is sung as the nuns move from the interior of the convent toward the central garden to start the celebration of the Feast of St. John the Baptist. It introduces the four convent leaders (Prioress Francisca do Sacremanto, Subprioress Joanna de Santa Rosa, First Prelate Mother Izabel de Aprezentação, and Second Prelate Mother Britis de Trindade), the novices, the postulants, the lay sisters, and lastly, the Augustinian friars. The "most exquisite flowers" (v. 2) are the sisters themselves, and the floresta (v. 3) is the "flower-garden" at the center of the convent.[95] This central garden, known as "the Valley of the Lilies,"[96] was

---

91. The fólia is explicitly mentioned once in the *Entrada* (v. 11) and four times in the *Cartepaço* (vv. 4, 118, 141, and 182). Cotarelo y Mori, *Colección de Entremeses*, ccxlv, provides a number of theories on the origins of the fólia, but he and others seem to favor Portugal.

92. See Richard Hudson, "The 'Folia' Dance and the 'Folia' Formula in 17th Century Guitar Music," *Musica Disciplina* 25 (1971): 199–221; and Richard Hudson, *The Folia, the Saraband, the Passacaglia, and the Chaconne: The Historical Evolution of Four Forms That Originated in Music for the Five-Course Spanish Guitar* (Rome: American Institute of Musicology, 1982), xi.

93. Cotarelo y Mori, *Colección de Entremeses*, ccxlv, cites the great Spanish lexicographer Sebastián Covarrubias's 1611 *Tesoro de la Lengua Castellana o Española*, "[f]ólia es una cierta danza portuguesa de mucho ruido; porque resulta de ir muchas figuras á pie con sonajas y otros instrumentos."

94. Flowers mentioned in the text include: roza (rose), lirio (lily), sulena, mistiça, clovina, angelica, giroçol (sunflower), espadana (cattail), madresilva (honeysuckle), jasmin (jasmine), açusena, dedia, and bonina (daisy), all of which must have been growing in the convent garden.

95. The convention of ascribing moral qualities to flowers and birds is found in the late-seventeenth and early-eighteenth-century works of the Clarissa Sister Maria do Céu (1658–1753), who wrote from the Convento de Nossa Senhora da Piedade da Esperança de Lisboa. Although her *Metáforas das Flores* was only posthumously published in 1873, her popular *Aves Ilustrada: Avisos para Server as Religiosas os seus Officios dos Mosteiros*, was published in 1734. For excerpts of Sister Maria do Céu's work, see Vanda Anastácio, ed., *Uma Antologia Improvável: A Escrita das Mulheres, Séculos XVI a XVIII* (Lisboa: Relógio D'Água Editores, 2013): 365–71.

96. The name, "The Valley of Lilies," was given to the garden by Fr. Diogo de Santa Anna in part III of his 1628 description of the convent, "Regimento do Culto Divino é Observancias deste Insigne Mosteiro de Nossa Senhora Madre Santa Monica de Goa, feito em conformidada da Sagrada Constituição do mesmo Mosteiro & quasi como, em, interpretação do religioso instituto delle, segundo o clima da terra & a possibilidade dos sogeitos que o professou," 1627, 167r.–275v., Biblioteca Pública de Évora, G.R. arm. III e IV, Nº 24. Part III was reprinted as "O Mosteiro de Santa Monica de Goa,"

divided into 128 flower beds, and the flowers it produced were used to decorate the convent's altars, adorning them with beauty and fragrance.

Song 2, 16–19: *Convida a Reverendissima Madre Prioreza as religiosas para hir a horta*

This song, a rondo consisting of a refrain and three verses all in quatrain, is an invitation from the Prioress to the whole community to come to the garden and celebrate the Festival of St. John. The number of community members—servants, cooks, slaves, and others—would have numbered more than two hundred.

Song 3, 20–26: *Cantigas a São João*

In this rondo, this time with a refrain and six verses all in quatrain, the heavens (the celestial bodies) also show their praise of St. John by shining brightly and dancing. The song ends by stating that the convent itself is the place where St. John is most honored.

Song 4, 27–30: *Outra cantiga a Madre*

The first of three rondos written in Spanish all with the same structure: a refrain in quatrain followed by three sextains. In this first rondo, Prioress Francisca do Sacramento is honored.

Song 5, 31–34: *Cantiga a Madre Suprioreza*

The second rondo in Spanish honors the Subprioress Mother Joanna de Santa Rosa.

Song 6, 35–38: *Cantiga para o Santo*

The last in the series of three rondos written in Spanish. This song is dedicated to St. John the Baptist himself. Interestingly, like the Mónicas themselves, St. John is compared to a flower "giving of fragrant scents" (v. 38).

Song 7, 39–46: *Cantiga a Madre Prioreza*

The songbook returns to Portuguese, and this song honors Prioress Francisca do Sacramento. Her ideas shine more brightly than the sun's rays, and her eloquence rivals that of Homer and Cicero. Whether this means the nuns actually read ancient Greek histories and epics or that they only knew about them, we do

---

O Chronista de Tissuary 1, no. 8 (Agosto) (1866): 215–19. Diogo de Santa Anna's description of the flower garden is as follows:

> All the four choirs of this floor it will collectively be called the *Lower Choir*, and the middle of all of it [shall be called] the *Valley of the Lilies*, and the flower beds, *Flower Beds of the Lilies*, and the walkways, the *Streets of the Lilies*, and the well house, *Fountain of the Lilies*, and its well, *Fountain of the Savior*. (217)

not know. But the song ends with the nuns declaring that the prioress has defeated these two by having greater wisdom and learning.

Song 8, 47–50: *Cantiga para Madre Supriorez*a

A short rondo in Portuguese (refrain and verses in quatrain) that honors the Subprioress.

Song 9, 51–82: *Cantiga para as Madres Ofiçiaes*

A long song made up of quatrains that honor fourteen nuns who hold important offices, including members of the convent council, gatekeeper, manager of the granary, mistress of the works, sacristan, manager of the garden, vicar of the choir, manager of the laundry, teacher of the novices, teacher of the postulants, mistress of the novices, mistress of the girls (postulants), and provisioner. The verses dedicated to Mother Senhorinha de Jesus are notable as they contain an allusion to her love of food, just as the *Entrada* (v. 108) does:

58	Convem louvar a esta	It is fitting to praise the
	Madre Mestra das Obras	Mother Mistress of Works
	venha colher desta festa	who has come to gather from this feast
	nas abundançias sobras	the abundant leftovers.

Song 10, 83–85: *Cantiga para Madre Escrivam*

This short rondo, consisting of a refrain and two verses in quatrain, honors the convent Scribe.

Song 11, 86–88: *as Madres Depozitarias*

This rondo is in Spanish and consists of a refrain in quatrain followed by two sextains, mirroring the structure of songs 4–6. This song honors the two keepers of the depository.

Song 12, 89–102: *Cantiga dos Padres*

This song is dedicated to the Graçianos, the Augustinian priests who inhabit the Convent of Nossa Senhora de Graça, located just across the street from the Mónicas' convent. They are described as "most beautiful," "storehouses of perfection," and more wonderful than angels. They are compared to gold and other gemstones. In verses 95–96, the poetess declares that she will not say anything inappropriate, but then proceeds to call them "passionate lovers" who "know how to steal the heart." As Anna Weerasinghe writes, "while these lyrics do not necessarily refer to actual love affairs—highly emotional, even erotic language is typical of Baroque poetry—they illustrate a close relationship between the Sisters of Santa Mónica and their Augustinian neighbors."[97]

97. Anna Weerasinghe, "Sister Mariana's Spyglass."

Song 13, 103–10: *Cantiga de Cupido*

This song cautions the sisters against the destructive nature of Cupid's love, or secular love. The first quatrain describes the disorienting effects of such love, driving one mad and creating confusion. Following this first quatrain, what appears to be a stage direction indicates that one should "take her from there [and] send her over here." Without additional context, the meaning is obscure, but it may refer to the process of bringing a lovestruck woman abandoned in one of the Recolhimentos to the convent and educating her in the religious life. Or, it could be something performed during the festival, such as a directive for the poem's subject to move from one location to another. Regardless, the song continues, alternating between addressing the unfortunate lovestruck woman and describing Cupid. The victim of Cupid's arrows is clearly mad: her emotions quickly shift from passion to rage, she loses her sense of reason, and she transforms into a madwoman, weeping then laughing, singing then shrieking. However, Cupid also meets an unfortunate end. After mocking his victims, he becomes a prisoner: his wings are broken, his broken bow no longer shoots arrows, he stumbles through the streets in despair, and he ends up with shackles on his feet. The song leaves us in suspense regarding the madwoman's and Cupid's fates. It is resolved many pages later in song #17.

Song 14, 111–14: *Outra Cantiga*

A short song praising Mother Barbora, the nun responsible for providing the lavish meal.

Song 15, 115–88: *Cantiga de Comunidade*

This section, the centerpiece of the celebration mirroring the Community Hymns from the *Entrada*, contains eighty-two quatrains, each one dedicated to a female religious in the community: thirty-six nuns of the black veil, six novices and/or postulants, and forty nuns of the white veil. The nineteen officeholders are not included in this section as they received their honors earlier.[98] There were sixteen nuns alive both in 1740 (the date of composition of the *Entrada*) and in 1766 (the date of composition of the *Cartepaço*), all of whom appear in both manuscripts except for one: Mariana de Jesus (professed 1717, died 1770), who does not receive a quatrain in the *Cartepaço*. Mother Mariana de Jesus was the very nun who was punished by Archbishop Ignácio de Santa Teresa in 1721 for passing love notes and sweetmeats with a particular Augustinian friar,[99] so perhaps this behavior was repeated at a later date and she was not considered a full member of the community anymore? If this was so, why was she not purged from the *Book*

---

98. There were thus ninety-five professed nuns, fifty-five choir nuns and forty lay nuns, and six novices and postulants in the convent.

99. See in this introduction, pp. 37–38.

of Professions, as it is recorded in that book that she died as a nun in 1770? There are no further hints as to the status of Mother Mariana de Jesus, so the answers to these questions remain unknown.

The overall tone and purpose of these quatrains are the same as those in the *Entrada*. Each quatrain in this section acts as a thread that weaves together a tapestry of the community, reflecting the individual's character, traits, habits, and achievements, fostering a lighthearted entertainment that reinforces the community's identity and unity.

(--), 189–90: [*Song to the Nurse*]

Verses 189 and 190 are set apart from both the preceding verses by the insertion of two crosses and the succeeding verses by the insertion of a large space on the manuscript page. The most likely explanation is that whoever penned this copy of the manuscript left these two verses out of song #9 *Cantiga para as Madres Ofiçiaes*, realized the mistake, and inserted them here. The verses praise the nurse (*enfermeira*) for her skill in healing the sick.

(--), 191–96: [*Farewell*]

This song ends the evening celebrations, expressing the hope that the prioress has been pleased by the festivities. The final verse (v. 196) uses similar language to that for the farewell in the *Entrada* (v. 269).

*The manuscript does not end here, and a further seven songs are provided.

Song 16, 197–200: *Cantiga de Amor*

The "Song of Love," a song in four sextains, warns us of the fickle nature of secular love. The poet asks the Beloved to forgive her unruly heart: love's passion leads to suffering, the offense of ingratitude, and unnecessary troubles. However, the identity of this Beloved is ambiguous: certainly, this song can be read as a love song to the Lord, but it could also be read as a meditation on the vicissitudes of love in general.

Song 17, 201–12: *Cantiga de Cupido*

This song continues the story begun in song #13, the earlier *Cantiga de Cupido*, where Cupid was unceremoniously dragged through the streets and shackled. At the beginning of this song, Cupid's hands and feet are still bound, now with a cord, and a proclamation against him is read aloud. We then get more details into his punishment: his eye has been plucked out, his wings have been cut off, his bow has been broken, he has been whipped as he was forced to crawl through the city streets, and he has been beaten. The proclamation/decree calls for his death by hanging, and a noose is put around his neck. But he is saved by the king, who stops the execution. Cupid escapes death, but he is left to live a miserable life.

Song 18, 213–19: *Cantiga da Madre Suprioreiza*
A song honoring the Subprioress, Sister Joanna de Santa Rosa, for her organization of the Festival of St. John.

The next three songs, all eight quatrains long, form a unit. They honor three sisters who, at first reading, do not seem to hold any special significance in the convent. They are not among the four leaders of the convent, nor are they among the longest professed nuns in the convent. Rather, they are singled out for their financial support for the festival.

Song 19, 220–27: *Cantiga da Madre Ignaçia*
This is a song of thanks to Sister Mother Ignaçia de Encarnação, the mistress of the postulants honored in verses 73–74. The poet suggests that Mother Ignaçia de Encarnação, or her family, provided extra funds for the feast:

223	Sem reparar nos dispendios	With no regard for expense
	em tenpo de tanta pobre	in a time of such poverty,
	fiz estes hum recreijo	you have put on an event
	mostrates vossa grandeiza	that demonstrates your greatness.

Song 20, 228–35: *Cantiga de Madre Bibiana*
Similar to the previous song, Mother Bibiana de São Miguel is praised for overcoming the poverty of the convent to put on this feast:

231	Em tempo de tanta penuria	At a time of such penury
	esta grandeza quizestes fazer	you wanted to make this great [feast] happen
	sem repararinos gastos	taking no notice of the expense
	que nelle havia de ter	that would be incurred.

Song 21, 236–43: *Cantiga de Madre Barbora*
And in the final song of this triad, Mother Barbora de Jesus Maria is also honored for providing funds for the meal:

239	Em tenso de tanta pobreza	Under the stress of such poverty,
	quis mostrar generoza	she wanted to show generosity;
	dan ao hum jantar	she put on a dinner
	tão rica e grandioza	so bountiful and grandiose.

Song 22, 244–47: *Cantiga a Madre Prioreza*
This short, four-verse song is dedicated to the prioress. Its purpose is linked to the last two lines:

247   ...
  Jannona e Clarinha desvelada Jannona and Clarinha unveiled
  e bem lhes podeis perdoar you can surely forgive them.

The diminutives Jannona and Clarinha might refer to the young girls Joanna do Nascimento and Joaquina de Madre de Deus, who in 1766 were both novices. Perhaps these two girls, preparing to take on full profession, had broken some of the convent's rules. This poem is asking the prioress to forgive them and allow them to profess, which they both do.

Index to Songs

  The manuscript ends with an index to the songs. Each song is identified by its first few words, and then that is followed by the key in which it is to be sung: *gesolreut* (G), *delasolreut* (D), or *çesolfaut* (C).[100] The index does not match the manuscript exactly, as it lists only twenty of the twenty-two songs, and another song is listed out of order.

A Note on the Translations

Translation is a difficult task, and translating song lyrics only adds to the complexity. Our translations do not attempt to creatively reproduce the rhymes and cadences of poetry and song. We believe that doing so would result in our voices replacing those of the Mónicas. At times, this results in infelicitous translations; however, we hope that the reader will consult the Portuguese original to get a sense of its musicality. Even with this conservative translation strategy, we had to make numerous decisions. The Mónicas subordinated proper spelling and grammar to the demands of rhyme and cadence, forcing us to contend with inconsistencies in just about every verse. They used particular vocabulary and turns of phrases that partook of an eighteenth-century Indo-Portuguese milieu that we could not always access. We include explanatory notes only when we believe our choices may be of interest to the reader.

  The physical condition of the manuscripts added another layer of complexity to the task. The *Entrada* was hastily copied in simple black ink on undecorated pages held together at its "spine" by string.[101] It has undergone numerous revisions

---

100. This musical notation comes from Latin. The first letter is the key in which the song is to be sung, G, C, or D, and it is followed by the set of syllables—do (or ut), re, mi, fa, sol, la, si—to which the song is sung, see *Oxford English Dictionary* entry on "gesolreut."

101. The manuscript was copied in 1766 at the same time that the *Cartepaço* was written. There is a "cover page" to the *Entrada* upon which two names are written in the same simple black ink: *Fr. Jozé de St.º G.* and *M.ᵉ Fran.ᶜᵃ de Sacram.ᵗᵒ*:

  (1) *Fr. Jozé de St.º G*.: Fr. Jozé de S. Guilherme, Prior of the Convento de Nossa Senhora da

throughout its history, and several passages of text have been crossed out, revised, and even covered over and replaced with glued scraps of paper.¹⁰² In addition, the manuscript has seen better days: significant portions of the text are illegible due to worm damage and smudged or runny ink. The *Cartepaço* is in comparatively better condition. Only a few words are obscured by worm damage, and the main text is neatly written in black ink. Each page has an intricate border decoration of red triangles with a green dot in the middle. The title page has a few abstract designs and a crude drawing of the Lamb of God holding the Primatial Staff with a Resurrection banner emblazoned with a cross. There are also a few illuminated initials scattered throughout. In working with both manuscripts, we encountered occasions when we were sufficiently assured to provide the missing text; however, there were also situations when we deemed it prudent not to. We mark these instances with asterisks (*) to indicate that we did not attempt to supply the missing text, or with a question mark surrounded by square brackets [?] to indicate that we attempted an emendation but were uncertain of its accuracy.

Lastly, we have standardized the spellings of names in the manuscripts. Due to illegibility or scribal errors, names are often spelled inconsistently within the texts. Additionally, modern spellings frequently differ from those found in the manuscripts. We have addressed these variations by adopting the most common form when multiple spellings exist in the source material, and by retaining original forms when they differ from modern conventions. For instance, the modern Portuguese name "Isabel" appears as both "Izabel" and "Isabel" in the manuscripts. Since 'Izabel' is more prevalent, we have used it consistently throughout our work. Conversely, where manuscript spellings differ from modern conventions, as with

---

Graça from May 18, 1766 to November 18, 1768; see Fr. Manuel da Ave-Maria, "Manual Eremítico da Congregação da Índia Oriental dos Eremitas de Nosso Padre Santo Agostinho," in *Documentação para a História da Missões do Padroado Portugués do Oriente*, ed. Antonio da Silva Rego, vol. 11 (Lisboa: Fundação Oriente: Comissão nacional para as Comemorações dos Descobrimentos Portugueses, 1954), 114.

(2) M.ᵉ Fran.ᶜᵃ de Sacram.to: Mother Francisca do Sacramento, prioress of the convent from February 9, 1764 to February 9, 1767 (see *Book of Elections*, 111; she actually began her governance two weeks earlier as the Vigaria Prioressa, the unelected prioress elevated to the position upon the death of Prioress Mother Sister Luiza da May de Deos on January 24, 1764).

102. After the text of *Entrada* ends, there are two more pages. Part of one page is missing, and the text that remains is crossed out and mostly illegible. However, the title on the first page is legible, and it tantalizingly reads "Chacotes." A chacote is a vulgar song, as Victor Coelho, "Music in New Worlds," in *The Cambridge History of Seventeenth-Century Music*, ed. Tim Carter and John Butt (Cambridge: Cambridge University Press, 2005), 103–4, writes: "In 1591, Fr. Nuno Rodrigues wrote him [the Jesuit General of the Sociey of Jesus Claudio Acquaviva] a letter highly critical of an instance when instrumental music and 'cantigas' had been performed at the Saturday morning service at the college, including 'other vulgarities, which in Portuguese is called *chacota*.'" The letter is reprinted in Josef S. J. Wicki, *Documenta Indica: Missiones Orientales* (Rome: Institum Historicum Societatis Iesu, 1948–1988), 15:715–23.

"Anunçiação" in the source material (modern spelling: "Anunciação"), we've preserved the original form. This approach maintains fidelity to the original texts while providing consistency for readers.

Figure 1. Holy Water Font and Sprinkler. Provenance: Donation of Mr R. Roy, Mumbai. Image Credits: Antonio Cunha under the commission of the Calouste Gulbenkian Foundation. ©Museum of Christian Art, Goa.

Figure 2. Incense Boat. Provenance: Old Goa, Basilica of Bom Jesus. Image Credits: Antonio Cunha under the commission of the Calouste Gulbenkian Foundation. ©Museum of Christian Art, Goa.

Figure 3. Angel Gabriel. Provenance: Old Goa, Convent of Santa Monica. Image Credits: Antonio Cunha under the commission of the Calouste Gulbenkian Foundation. ©Museum of Christian Art, Goa.

Figure 4. Statue of St. John the Baptist. Provenance: Old Goa, Church of Santa Monica. Image Credit: Clive Figueiredo. ©Museum of Christian Art, Goa. The inscription reads SIOAOMB: S[ÃO] IOÃO M[ÁRTIR] B[ATISTA], "St. John the Baptist, Martyr."

Figure 5. Chalice and Paten. Provenance: Old Goa, Basilica of Bom Jesus. Image Credits: Antonio Cunha under the commission of the Calouste Gulbenkian Foundation. ©Museum of Christian Art, Goa.

Entrada de Bonifrate para Festa dos Reis

1 recto

	Entrada de Bonifrate para Festa dos Reis	**The Arrival of the Puppets for the Feast of the Kings**
	Sai Mestre Malavar Caneri Cafre	*Enter*[1] *the Master, the Malavar, the Canarim, the Cafre.*[2]
1	Mestre	Master
	Boas noites de Feliçidades tenha Senhora Prioreiza	May the Senhora[3] Prioress have a fine evening filled with joy.
2	Malavar	Malavar
	E toda real nobreza desta Santa Comunidade	And also all the Royal Nobility of this Holy Community.

---

1. Early modern Iberian dramatists used the verb *sair* (Spanish: *salir*) to indicate that the performer "leaves" the offstage wings and comes out, or "enters," onstage. The *Entrada* uses both *sai* and *entra* to indicate a character has joined the action.

2. The Malavar represents a native of the Malabar coast. Canarim is a derogatory term for a native Goan. The Cafre represents an African slave. See introduction, pp. 21–22.

3. The translation of the conventions used for titles of address is always tricky. What sounds natural in one language sounds quite peculiar in another. Therefore, the translation of Senhora Prioreza" as "Lady Prioress" sounds a bit off. In fact, "Senhora" and "Senhor" are terms well known in English as titles of respect; therefore, we have left the Portuguese "Senhora" and "Senhor" untranslated when referring to a person. When "Senhora" and "Senhor" are used to address Mary, Jesus, and God, however, we translate them as Lady and Lord, as in English titles such as "Our Lady of Guadalupe" and addressing God as "Lord." For a discussion of the difficulty in translating Portuguese titles of address, see Malcom Coulthard, "Translation: Theory and Practice," in *Theoretical Issues and Practical Cases in Portuguese English Translations*, ed. Patricia Anne Odber de Baubeta and Malcom Coulthard, 12–13 (Lewiston: Edwin Mellen Press, 1996).

58 Entrada de Bonifrate para Festa dos Reis

3 Caneri   Canarim

Senhoras para assestir   Senhoras, we have come in order
nesta festa viemos   to participate in the festival.
o bonifrate fareimos   We shall perform a puppet show
para em tudo vos servir   to suit you all.

4 Mestre   Master

De Madre Prioressa   We have all been invited
todos somos convidados   by the Mother Prioress[4]
para recrear a Vossa Reveren-   to entertain Your Reverence,[5]
dissima   and we have come with great pleasure.
viemos com muito agrado

5 Caneri   Canarim

Eu para minha Senhor   I have also come
tambem ia vi iuda   to serve my Lord,
para fazer su gosto   and in order to do his bidding [to please him],
baila tagei canta   I shall dance, play instruments, and sing.

6 Para mi ia pidi rugar   For my part, I have already prayed
para eu graça fazei   that I may entertain
para qui tudo Madre Mestre   all the Mothers;
para mi grande bem querei   I wish [them all] to have a good time.[6]

7 Cafre   Cafre

O Canari mintirouzo   O dishonest Caneri,
Aqui tanta mintira parar   Stop with such lies here and now!
vosso ia nesta festa   You have come to this festival
serião para rebentar   only to cause trouble.[7]

---

4. The original manuscript reads "S̶u̶b̶prioressa."

5. The Padre Confessor, an Augustinian friar from the neighboring Convento de Graça.

6. In these two verses, the Canarim attempts to enhance his reputation in the eyes of the Prioress and the Prior.

7. Here, the Cafre is playing on the word *rebentar* (*arrebentar*). The first, more common, meaning of *rebentão* is related to flowers: to burst forth, or to flower, from *arrebentar* (see *Vocabulario Portuguez*, 1:552). Its second meaning relates to Satan, gentiles, and wine; it means to flourish but in a negative

8	Mestre	Master

Ora Senhores meus compan-   Now, Senhores, my friends,
heiros   Stop this bickering already!
Sesse logo a porfiar   Take up your instruments,
toma seus intrumentos   and cry out the revelries.
e corriesa a fuliar

assenta todos   everyone sits down

9	Mestre	Master

Ora saia saia   Now, settle down, settle down,[8]
Lindos chicoteiros   lovely jokesters;[9]
Cantarei com vosco   I will sing with you
este noita inteiro   throughout the night!

1 verso

10	Todas	All

Esta noita inteiro   Throughout this
de muita alegria   joyful night,
apostai com nosco   join with us
cantar á porfia[10]   in singing our hearts out.

---

sense (*Supplemento ao Vocabulario Portuguez*, pt. 2:73). We interpret this phrase as meaning "to cause trouble."

8. *saia*: "so be it" or "come, come." The Master is saying, "Let's stop arguing and move on with the evening." In other words, the Canarim and the Cafre are competing to be the most deferential to the Master, and the Master is telling them that they need not compete because she will sing with them both.

9. *chicoteiros* (*chacoteiros*): o que canta chacotas [one who sings *chacotas*] (*Diccionario da Lingua Portugueza*, 1:260); *chacotas*: vulgarities (see introduction, p. 50, n. 102, or less forcefully, "fazer trovas, burlescas, e satíricas [to perform folk songs, burlesques/comedies/farces, and satires]" (*Dicionário Priberam*).

10. *porfia*: "com emulação desejo de fazer alguem huma causa melhor que outra [trying to outdo one another while copying each other]" (*Vocabulario Portuguez*, 6:620).

    Here is an example of its usage from a traditional song from Léon:

Canta, compañero, canta,   Sing, my friend, sing
cantaremos a porfía,   We will sing our hearts out,
tú le cantas a tu novia   You sing to your girlfriend
yo le cantaré a la mía.   I'll sing to mine.

	Baila o anel	The Dance of the Ring
11	Mestre	Master
	Tocai companheiros fazei a fulia que meu anel quer bailar neste dia	Play, my friends, and perform the fólia,[11] for my ring wants to dance today.
12	Malavar	Malavar
	Vinde Madres minhas vinde ver prinçeizas bailar o anel com tanta destreiza	Come, my Mothers, come see, Princesses, the ring that dances with such dexterity.[12]
13	Caneri	Canarim
	Veide bem Senhoras esta sutileiza anel de tambaque bailar nesta meiza	Look closely, Mothers, at the subtlety with which the brass ring[13] dances on this table.
14	Cafre	Cafre
	Esta anel deive ser mui estimado tendo lhe no deido com muito cuidado	This ring ought to be greatly prized; put it on your finger after much thought.[14]
	Parte sete papeis pintado	Bring out Seven painted paper [figures][15]

11. *fulia*: a raucous form of song and dance; see introduction, p. 43, n. 92.

12. *destreiza* → *destreza*, "a fazer com agilidade e perfeção . . . dexteritas [with agility and perfection . . . dexterity]," (*Vocabulario Portugu*ez, 3:177).

13. *tambaque*: alloy of copper and zinc; tombak, brass (*Glossário Luso-Asiático*, 2:346).

14. The ring here is a wedding band. The nuns are asked to carefully consider their vows to become "brides of Christ."

15. *parte sete papeis pintado*: These must be painted (*pintado*) paper (*papeis*) likenesses of the seven individuals addressed in the following fourteen quatrains: Confessor, Procurator, Prioress, Subprioress, Sister Emerençiana, Sister Bitona, and Sister Izabel de Madre de Deus. They are "set out" (*partir* has

15	Mestre	Master
		[Addressing the paper figure of the]
	Padre Confessor	Father Confessor
	Aguia com coroa	O Father Confessor,
	insigne real	I want to give to you
	Padre Confessor	a royal symbol:
	eu vos quero dar	an eagle with a crown.[16]
16	Malavar	Malavar
	Anda remotado	Your feelings
	os vossos sentidos	have risen high;
	como esta aguia	like this eagle,
	tens o çeo subido	you have reached the Heavens above.
17	Mestre	Master
	Padre Procurador	Father Procurator
	Por bello planeita	I give you this sun,
	vos dou este sol	such a beautiful planet,
	sendo que vos sois	since you are
	o melhor farol	the brightest beacon.[17]

---

the sense of establish, set out; a synonym is *establecer*) or "brought out" one at a time, and the puppets sing two quatrains to each figure.

16. *aguia com coroa*: This is the emblem of the Habsburg dynasty: an eagle with a crown. Unless it is functioning simply as a symbol of sovereignty, it is odd that this is the symbol and not that of the Braganças.

17. Since there is only one other print publication that analyzes the *Entrada* and the *Cartepaço* (Castel-Branco's 2000 article translated by Charles J. Borges, SJ), in these notes we have included Borges's translations for comparison with our own. Their inclusion is in no way intended as a criticism; rather, it provides the reader with an alternative interpretation of these extremely challenging quatrains.

> For the beautiful planet
> I give you this Sun
> For you are
> The best lighthouse.
>> (Borges translation in M. Carmen d'Assa Castel-Branco, "The Presence of Portuguese Baroque in the Poetic Works of the Sisters of Santa Monica in Goa," in *Goa and Portugal: History and Development*, ed. Charles J. Borges, Óscar G. Pereira, and Hannes Stubbe, trans.

18	Caneri	Canarim

Este sol dorado	This golden sun,
Padre Procurador	Father Procurator,
a vossa vista	pales in comparison
perde seu valor	to the sight of you.

19	Mestre	Master

Madre Prioressa   Mother Prioress
Mother Catharina do Sacramento: 1689–1743

Palma e coroa	I give you this martyr's crown,[18]
Senhora Prellada	Madame Prelate,

2 recto

vos dou ** contento	content [to know]
por seres de vos amada	that you will adore it.

20	Cafre	Cafre

As vossas vertudes	Your virtues
e fama pregoa	and fame are preached [far and wide];
com rezão vos coube	it is natural that this martyr's crown
a palma e coroa	fits you perfectly.

21	Mestre	Master

Madre Subprioreiza   Mother Subprioress
Mother Anna de Jesus: 1698–1750

So vos mereçeis	Only you are worthy
perolas que a qui vão	of these pearls [I put before you],
com vos ia tres são	three of which are yours,
se as contas fazeis	should you count them.[19]

Charles J. Borges, 252 [New Delhi: Xavier Centre of Historical Research, 2000])
18. *palma e coroa*: a symbol of victory over death.
19. *fazer contas*: to do arithmetic, to do sums, to count.

22	Malavar	Malavar

        Perolas sem valimento
        roza nacarada
        sois toda engraçada
        e bello protanto

        The pearls, pale
        pink, are worthless.
        You, however, are utterly delightful
        and beautiful as well.

23   Mestre   Master

        Madre Mareçiana

        [Addressing] Mother Mareçiana
            Mother Emerençiana de Santa Maria: 1689–1743

        Foi meu intento
        coroar vos para Rainha
        esta de espinhos
        será do vosso contento

        It was my intention
        to crown you queen;
        [but] you will have to be content
        with this crown of thorns.

24   Caneri   Canarim

        No teu coração ditouzo
        esta prenda guardai
        e sempre venerai
        como do esposo

        Keep this gift
        in your blissful heart
        and revere it always,
        as if it were your spouse's.[20]

25   Mestre   Master

        Madre Bitona

        [Addressing] Mother Bitona
            Mother Bitona do Sacramento: 1690–1757

        Açucena he flor
        que esplica pureiza
        nella tão bem denota
        a vossa singileiza

        The azucena[21] is a flower
        that signifies purity;
        it also denotes
        your innocence.

---

20. *esposo*: the spouse is Christ.
21. *açucena*: the azucena flower, also called the garden lily.

64 Entrada de Bonifrate para Festa dos Reis

26   Cafre   Cafre

      Esta flor coube   This flower is worthy
      a vossa pessoa   of your person;
      estimai Senhora   Appreciate, Senhora,
      que he couza bom   that this is a good thing.

27   Mestre   Master

      Madre Izabel de Madre de Deus   [Addressing] Mother Izabel de Madre de Deus
                                             Mother Izabel de Madre de Deus:
                                             1691–1744

      Venos por fermosa   Venus goes in search of
      vos veio buscar   your beauty;
      **** graçiosa   you are all the more unique
      sois mais simgular   [for being so] graceful.

28   Anda esta mulher   This woman goes about
      por vos perdida   lost in you [Christ];
      promete vos servir   she promises to serve you
      toda a sua vida   her entire life.[22]

      Fogo na purçula   A fire starts in the theater box[23]

---

22. This woman
    Mad about you,
    Promises to serve you
    For her whole life long.
        (Borges translation in Castel-Branco, "The Presence of Portuguese Baroque in the Poetic Works of the Sisters of Santa Monica in Goa," 256)

23. *purçula*: a box at the opera or theater, also known as *a risa de teatro*.

29	Mestre	Master

    A agoa e fogo   Water and fire,
    que contrarias são   what opposites they are—
    ambos se unirão   the two of them unite
    nesta ocasião   on this occasion.[24]

30   Malavar   Malavar

2 verso

    Sendo tão contrario   They are such opposites,
    como he sabido   as is well-known;
    assista na festa   [but] see them here at this festival,
    ambos mui unidos   united as one.

31   Caneri   Canarim

    Fogo na agoa   The fire is in water
    sem ser apagado   without being quenched—
    eu nunca tal vi   I have never seen such a thing.
    estou espantado   I am astonished!

32   Cafre   Cafre

    Fogo do valor   A lively fire,
    e esta por serto   this is certain—
    vinde ver Senhoras   come and see, Senhoras,
    chegai bem perto   come close.

    Toca assubio entra tamborreiro   A whistle blows;[25] enter a tambourine
    e trobeiteiro   player and a trumpeter

---

24.   Water and Fire
      Opposite they are
      Both will unite themselves
      On this occasion.
      (Borges translation in Castel-Branco, "The Presence of Portuguese Baroque in the Poetic Works of the Sisters of Santa Monica in Goa," 253)

25. *assobio*: this is spelled differently throughout the manuscript; in modern Portuguese, *asubio*, meaning "whistle."

66 Entrada de Bonifrate para Festa dos Reis

	Toca assubio entra cafre com alquitifa canta Aie Aie	A whistle blows; enter a cafre with a decorative stage curtain,[26] singing "Woe, Woe"[27]
	Toca assubio entra malim canta Mãe Felipa *****	A whistle blows; enter the *malim* [gardener?] singing "Mother Felipa ****"
	Toma sete papeis	Take up the seven paper [figures again][28]
33	Mestre	Master
	Padre Confessor	[Addressing] the Father Confessor
	Dando vos eu Aguia com todo cuidado trocosse em mitra meu sol dorado	Having given you the Eagle with great consideration, might you exchange your mitre for my golden sun?
34	Malavar	Malavar
	Padre Procurador	[Addressing the] Father Procurador
	Sifra da Agostinho He o Sol dorado em espirito Santo vos saio trocado	The sign of St. Augustine is the golden sun; in the name of the Holy Spirit, the exchange is done.

---

26. *alquitifa*: a carpet or rug. In the context of the Convento Real de Santa Mónica, an *alquitifa* (or *alcatifa*) was one of the many items used to decorate the altars during festival days (see Michon and Smith, *To Serve God in Holy Freedom*, 133–35). So, perhaps rather than a "rug," it should be thought of as a "decorative cloth" that is used as a stage curtain to conceal any activity taking place in the front while the Cafre sings a woeful tune.

27. *ai*: a cry of "woe"; see Juliet Perkins, "Translating António Da Silva's *O Judeu*," in *Theoretical Issues and Practical Cases in Portuguese English Translations*, ed. Malcom Coulthard and Patricia Anne Odber de Baubeta (Lewiston: Edwin Mellen Press, 1996), 99.

28. These are the same seven painted figures that were used previously.

35	Caneri	Canarim
	Madre Prioreiza	[Addressing the] Mother Prioress
	Palma e Coroa vos dei com cuidado vem em vossa busca Jesus **amentado	With consideration I gave you a martyr's crown; Jesus will seek you out **
36	Cafre	Cafre
	Madre Subprioreiza	[Addressing the] Mother Subprioress
	Perolas de valor vos dei que estremada como ovelha amada levai [?] o bom Pastor	I gave you the choicest valuable pearls; like a beloved sheep led by the good Shepherd.
37	Mestre	Master
	Madre Emerençiana	[Addressing] Mother Emerençiana
	Retrato fermozo por coroa sae [?] no coração guardai que he do espouzo	The martyr's crown makes for a beautiful portrait; keep in your heart that which comes from your spouse.
38	Malavar	Malavar
	Madre Bitona	[Addressing] Mother Bitona
	Pois de contino cuidais no espozo o papel ditozo *** ecce homo divino	Because of the little tale, [since you continuously care for your spouse] you entrust in your spouse; the happy role *** behold the divine man!

39	Cafre	Cafre
	Madre Izabel	[Addressing] Mother Izabel
	Venus com favor vos buscou com cuidado Cupido desfarçado sahe o divino amor	Venus, in her favor, carefully sought you out; Cupid, in disguise, brings forth the Divine love.
	Sae Donna Aldonça canta minina[29]	Enter Donna Aldonça singing "[Oh] little girl"
	Passaro de fogo	The Fire-Bird
40	Mestre	Master

3 recto

	huma maravilha quer vos mostrar passaro no fogo bailar e cantar	I want to show you a marvelous thing: a bird, on fire, that sings and dances!
41	Malavar	Malavar
	Serto minhas Madres estou espantado não morrer o pássaro no fogo abrazado	Surely, my Mothers, I am astonished, for the bird, scorched by flames, does not die.[30]

---

29. This stage direction appears in a different hand, suggesting that it was added later. For information regarding Donna Aldonça as a stock character in early modern *entremeses*, see introduction, p. 25, n. 69.

30. Surely, dear Beloved Mothers
    I'm really astonished
    For the bird doesn't perish
    Burnt in the fire.
    (Borges translation in Castel-Branco, "The Presence of Portuguese Baroque in the Poetic Works of the Sisters of Santa Monica in Goa," 254)

| 42 | Caneri | Canarim |

	O Senhoras minhas	O Senhoras of mine,
	estou espantado	I am astonished;
	este passaro he	this bird is,
	sem duvida emcantado	without a doubt, enchanted.[31]

| 43 | Cafre | Cafre |

	Eu mais serto creo	I most certainly believe
	para vida minha	on my life
	que este he arte	that this is the art
	de brites caninha	of the magician[32] Brites.

Faz Christandade — Becoming Christian[33]

Toca assubio entra Senhor
com negrinha canta vos
de mim para que fugi

A whistle blows: enter a Senhor
with the little black girl singing "why did
you run away from me?"

toca asubio entra Senhora — A whistle blows: enter a Senhora

Parte os papeis — Set out seven [painted] paper figures

---

31. Oh, dear Ladies
   Astonished I am
   This bird no doubt
   Is under a charm.
   (Borges translation in Castel-Branco, "The Presence of Portuguese Baroque in the Poetic Works of the Sisters of Santa Monica in Goa," 254)

32. *caninha*: The entry in *Glossário Luso-Asiático* (1:205) reads:
   CANIANE: canoniane (malaiala *kaṇiyān*). Astrólogo, feiticeiro no Malabar. V. *canaiate*.
   1606 — «Manda o sagrada Concilio que nemhuma pessoa se cure com *Curumbim* o Canoniane, ainde que sejão christãos». — Quinto Concilio de Goa in *Archivo*, iv, p. 265.
   Translation of *Glossário Luso-Asiático* entry above:
   CANIANE: canoniane (in Malayalam *kaṇiyān*). Astrologer, magician from Malabar. V. *canaiate*.
   1606 — "The Sacred Council mandates that no person should cure themselves with a Curumbim or Canoniane, even if they are Christians," Fifth Council of Goa in *Archivo*, iv, p. 265.

33. Quatrains 44–57: each quatrain describes how the nun came to her profession.

44	Mestre	Master
	Madre Antoca	Mother Antoca
Mother Antonia de Encarnação: 1696–1756
	A frecha perdeu Cupido
quando lhe foi a tirar
perdeose a frecha no ar
ficou o arco perdido	Cupid lost his arrow
when he shot it at you;
with the arrow gone missing in the air,
the bow was also lost.
45	Malavar	Malavar
	O Pregão tereis ovido
e a sentença está dado
e a forca aparelhado
para morrer Cupido	You have heard the decree,
and the sentence has been handed down;
the gallows are ready
to put Cupid to death.[34']
46	Mestre	Master
	Madre Ignaçia	Mother Ignaçia
Mother Ignaçia de Anunçiação: 1699–1752
	Com confiança
podeis asseitar
este surumgam[35]
que vos quero dar	You can accept
with confidence
this surumgam-flower
that I want to give to you.

---

34. You have heard the notice
　　The sentence is given
　　The gallows are ready
　　For Cupid to die.
　　　(Borges translation in Castel-Branco, "The Presence of Portuguese Baroque in the Poetic Works of the Sisters of Santa Monica in Goa," 255)

35. *surungam*: "small yellow flowers . . . extremely aromatic. The women of India use these flowers in garlands"; see Alberto Osório de Castro, *A Cinza dos Myrtos: Poemas* (Nova Goa: Imprensa Nacional, 1906), 199.

| 47 | Caneri | Canarim |

| | Por muito fermoza
vos dou esta fula
**** que pequena
he da muita dura | By great beauty
I give you this quatrain
**** so small
but it is a very difficult [enduring, it endures] |

| 48 | Mestre | Master |

| | Madre Paula | Mother Paula
Mother Paula de Espírito Santo: 1700–1763 |

| | O teu lindo corpo
para se lavar
este chafariz
he mui [singular?] | To bathe your
lovely body,
this fountain
is ideal. |

| 49 | Cafre | Cafre |

| | lavai minha [corpo?]
nesta agoa cheroza
que mandei trazer
para vos fermoza | Wash my [body?]
in this scented water
that I ordered brought
for you, O beautiful one. |

| 50 | Mestre | Master |

| | Madre Aninha | Mother Aninha
Mother Anna da Virgem Maria: 1700–1762 |

| | Ambar e nobreza
em ouro emgastada
tomar minha Roza
minha afeçuada | Take, my rose,
my affectionate[36] one,
amber and nobility
inlaid in gold. |

---

36. *affeiçoado*: affection (*Vocabulario Portuguez*, 1:152–53).

3 verso

51	Malavar	Malavar
	[Para] ambar a ençela*** **** bella flor na graça e amor vos dá preeminençia	For that ensconced in amber **** [like a?] beautiful flower; in grace and love you are preeminent.
52	Mestre	Master
	Madre Micaella	Mother Micaella *Mother Michaella da Conçeição: 1702–1749*
	Reçebei com amor os cravos que vai no coração emcravai e meditai com fervor	Lovingly receive carnations,[37] fix them in your heart, and meditate fervently.
53	Caneri	Canarim
	Meditei fermoza no coura e na lição que esta he a ***** da vida ****	Contemplate, o beautiful one, in the choir and during lessons, that this is the **** of life ****
54	Mestre	Master
	Madre Antonia	Mother Antonia *Mother Antonia do Sacramento: 1703–1761*
	Meu bello painel esplica seu coração vossa grande afeição nessas cravos de Arrochel	My beautiful painting[38] explains your heart; your great affection is in these carnations of Arrochel.

---

37. *cravos*: (1) a carnation; (2) a spice, clove (*cravo-da-india*, spice of India); (3) a nail. This could be a play on the meanings of flower and nail.

38. *painel*: perhaps the Master points to a panel or painting in the room, and it serves as a visual aid for the quatrain.

Entrada de Bonifrate para Festa dos Reis

55	Malavar	Malavar

Vossa grande afeição
meu Rico Thesouro
achareis no couro
com toda consolação

Your great affection
is my valuable treasure;
Seek in the choir
all the consolation you need.

56   Mestre   Master

Madre Antica   Mother Antica
                                     Mother Antonia de Santa Roza:
                                     1705–1742

Muito pode hum afeição
ocultarse de maneira
esta flor do lanageira
levais por relação (?)

Affections can be hidden
in many ways;
take this orange blossom,
as an example.

57   Cafre   Cafre   ~~Malavar~~

r**cai coração
*m*i*nha bunina
p** perengrina
*** prendes e perfei*ç*ã*o

*** heart
****
****** pilgrim
***** perfection[39]

mostra roza quema tualha
tira agua do cheiro

A rose is displayed, and a cloth set on fire;
scented water is thrown

Toca asubio entra dois canarios
toca asobio entra dois
dizembargadores vate em***
quini canta geval [?]

The whistle blows, enter two Canarins
The whistle blows, enter two judges
**** enter ****
*** sings ***

toma sete papeis

Take out seven [painted] papers

---

39. Much of this verse is illegible.

58	Mestre	Master
	Madre Antoca	Mother Antoca
	A sua frecha vos deu o Cupido para sua grande afeição agora vos sai trocado a Senhora de Conçeipção	Cupid shot you with his arrow due to your great love; now you are transformed into the Lady of the Conception.
59	Malavar	Malavar
	Madre Ignaçia	Mother Ignaçia
	O que papel brioza em surumgam foi trocada Deos trino amado mereçestes por ditoza	What a lively role in exchange for a surumgam flower; The God of the Trinity loves you and you are deserving of good fortune.

4 recto

60	Caneri	Canarim
	Madre Paula	Mother Paula
	Olha faris com cuidado vos dei roza bella trocasse [?] ela [?] em Ceos estrellado	Look, and do so carefully: I gave you a beautiful rose exchange it [?] in the starry Heavens
61	Cafre	Cafre
	Madre Aninha	Mother Aninha
	Sifra de Jesus em trocada pella como espouza bella vos sae minha lux	Changed by the Sign of Jesus; like a beautiful wife, you will be my light.

62	Mestre	Master
	Madre Micaella	Mother Micaella
	Cravos[40] do teu espouzo dei para comtempla Senhora de Assumpção vos veio buscar	Carnations of your spouse, I gave to you to contemplate; the Lady of the Assumption, He has come to fetch you.[41]
63	Malavar	Malavar
	Madre Antonia	Mother Antonia
	Cravos de Arrochel vos dei meu coração Jesus no leito vos busca com afeição	Carnations from Arrochal[42] I gave you my heart; Jesus in his bed seeks you with affection.
64	Caneri	Canarim
	Madre Antica	Mother Antica
	Flor de larangeira vos dei com cuidado agora vos sahio Jesus crucificado [?]	I gave you, thoughtfully, an orange blossom; now you have gone to [see?] the crucified one.

---

40. *cravos*: (1) a carnation; (2) a spice, clove (*cravo-da-india*, spice of India); (3) a nail.

41. This verse implies that Mother Michaella da Conçeição was close to death. If she professed at the minimum age of fifteen, she would have been fifty-four years old in 1741; perhaps she professed at a more advanced age.

42. The phrase "cravos de Arrochel" is mentioned in the Jesuit Francisco de Azevedo's 1632 account of his journey to Tibet titled *Pera o Padre Antonio Freire, Procurador das Provincias da India da Comp. de Jesus em Portugal*, reprinted in appendix 1 of Cornelius Wessels, *Early Jesuit Travellers in Central Asia, 1603–1721* (The Hague: Nijhoff, 1924), 297.

76 Entrada de Bonifrate para Festa dos Reis

	Pella na tualha	Ball in a cloth
65	Mestre	Master

	Vinde ver Senhoras	Come and see, Senhoras,
	faça laia laia	the way in which
	asande a pella	the flaming ball
	não quemar tualha	doesn't burn the cloth.

| 66 | Malavar | Malavar |

	Este fogo uza	Take great care
	da grande cautella	with this flame;
	sendo ella asseiza	despite being on fire,
	não des*fas a pella	the ball is not destroyed.

| | Bolas de Fogo | Balls of Fire |
| 67 | Mestre | Master |

	Vei de bem Senhoras	Look well, Senhoras,
	que vos quero mostrar	at what I want to show you:
	bollas de fogo	balls of fire
	no ar paçear	passing through the air![43]

| 68 | Malavar | Malavar |

	Eu nunca tal vi	I never saw,
	minha princeiza	my Princess,
	bolas de fogo	balls of fire
	andar sobre a meiza	pass over a table.

---

43. Look well dear Ladies
 What I want to show you
 Balls of fire
 In the air moving.
  (Borges translation in Castel-Branco, "The Presence of Portuguese Baroque in the Poetic Works of the Sisters of Santa Monica in Goa," 254)
 Castel-Branco suggests that this is a skin-covered ball.

69 Caneri

    Esta bolla tem
    grande valia
    ** **** grande
    pareiçe ****

Canarim

This ball is
of great value,
**** big
it seems ****

70 Cafre

    Esta maravilha
    nos cauza espanto
    he serto Senhora
    que he do emcanto

Cafre

This marvel
astonishes us;
it is certain, Senhora,
that it is enchanted.

    toca asobio [en]tra dois cafres
    de Angloa canta maraquita
    toca asubio entra langara
    jamgoma

A whistle blows; enter two Cafres from
Angola singing a maraquite
A whistle blows; enter Langara Jamgoma

71 Mestre

Master

4 verso

    Langara Jangoma
    home primarouzo
    dançai meu amigo
    que **br[?]indes briouzo.

Langara Jangoma,
man of distinction!
Dance, my friend,
and be lively [?].

72 Malavar

    Langara Jamgoma
    meu camarado
    de Madre Suprioreiza
    sois a convidado

Malavar

Langara Jangoma,
my friend,
you are a guest
of the Mother Subprioress.

    Fas seu testamento mostra
    trigo fas rulão bolo frege
    ovos tira vinho de cabeiça
    de Malavar

Make your recipe:[44] bring out
the wheat, make a rulão cake,
fry the eggs, and take wine
from the head of Malavar.

---

44. *testamento*: as suggested by its English cognate, the most accurate translation is "testament." However, what follows is a recipe.

Entrada de Bonifrate para Festa dos Reis

73 Mestre | Master

Sem ser padeiro / Without being a baker,
quero fazer bolo / I want to make a cake,
bollo jagra couco / a jaggery and coconut cake
que não tenho miolho / that is unleavened.[45]

74 Malavar | Malavar

Dai nos meu Mestre / Give us, O Master of mine,
hum bollo quente / a hot cake
de jagra e couco / of jaggery and coconut
muito ençendente [?] / that is piping hot.

75 Mestre ~~Caneri~~[46] | Master

Vos *** cadeia / ***
podeis apreçar / make haste
asar este bollo / in grilling this cake
para nos sear / so that we may have it for supper!

76 Cafre | Cafre

Fassamos a seia / We shall make it
sem nenhum demora / without delay;
os meus companheiros / my friends,
comamos agora / let's eat it now!

toca asubio entra duas mistiças / A whistle blows; enter two mestizos singing,
canta hum perro **** / a dog ****
toca asubio entra caferinho / A whistle blows; a little cafre enters
**** / ****

---

45. Without being a baker
    I want to make a cake
    Of jaggery and coconut
    Which is not fluffy.
     (Borges translation in Castel-Branco, "The Presence of Portuguese Baroque in the Poetic Works of the Sisters of Santa Monica in Goa," 255)

46. Caneri is crossed out in the manuscript.

Entrada de Bonifrate para Festa dos Reis

	Cantiga de Cafrinha	Song of the little Cafre
	~~bainea~~ ai minina menina[47]	Oh little one [?]
77	Andando para hum caminho encontrei com hum Padre Sentado na huma pirão perezando[?]com tudo gente	I was walking along the road when I ran across a priest, sitting by a funeral pyre praying[48] [?] with everyone.
78	Eu entrei com huma paravrinha doço bazaruco de peixe frito hum gargõ de cura quente coração fazei chaça chaçu praza Deus que venha mais lenhos	I entered saying little,[49] [carrying] sweet fried fish-coins and a mug of warm *cura*;[50] the heart goes pitter-patter, praise God to bring more firewood.
79	Mais demazia chi farei minha filha chi farei bazaruco *** tem jagra branco sa vem**	But you make too much my daughter who makes it, the sweet coins *** white jaggery ***
80	Queimarinho ia perde hum pano de cabeçeira doçu panno de tabareira araca com elle	Already lost to the quemarinho [are] the head cloth [containing the cake?] Sweet bread of [?] and arrak with him.[51]

---

47. The phrase "~~bainea~~ *ai minina menina*" was added by a different hand. This "ai" appears to be the same as the previously mentioned "Aie Aie" (see note 27) with the meaning of "Woe." This song is thus a lament sung by a young slave girl.

48. *perezando*: possible corruption of *rezando*, derived from the verb *rezar*, to pray. It would be scandalous for a priest to preside over the Hindu ritual of cremation. Here is an example of the Catholic and Hindu worlds coming together. Or, *perezando* could be a corruption of the verb *prezar*, which means to appreciate or cherish; however, this interpretation does not make sense in the context of the song. The *prezar/rezar* issue reappears in the following verse.

49. *paravrinha*: possible corruption of *palavrinha*, a quick word or a moment. We translate the phrase as "saying little" to convey that what is occurring is improper. However, this seems to contradict the rest of the verse, in which the little slave girls appear to be bringing food and drink. Therefore, it is possible that a *paravrinha* is a small platter used to serve food and drink, but we have no evidence to confirm or refute this.

50. *cura*: a curative or a remedy (*Vocabulario Portuguez*, 2:639).

51. This verse is very difficult to translate, but perhaps the *queimarihno* (the bailiff) has come and taken the cakes, sweet breads, and arrak away from them.

Entrada de Bonifrate para Festa dos Reis

81	Hum piou cata/lata piou	a drink
	por vida vossa madrinha	for life your godmother
	forogo confessa cafrinha	the cafrina confesses in court
	*****	

5 recto

    Baila de Milhano   Dance of the Kite

82	Mestre	Master
	Choquei hum galinha	A chicken laid an egg [I hatched a chicken]
	saio quinza pinto	and out came fifteen chicks;
	dai levou milhano	The kite struck and carried some off,
	eu ficou com sinco	and I am left with five.
83	Malavar	Malavar
	Criei sinco pinto	Five chicks
	com grande cuidado	I very carefully raised;
	todos levou milhano	but the Kite took them all
	por meus pecados	because of my sins.[52]
84	Caneri	Canarim
	Com graça e ar	O kite, dance
	milhano dançai	gracefully in the air;
	vossa abelidade	show your abilities
	a todos mostrai	to everyone.[53]

---

52. Five little chicks
    Very carefully I bred
    The kite lifted them all
    by (...)
    (Borges translation in Castel-Branco, "The Presence of Portuguese Baroque in the Poetic Works of the Sisters of Santa Monica in Goa," 255)

53. Gracefully
    You kites dance
    Your skill
    To everybody you show.
    (Borges translation in Castel-Branco, "The Presence of Portuguese Baroque in the Poetic

	dis todos	They all say
85	Milhano miouto[54] minha ovo milhano miouto; comonidade	[the] community [sings]: kite thief my kite thief-of-eggs
	toca asubio entra buneca de sima mercador com roupa cachorro ladrão mirinho com forca infurcando com cafre	A whistle blows; from above enter [the following] puppets: a merchant with clothing, a dog, a thief, a bailiff with a slave with a noose around his neck
	Depois de sair todas entra Donna Aldonça dedó [?] papel de pedi*ume [?]	After they all leave Donna Aldonça[55] arrives [saying] give me a paper for each[56]
	toca asubio entra dois malavar *canta com muita vénia[?]*	The whistle blows; enter two Malavars *singing with great courtesy*
	Copo lenvanta alamoferis	Raise a large iron cup[57]

Works of the Sisters of Santa Monica in Goa," 256)

54. *miouto*: *mioto*, *mihafre* (raptor), as well as a thief, a robber.

55. For the importance of Donna Aldonça, see introduction, p. 25, n. 69.

56. The phrase *papel de ped[i]*ume* also appears immediately preceding v. 166. Both of these phrases were added to the original text by a different hand. In addition, they both occur before a series of eighty quatrains. It is unclear what this phrase means, but it may mean "bring out a picture of each"; see pp. 60–61, n. 15.

   In vernacular Marathi and Hindi, *dedo* is a formal way to request something, as in "give [to me]." For example, one might say *apka telefone-number dedo*, "Give [to me] your telephone number." Here we see a mix of local Indian languages combined with Portuguese.

57. It is odd that a cup (*copo*) and a mortar and pestle (*almofariz*) would be raised. There is no doubt that an *almofariz* is, literally, a mortar and pestle, as the word is derived from the Arabic, and it refers to "an iron vessel in which one crushes or pulverizes various ingredients" (see *Vocabulario Portuguez*, 1:274, "derivase do Arabico *Almiberiçum*, ou *Milereçum*, que quer dizer cousa, en que se moe ou piza qualquer materia; & almofariz he hum vaso de metal, em que se pizão various ingredientes"). However, perhaps the *almofariz* is used here just to describe the kind of cup that is to be raised, and we can understand *almofariz* as a kind of *almofia*, or "big vessel, ordinarily of glazed clay or tin, which has the form of a bowl" (see *Vocabulario Portuguez*, 1:274: "vaso grande, ordinariamente de barro vidrio, ou estanho, tem feitio de tigela"). This interpretation is consistent with v. 86, which describes the cup exactly in this manner.

86 Mestre | Master

Senhoras minhas
estou espantada
levantar o copo
ferro tão pezado

My Senhoras,
I am astonished
to lift such a heavy
iron cup.

Padre Confessor | Father Confessor

87 Mestre | Master

Dignissimo Confessor
cuia brandura e bondade
reconheçe toda freira
venera todo frade

Most worthy Confessor,
whose gentleness and kindness
is recognized by all the nuns,
[and] venerated by all the monks.

88 Malavar | Malavar

Father Procurator[58]

Lovar agora he justo
ao Reverendissimo Procurador
por ser em tudo hum protanto
he digno de todo lovor

It is right to now give praise to
the Most Reverend Procurator;
for, being talented in all things,
he is worthy of all praise.

89 Caneri | Canarim

*Mother Catharina do Sacramento:
1689–1743*

Reverendissima Prioreza
todas lha no coração
com rezão vos deive
toda estimação

Most Reverend Prioress
keeps everyone in her heart,[59]
it is right to give you
all esteem.

---

58. In verses 88–165, we have added the names and dates of the verse's subjects in italics. These names and dates do not appear in the original manuscript.

59. alternative translation of line 2: "everyone loves you in their heart."

90	Caneri	Canarim

Mother Anna de Jesus: 1698–1750

	Madre Subprioeiza	Mother Subprioress
	é com singular cuidado	it is with special care
	roga nel coro dos Anjos	that [you] pray in the Choir of Angels
	de serafim hum renado	for the Kingdom of the Serafim.
91	Mestre	Master

Mother Emerençiana de Santa Maria: 1689–1743

	De Santa Maria ****	You are called Emerençiana
	chamarse Emerençiana	"of Saint Mary" ****
	porque a Santa Maria	because you burn with love
	com grande açesso ama	for the Blessed Mary.
92	Malavar	Malavar

Mother Brites do Sacramento: 1690–1757

	Sois Brites tão perfeita	You are Brites, so perfect,
	que sacramento vos convida	that the "Sacrament"[60] invites you
	para çeo donde mora	to the heaven where you [will] live
	para ser sua escolhida	to be his chosen one.

5 verso

93	Cafre	Cafre

Mother Isabel de Madre de Deus: 1691–1744

	Izabel de Madre de Deus	Izabel de Madre de Deus
	cuia suma gravidade	whose great dignity
	confunda todo juizo	confounds all judgment
	cativa toda vontade	and captivates every will.

---

60. Here, the sacrament, which is the body of Christ, is personified.

94	Caneri	Canarim

Mother Antonia de Encarnação: 1696–1756

Diria he do lovor Antonía da Emcarnação pois tem por simblo preçipio de redenção	I would say that Antonia "of the Incarnation" is worthy of praise because she has for her symbol the cradle of redemption.

95	Mestre	Master

Mother Ignaçia de Anunçiação: 1699–1752

Quem duvida minha roza vossa grande devoção por isso vos chamasteis Ignaçia de Anunçiação	No one doubts, my rose, your great devotion; that is why you are called Ignaçia "of the Annunciation."

96	Malavar	Malavar

Mother Paula de Espírito Santo: 1700–1763

Paula ***mo do prado Espirito Santo invocai o favor ao çeo repetidas graças dai	Paula *** of the meadow, by invoking the "Holy Spirit" the favor of Heaven bestows upon you many graces.

97	Caneri	Canarim

Mother Anna da Virgem Maria: 1700–1762

Anna da Virgem Maria por iço mais galante bem sera que em seu ama mostra sempre constante	Anna da Virgem Maria, for this reason you are so graceful; it is well established that in your love you always demonstrate constancy.

98	Cafre	Cafre

Mother Michaella da Conçeição: 1702–1749

Micaella sois roza	Micaella, you are a rose
do jardim da perfeição	from the garden of perfection,
e por mais bizarria	and for your elegance,
tendes a assupção	"the Assumption" is yours.

99	Mestre	Master

Mother Antonia do Sacramento: 1703–1761

Antonia do Sacramento	Antonia do Sacramento,
quem ignora seu primor	who could ignore your excellence?
o çeo lhe des sempre	Heaven's love for her
aumento do seu amor	is ever increasing.

100	Malavar	Malavar

Mother Antonia de Santa Roza: 1705–1742

Antonia com grande asertos	Antonia, with great assurances
vos chama de Santa Roza	you are called "of the Holy Rose";
esta que o seu espouzo	because of this, your spouse
escolheu por mais fermoza	deems you as the prettiest.

101	Caneri	Canarim

Mother Maria de Ressureição: 1705–1744

Maria de deos amante	Maria, the lover of God,
de ressureição quis chamar	wanted to be called "of the Ressurection,"
pedindo lhe o amore perfeito	asking for his perfect love
para com ella triunfiar	to triumph over her.

102 Cafre

Cafre

Mother Clara de Jesus: 1706–1768

Na Clara se consiste	In Clara resides
toda lux e claridade	all light and clarity;
que com Jesus estais sempre	may you always be accompanied
de luzas acompanhada	by the light "of Jesus."

103 Mestre

Master

Mother Antonia de Madre de Deos: 1707–1755

E digno de lovor
vosso bem proçedimento
Antonia de Madre de Deos
nesta Real Convento

Your good behavior
is worthy of praise,
Antonia de Madre de Deos,
in this Royal Convent.

104 Malavar

Malavar

Mother Holaya de Jesus Maria: 1708–1743

Duas cosas tendas olaia
por estas duas fermozas
sois de Jesus e Maria
por iço mais venteroza

Holaya has two things,
both of which are beautiful;
you are "of Jesus and Mary,"
thus all the more fortunate.

105 Caneri

Canarim

Mother Antonia de Santo Agostinho: 1710–1758

Antonia de Santo Agostinho
sugeito da estimação
freira que tem ia emtregue
a Deos seu coração

Antonia de Santo Agostinho,
person of great esteem,
a nun who has already
given her heart to God.

| 106 | Cafre | Cafre |

Mother Teresa do Sacramento: 1710–1766

	Thereiza do Sacramento	Teresa do Sacramento,
	dizem que tem apostado	they say that you have the commitment
	dar por amor de Deos	to give, for the love of God,
	samgue do proprio lado	blood from your own side.

6 recto

| 107 | Mestre | Master |

Mother Izabel de Aprezentação: 1711–1767

	Jesus **** Izabel	Jesus **** Izabel,
	mas esta sabe levar	but this one knows to take
	ventage em serto modo	advantage in a certain way,
	por aprezentação chamar	that is why she is called "of the Presentation."[61]

| 108 | Malavar | Malavar |

Mother Senhorinha de Jesus: 1712–1774

	A Jesus troxe Maria	Mary carried Jesus
	nova mezes em seu ventre	in her womb for nine months;
	mais grossa sinhorinha	Senhorinha, who is fatter,
	he de Jesus para sempre	is always with "Jesus."

---

61. This verse plays on a particular detail of the Presentation of the Blessed Virgin Mary. When God asked Mary to bear the Christ child, she was given free choice to accept or reject the gift. Without knowing what this would bring, she said yes. Perhaps Izabel de Aprezentação, too, made faithful decisions without knowing all the consequences beforehand.

109 Caneri

Canarim

Mother Brites de Trindade: 1713-1766

Mal se pode esplicar	One can hardly explain
a graça de Beatris	Britis's grace
que para ser mais engraçada	except by the fact that the "Trinity"
para si a Trinidade quis	wanted her to be so infused with grace.

110 Cafre

Cafre

Mother Anna de Transfiguração: 1714-1749

Repiquece os sinos
venhão todo cortezão
aplaudir a Anna
esta de Transfiguração

Ring out the bells,
come all you courtiers,
praise this Anna
de Transfiguração.

111 Mestre

Master

Mother Francisca de São José: 1715-1776

Francisca hunico estremo
de São Joseph quis chamar
para com o mesmo nome
o que he significar

Francisca, one of a kind,
wanted to be called "of Saint Joseph";
she wanted to be known by this very name
and what it signifies.

112 Malavar

Malavar

Mother Maria de Trindade: 1715-1756

Maria de Trindade
Jesus que graça tem
não sei que trazeis en vos
que todos vos querem bem

Maria de Trindade,
who has the grace of Jesus,
I don't know what it is that is within you
that [prompts] all to wish you well.

113 Caneri

Canarim

Mother Izabel da Virgem Maria: 1715–1756

Afirmeiza de Izabel
aplauda hoie constante
por ser Virgem Maria
e ser della muito amante

Izabel's steadfastness,
for being [called] "Virgin Mary"
and being such an admirer of Her,
is constantly praised nowadays.

114 Cafre

Cafre

Mother Lionarda de Trindade: 1716–1742

Lionarda de Trindade
engraçada contento
bem pode repetir ia
venha cá esta protento

Lionarda de Trindade,
witty, delightful;
we would do well to have another marvel
such as she come here again.

115 Mestre

Master

Mother Anna de Trindade: 1716–1746

Anna de Trindade
hum anio no natural
que a todos fará bem
não fazendo a ninguem mal

Anna de Trindade
an angel by nature,
[she is] one who will do good by all
and do harm to none.

116 Malavar

Malavar

Mother Luiza dos Querubins: 1717–1747

Da qui sará vos digo
Luiza dos Querobins
sois na graça fermazura
hum mais lindo rubim

What shall I say about you,
Luiza "of the Cherubims";
you are beautiful in your gracefulness,
a most beautiful ruby. [cherub]

117 Cafre

Cafre

Mother Mariana de Jesus: 1717–1770

Vos sois manona	You are Manona,[62]
hum lindo querobim	a pretty Cherubim;
de Jesus chamada	you are called "of Jesus,"
sois hum serafim	[and] you are a Serafim.

118 Caneri

Canarim

Mother Arcangela de Gloria: 1717–1744

Arcangela de Gloria	Archangela de Gloria
he huma linda rosa	is a gorgeous rose;
a mais a Deos **n**	the more [you praise] God,
sereis mais fermoza	the more beautiful you become.

119 Mestre

Master

Mother Maria dos Gerarguias: 1718–1745

Alegreçe todos prezente	Everyone here is pleased
com muzica e armonia	with music and harmony
que assiste aqui com nosco	because attending [this festival] with us
Maria de Gerarguia	is Maria de Gerarguia.

120 Malavar

Malavar

Mother Luiza de Madre de Deus: 1721–1764

De mai de Deos	Luiza "of the Mother of God,"
sois Luiza huma flor	you are a flower
pois della sois amada	because you are beloved by Her;
servirlhe com amor	you serve Her with love.

---

62. Manona is a nickname for Mariana.

6 verso

121 Cafre

        Cafre

Mother Francisca do Sacramento: 1723–1776

Francisca do Sacramento
cuia gala e bizarria
ha de vir a ser aumento
desta nossa companhia

        Francisca do Sacramento,
        whose refinement and elegance
        will come to enhance
        this company of ours.

122 Mestre

        Master

Mother Luiza de Assumpção: 1724–1742

Luiza de Assumpção
flor do nosso jardim
he na graça e donaire
na terra hum querobim

        Luiza de Assumpção,
        a flower from our garden,
        is in grace and elegance,
        a cherubim on earth.

123 Caneri

        Canarim

Mother Anna de Madre de Deos: 1726–1764

Anna de Madre de Deos
nome do seu contento
em o amor divino
constante a todo tempo

        Anna "of the Mother of God,"
        the name of your contentment
        in the Divine love
        remains for all time.

124 Malavar

        Malavar

Mother Eufrazia de Ressurreição: 1727–1750

Eufrazia de Ressurreição
devota sobre maneira
tanto que neste ponto
bem pode ser primeira

        Eufrazia de Ressurreição
        devotes herself in such a way
        that, at this point,
        she could very well be the best (devotee).

125   Cafre   Cafre

                                         Mother Maria de Assumpção: 1728–1788

      Fermoza emgraçada   Beautiful, delightful,
      sois de Assumpção Maria   you are Maria "of the Assumption,"
      e por isso come rezão   and for this reason
      vos louve nesta dia   we praise you on this day.

126   Caneri   Canarim

                                         Mother Brites de Santa Anna: 1728–1762

      Brites de Santa Anna   Brites de Santa Anna,
      bem ornado jasmin   well-adorned jasmine,
      tão bem simples mosqueta   just like a simple mosquito
      repita todos sim sim   you repeat all the time, yes yes.

127   Mestre   Master

                                         Mother Joanna de Santa Rosa: 1729–1773

      De Santa Roza sois Joanna   You are Joanna "of the Holy Rose,"
      vos de graça superior   and you are the most graceful
      roza desta jardim   rose from this garden,
      he digna de todo lovor   worthy of all praise.[63]

128   Malavar   Malavar

                                         Mother Maria de Annunciação: 1729–1754

      Maria de Anuçiação   Maria de Anuçiação,
      bem mostra por serto   it is evident indeed
      pois andando cá na terra   to those here on earth
      pareçe hum çeo aberto   that you are like a clear sky.

---

63. You are Joan of St. Rose
    Your beauty is beyond words
    The rose of this garden you are
    Most praiseworthy.
        (Borges translation in Castel-Branco, "The Presence of Portuguese Baroque in the Poetic
        Works of the Sisters of Santa Monica in Goa," 253)

129	Cafre	Cafre
		Mother Francisca de Annunciação: 1730–1741
	Francisca de Anunçiação mostrais sempre constante para com vosso espouzo sede firme amante	Francisca de Anunçiação you always show constancy; be steadfast in your love toward your husband.
130	Caneri	Canarim
		Mother Margarida de São Jozeph: 1738–1750
	Margarida da Santa Joseph se sois de Deos amante aveis da preçuerar em seu amor constante	Margarida da Santa Joseph, if you are a lover of God, you will abide in his steady love.
131	Mestre	Master
		Mother Caetana de Jesus Maria: 1738–1766
	Esta Caetana Senhora que assiste com alegria e por ser mais emgraçada tras a Jesus e Maria	This Senhora Caetana, who happily participates [in our community], and even more delightfully, she brings along "Jesus and Maria."
132	Malavar	Malavar
		Mother Anna de Ressureyçião: 1738–1747
	De ressurreição sois Anna com rezão segui o Santo caminho e amai a perfeição	Anna, for good reason you are "of the Resurrection"; you follow the saintly path and love perfection.

133 Cafre

Cafre

Mother Maria de São Joachim: 1738–1796

Maria de São Joquim	Maria de São Joquim,
chamada quis ser	you wanted to be called this
para assim a este Santo	so that this Saint
em sua defença ter	would defend you.

134 Mestre

Master

Mother Jozepha de Santo Agostinho: 1739–1775

De Santo Agostinho	Josepha [is a] faithful daughter
Jozepha fiel filha	"of St. Augustine,"
por isso he do mundo	and thus she is a true marvel
encelente[64] maravilha	of this world.

7 recto

135 Caneri

Canarim

Mother Roza de Assumpção: 1739–1781

Senhora Roza	Senhora Roza
esta de Assumpção	is "of the Assumption,"
temos nella maravilha	and in her we have
deposta de sobre mão	a carefully attested marvel.

136 Malavar

Malavar

Mother Maria de São Guillierme: 1739–1763

Maria aquelle protente	This amazing Maria
de São Guilherme que graça tem	de São Guilherme has such grace;
Maria huma Roza	Maria is a rose,
resonda todos amen	and all reply Amen.

---

64. Emend *encelente* → *excelente*.

| 137 | Caneri | Canarim |

Mother **** de São Jozeph[65]

	***** que por ventura	**** has the good fortune
	por São Jozeph e chamada	of being named after "St Joseph";
	quem duvida ser ella	none doubt that
	quanto basta engraçada	her grace is more than sufficient.

| 138 | Mestre | Master |

Novice Bibiana de São Miguel: 1742–1775

	Bibiana sois chamada	Bibiana, you are called
	de São Miguel com rezão	"of Saint Michael" for good reason;
	que sois bunitinha	who would not say
	quem dirá que não	that you are a lovely little thing.

| 139 | Malavar | Malavar |

Novice Anna de São Jochim: 1742–1776

	Vos minha anona	You, my Anona,
	de São Joaquim	de São Joachim,
	sois huma bonina	you are a daisy
	de nosso jardim	from our garden.[66]

---

65. There is a mistake either in the *Book of Professions* or in the *Entrada*, as a **** de São Joseph who professed circa 1737–1740 is not recorded. However, there is a Sister Joseph de Santo Joaquim, 1738–1796 (entry #380) in the *Book of Professions*, and since it does contain a number of errors, we assume that her name has been miscopied.

66. You my sweetsop
   of Saint Joachim.
   You are the most lovely daisy
   From our garden.
   (Borges translation in Castel-Branco, "The Presence of Portuguese Baroque in the Poetic Works of the Sisters of Santa Monica in Goa," 252)

Borges translates *anona* as "sweetsop," but there are two other possibilities: (1) Anona could be a diminutive for Anna, as in Antonia → Antoca (v. 44); Anna → Aninha (v. 50), or (2) *Annona squamosa* is the Goan custard apple.

140	Cafre	Cafre

Postulant Juliana de Querobim

Sois hum fetiço	You are an enchanting
menina Juliana	little girl, Juliana,
rico querobim	a splendid "Cherubim"
em tudo soberano	sovereign in everything.[67]

141	Mestre	Master

Lay Sister Luiza de Serafim

Luiza vossas façoens	Luiza, your features
vença os mesmos jasmin	conquer those of jasmine itself;
quem sabe se por isso	perhaps this is why
vos chamais do Serafim	you are called "of the Seraphim."[68]

142	Cafre	Cafre

Lay Sister Magdalena de Jesus

Magdalena de Jesus	Magdalena de Jesus,
aqui pareçe esta ella	here it seems that this one
mereçe por primaroza	deserves, for being the first among
de flores rica capella	flowers, a rich chapel.

143	Mestre	Master

Lay Sister Joanna de Jesus Maria

Da todo coração Joanna	With all your heart, Joanna,
invocais a Jesus Maria	you invoke "Jesus and Maria"
que vos livres da todo mal	so that you may be free from all evil;
vos dai pax e alegria	you bestow peace and happiness.

---

67. Perhaps lines 3–4 could be more felicitously translated as "a splendid cherubim in all your glory."

68. The white flowers of Arabian Jasmine (*Jasminum sambac*) resemble angel's wings. For the importance of jasmine in Goa, see S. A. Safeena, S. Priya Devi, and M. Thangam, *A Catalogue of Jasmine Accessions in Goa*, Technical Bulletin, no. 58 (Old Goa: Horticulture Science Section, ICAR-Central Coastal Agricultural Research Institute, Indian Council of Agricultural Research, 2016), 1–42.

144 Malavar

Malavar

Lay Sister Izabel de Santo Christo

Izabel de Christo tem
ventura tão singular
que por espouza de Christo
se empenha ****

Izabel "of Christ," you have
the singular good fortune
to be pledged ****
as a bride of Christ.

145 Caneri

Canarim

Lay Sister Roza do Paraizo

Roza do Paraizo
do jardim da gloria
com este rico nome
lograis a vitoria

Roza "of Paradise"
from the garden of glory,
with this rich name,
you will attain victory.

146 Cafre

Cafre

Lay Sister Maria de Consolação

Maria todas de vos
fazem muito estimaças
mais que muitos se lograis
nome de Consolação

Maria, everyone holds you
in high esteem;
more than most you have earned
the name "of Consolation."

147 Mestre

Master

Lay Sister Caetana de Jesus

Caetana pello deveras
tendas mui grande ventura
pois trazeis sempre con vosco
de Jesus a fermazura

Caetana, truly,
you have great fortune
because you bring with you
the beauty that comes from the name "of Jesus."

148 Malavar

Malavar

Lay Sister Maria de Jesus de Nazareth

Jesus de Nazaret	Maria has the name
tendes o nome a Maria	"of Jesus of Nazareth";
gozais deste nome	enjoy this name,
que he de mutia valia	which is of great worth.

7 verso

149 Caneri

Canarim

Lay Sister Ignes de Purificação

Ignes por varios modes
chamase de purificação
tenda pura a alma
juntamento o coração

Ignes, in various ways,
you embody the name "of Purification";
you have a pure soul
along with a pure heart.

150 Cafre

Cafre

Lay Sister Joanna de Baptista

Nossa Joanna Bautista
tem guarda do valor
que leva por companheiro
de Christo o procunçor

Our Joanna "of the Baptist"
safeguards the value,
which she brings as the companion
of the proclaimer of Christ.[69]

151 Mestre

Master

Lay Sister Micaella de Anjo

Micaella anda sempre
de anio a companhada
o que grande ventura
desta freira na verdade

Micaella always goes about
accompanied by "an angel";
this is the great fortune
of this nun, truly.

---

69. St. John the Baptist proclaimed the imminent arrival of Jesus Christ. The other text translated in this volume, the *Cartapaço da Muzica*, is a collection of songs to be performed on the celebration of his day of birth, June 24.

152 Malavar

Malavar

Lay Sister Izabel do Sacramento

Izabel do Sacramento
aquella que todos sabe
ser sugeito emgraçada
que todo lovor lhe cabe

Izabel do Sacramento
is she who is known to all
to be a person of grace
befitting of all praise.

153 Caneri

Canarim

Lay Sister Rozalia de Madre de Deus[70]

Rozalia de Madre de Deos
esta nome invocais
que tendes rico tezouro
no teu coração guardeis

Rozalia "of the Mother of God,"
you invoke this name,
which contains a splendid treasure
that you safeguard in your heart.

154 Cafre

Cafre

Lay Sister Maria de Piedade

O que grande nome
Maria de Piedade
a vos nos convem
lovar na verdade

What a great name,
Maria "of Piety";
it truly suits us
to praise you.

155 Mestre

Master

Lay Sister Senhorinha de Purificação

Não se pode chamar Senhora
nenhum junto rainha
vos por purificação
sois Senhora e Sinhorinha

None who are near a Queen
cannot be called Senhora;
you, "by purification,"
are both a Senhora and a Senhorinha.

---

70. In 1732, Rozalia de Madre de Deus signed the *Relação* as a postulant. However, she never became a full choir nun, and she must have chosen to become a lay sister instead.

156 Malavar

Malavar

Lay Sister Maria de Christo

A devoção da Maria	The devotion of this Maria
he asombro nunca visto	is an astonishing thing never seen before,
pois quis tomas para si	for she wanted to take for herself
o renobre de Christo	the renowned name "of Christ".

157 Cafre

Cafre

Lay Sister Francisca de Assumpção

Francisca com muita cauza
vos chamase de Assumpção
pois sabe a natureiza
fazer vos de sobre mão

Francisca, for good reason
you are called "of the Assumption,"
because it is known that your character
was well formed.

158 Caneri

Canarim

Lay Sister Jozepha de São Miguel

Jozepha linda menina
que chamarçe de São Miguel
por devoto deste anio
na boca lhe sabe o mel

Jozepha, beautiful girl,
who is called "of St. Michael,"
her devotion to this angel
tastes like honey in her mouth.

159 Mestre

Master

Lay Sister Mónica de Jesus Maria

Bem posso afirmar
he monica com rezão
pois mostra ser muito pura
e limpa do coração

I can assuredly attest
that she is rightly named "Monica,"
because she shows herself very pure
and clean of heart.

160 Malavar

Aura dos Çeos
menina muito amante
por isso he sempre
ostemtarçe triunfante

Malavar

Lay Sister Aurea do Çeos

Aura "of the Heavens"
is a very loving girl;
thus she always
shows herself to be radiant.

161 Caneri

Maria aquella que
de Salvador nome tem
aplaude seu naçimento
que he do mundo maior bem

Canarim

Lay Sister Maria do Salvador

Maria, she who
has the name "of the Savior,"
praises his birth,
which is the world's greatest gift.

162 Cafre

Paschoa de Assumpção
sobre nome graçioso
sois qual lirio
sobre maneira cherozo

Cafre

Lay Sister Paschoa de Assumpção

Paschoa de Assumpção,
beyond your graceful name
you are an exceedingly
fragrant lily.

163 Mestre

Anna de Santa Maria
Maria vos há de valer
quando vossos inimigos
quizerdes minina vençer

Master

Lay Sister Anna de Santa Maria

Anna "of the Blessed Mary,"
Mary will be there for you
when your enemies
seek to conquer this girl.

164 Malavar

Feliçia vos sois felix
pois de Jesus Maria
trazai sempre na memoria
nella para vossa guia

Malavar

Lay Sister Filiçia de Jesus Maria

Feliçia, you are felix
because [you are] "of Jesus and Mary";
always carry them in your memory
as your guide.

165 Caneri	Canarim
	Lay Sister Rozalia de Santa Rita[71]
Rozalia de Santa Rita Rico nome de devoção elle vos dará a lux para o caminho de Salvação	Rozalia "of Saint Rita," whose name is rich in devotion, she will be the light on the road to Salvation.

8 recto

para	stop
papel de ped*ume	ask for each paper [to be brought out again]
166 Arco Fracha	Bow and Arrow
Rigaroza frecha lança pello o ar o cruel Cupido para vos matar	A well-aimed arrow flies through the air [shot by] the cruel Cupid in order to kill you.
167 Torre	Tower[72]
Sem rezão do amor mostrais apartada sempre de contino[73] preza e ferrolhada	Wrongly, in spite of love,[74] you are taken away, always and forever imprisoned and chained.

---

71. Irmã Rozalia de Santa Rita signed the *Relação* as a postulant in 1732. It is unknown why she did not become a choir nun; perhaps she lacked the necessary dowry.

72. The tower is like a prison.

73. *contino*: *continuamente* (*Vocabulario Portuguez*, 3:500).

74. Alternative translation to line 1: Wrongly separated from love.

168 Trombeita

    Festes e guerras publica
    essa trombeita exelente
    para o que for coniviniente
    ia este a caza vos fica

Trumpet

    Announcing feasts and wars,
    this excellent trumpet
    is suitable for anything,
    and it is at hand in the house for you.

169 Nao

    A nao que em si leva
    farol de esperança
    vai cortando as agoas
    em toda bonança

Ship

    The ship that bears
    a beacon of hope
    cuts through the water
    in the utter calm.

170 Lança

    A lança em que pintada
    he instromento penozo
    o teu peito animozo
    espoem a estas lançadas

Spear

    The spear that drips [with your blood]
    is an instrument of pain;
    your courageous breast
    exhibits these wounds.

171 Corrente

    Veio-nos leida e contente
    sem sobrozos nem temoras
    ignorando os rigoras
    que em si tras estas correntes

Current

    She came happy and content
    without gloom or fear,
    ignoring the rigors
    that these currents/chains bring.[75]

---

75. She came happy and content
    Without gloom nor fears
    Ignoring the rigors
    Which these currents bring.
        (Borges translation in Castel-Branco, "The Presence of Portuguese Baroque in the Poetic Works of the Sisters of Santa Monica in Goa," 253)
Corrente can be either a "current" or a "chain." Either works here, and we cannot determine which is indicated. It seems that current, as in the currents of the Mandovi River, is more likely, but there is no reason to reject a translation of "chain."

172 Cupido / Cupid

Val*** de os que vem
O rapas descomedido
para ferir atrevido
a quem ferir não [convem?]

*** who he sees
the immoderate youth
in order to arrogantly wound;
whoever is wounded is unworthy.[76]

173 Anzol / Fishhook

Lançai anzol ao mar
para buscar os pescados
levai a caza cuidados
para muita ***ustar

Cast your fishhook into the sea
to catch fish;
bring them home carefully
to enjoy[77] them very much.

174 Tanque / Cistern

Apurais os teus cuidados
no tanque do dezengano
que sustentar do engano
de tormento muy pessado

Examine your cares
in the cistern of disenchantment,
and may you pull yourself from the lies
of endless torment.

8 verso

175 Oculo / Spyglass

Se de parto quereis ver
a que a vista não alcança
podeis com grande confiança
desta instromento valer

If you wish to see up close
that which vision cannot reach,
you can with great confidence
rely upon this instrument.[78]

---

76. This verse was originally written in Spanish, but a later editor modified the letters to make it Portuguese. The original spelling seems to have been *herir* (wound), but the "he" was changed to an "fe" to create "*ferir*." Similarly, the last line originally read "a quien," but this has been changed to "a quem" by the editor. The word for "no" in Spanish is given a small tail/tilde, so it reads "não."

77. Emend ****ustar* → *degustar*.

78. This translation by Anna Weerasinghe cannot be improved upon, so it has been retained in its entirety. The interpretation of this verse by Weerasinghe is also quite convincing (see introduction, pp. 37–38).

176 Espada

Sorte em boa ocazião
essa espada oferesse
matar a quem mereçe
he pundanor e rezão

Sword

At the right moment,
this sword offers the chance
to kill those who deserve it;
this is honorable and right.

177 Bogio

Bugio he travesso
mais sabe dançar
bem podeis com elle
sempre recrear

Monkey

The monkey is mischievous
but knows how to dance;
you can always have
a good time with him.

178 Arpa

Resta minha roza
que canteis agora
que he para ouvir
vossa vos sonora

Harp

Stay, my rose,
and sing now
so I can hear
your sonorous voice.

179 Viola

Cantai de auzencia
lastimas sentidas
para ver se asim
divertas a vida

Guitar

Sing of absence,
of heartfelt sorrows,
and see if this makes
life enjoyable.

180 Copo

Senhora este **nho
he mui ençelente
para o chaque[79]
da que andeis duente

Cup

Senhora, this wine[80]
is most excellent
for the ailment
from which you suffer.

---

79. Emend *o chaque* → *o achaque*.
80. Emend ****nho* → *vinho*.

106 Entrada de Bonifrate para Festa dos Reis

181 Dados | Dice

Com dados podeis
gastar toda dia
livre de emfados
sem malenconias

With dice you can
pass the whole day
free from boredom
and gloom.

182 Galo | Rooster

Sirva vos o galo
despertador
com elle louveis
a teu creador

The rooster serves
as an alarm
to wake up and
praise your Creator.

183 Chave | Key

Pois tal privilegio
esta chave tem
desta grande dita
louves para bem

Since this key
grants so much privilege,
it is fitting to praise
this great thing.

184 Palmeira | Palm Grove

O senhora minha
tomai sem detença
hum rico palma
para vossa tença

O my Senhora,
take without delay
a rich palm grove
for your pension.[81]

185 Meiza | Table

Comei mana minha
pois o não hastes
esta bella ceia
que agora achates

Eat, my sister,
as if you don't [eat]
this beautiful meal,
then you will waste away already.

---

[81]. The use of palm groves as a source of income was quite common, and the convent owned numerous palm groves in the Northern Provinces. The fact that these land holdings were extremely profitable caused friction with other Portuguese in India, who were not as wealthy; see introduction, pp. 6–8.

186	Anel	Ring

    Este rico anel　　　　　　This magnificent ring
    de pesso sobido　　　　　of high value,
    posto em teu dado　　　　[when] placed on your finger
    fica mais luzido　　　　　becomes even brighter.

187 Abano　　　　　　　　　　Fan

    Com este abano　　　　　　With this fan
    Regulai minha alma　　　　 I relieve my soul,
    fugi das candeias　　　　　 [but] I flee from the candles
    que fazem mais calma　　　 to keep them from flickering.

9 recto

188 Alegrete　　　　　　　　　Flower Bed

    Levais alegrete　　　　　　Fill the flower bed
    de diversas rozas　　　　　with many kinds of roses,
    se elles são bellas　　　　　and if they are beautiful,
    vos a mais fermozas　　　　then you are all the more lovely.[82]

189 Angelica　　　　　　　　　Angelica[83]

    Por anio vos tem　　　　　You rightfully have
    todos com rezão　　　　　 everyone as your guardian angel;
    anio sois no rosto　　　　　you are angelic in your features,
    no juizo e condição　　　　judgment, and character.

190 Estrella　　　　　　　　　　Star

    As estrelas perdem　　　　Stars lose
    o seu valimento　　　　　 their shining light
    vendo o brilhante　　　　　when they see
    do teu luzimento.　　　　　your brilliance.[84]

---

82. The flower bed represents the convent, and the roses represent the nuns. If you populate this beautiful convent with nuns, it becomes even more stunning.

83. *angelica*: wild celery (*anjelica achangela*)? Or another name for a flower?

84. Stars lose
    Their shining light

191 Mão com frecha   Hand with an Arrow[85]

      A hum peito livre   Arrows shot at
      inzento do amor   a free heart
      que frechas disparas   unencumbered by love
      cruel traidor   are a cruel betrayal.

192 Lirio   Lily

      Pureiza esplica   Purity accounts for
      lirio preçiozo   [why] the precious lily
      cheiro que agrada   [has] a smell that pleases
      a teu douçe espozo   your sweet husband.

193 Garça   Heron

      He garça real   The heron
      das a ves Senhora   is the Senhora among birds;
      entre damas bellas   among fine ladies,
      vos levais coroas   you take the garlands. [you wear the garlands?]

194 Espelho   Looking Glass

      En este espelho roza   In this looking glass, rose,
      comtemplai vossa belleiza   contemplate your beauty,
      e vereis que a natureiza   and you will see that nature
      te fes gala das fermozas   has made you the belle of the ball.

    Just as they watch
    Your golden aura.
        (Borges translation in Castel-Branco, "The Presence of Portuguese Baroque in the Poetic Works of the Sisters of Santa Monica in Goa," 252)

85. Clearly, this is Cupid's hand.

195 Cobra

    A cobra te segue
    com toda cautella
    descuidos te faz
    não fugir della

Cobra

    The cobra carefully
    stalks you;
    [if] you are careless,[86]
    you will not escape.

196 Canbalião

    Se cambalião
    sustento do vento
    tambem os amantes
    tem mesmo sustento

Drunkard [Weather Vane?]

    If the wind will hold up
    a drunkard,
    then those who love God
    will also be supported.

    [If the Weather Vane
    is sustained by the wind,
    so, too, lovers
    have the same support?]

197 Coroa

    Prendas da Rainha
    tem vossa pessoa
    com rezão te dã
    a sorte coroa

Crown

    You have
    the Queen's gifts;[87]
    they rightfully bestow upon you
    the blessed Crown.

198 Capella

    Sorte te oferesse
    para fermoza e bella
    dessas ricas flores
    a melhor capella

Chapel

    You are offered good fortune
    because of your beauty;
    these lovely flowers
    make for the finest chapel.

---

86. *descuido*: in vernacular Portuguese, means an unplanned pregnancy. Did it have the same meaning in early modern Portuguese? And if so, does this verse warn against the dangers of sex?

87. Queen of Portugal is Maria Anne.

199 Lua

    Desmaiada a Lua
    perde a valia
    competir não ousa
    com tal bizarria

Moon

    The vanishing [pale?] moon
    loses its luster
    and dares not compete
    with elegance such as yours.[88]

9 verso

200 Crux

    Na crux achareis
    toda dita e gloria
    pois he estandarte
    da major vitoria

Cross

    In the cross you will find
    all happiness and glory
    for it is the standard
    of great victory.

201 Azas

    Quem voar pretende
    com azas de esperanças
    não deive temer
    fortuna e mudança

Wings

    Whoever tries to fly
    on wings of hope,
    need not fear
    fortune and change.

202 Mundo

    O mundo blazona
    este vasallaie
    que de iuro paga
    a tão bella imagem

World

    This obedience [the world boasts]
    displays the world,
    which rightly pays interest
    to such a beautiful image [of Christ].

---

88. The vanishing moon
    Has no value
    And dares no competition
    With such a gallantry of yours.
        (Borges translation in Castel-Branco, "The Presence of Portuguese Baroque in the Poetic Works of the Sisters of Santa Monica in Goa," 252)

Entrada de Bonifrate para Festa dos Reis 111

203 Coração com azas

Alegres cuidados
venturoza dita
logreis em Jesus
glorias infinita

204 Serafim

Serafim humano
sois bella roza
em tudo descreta
em cabo fermoza

205 Frasco

Esta cor[dial]*
males não alivia
antes se redobra
as manlenconoias

206 Relogio

Penando cantais
relogios de auzencia
o ter*mo dilatão
faltão a paçiençia

207 Querobim

Meu cravo cherozo
meu bello jasmin
parelha com vosco
faz o querobim

Winged Heart

Be joyful, vigilant,
blissful, and fortunate:
you will find in Jesus
infinite glories.

Serafim

Human angel,
you are a beautiful rose,
discreet in all things
and beautiful to the end.

Flask

This cordial
does not take away maladies
but rather redoubles
one's sorrows.

Clock

You lament
the passing of time;
the interval expands,
clocks lack patience.

Cherub

My fragrant carnation,
my beautiful jasmine,
paired up with you
makes the Cherub.

208   Coração chorando   Weeping Heart

      Penoso chorais   In pain you weep,
      sem alívio a dor   your sorrow unrelieved,
      [. . .] que cruelmente   because love cruelly
      nos maltrata amor.   mistreats you.[89]

209   Lião   Lion

      Vençer ao amor   To conquer love
      he grande valentia   is a great feat;
      essa dita logra   by your gallantry
      vossa bizaria   you have achieved this good fortune.

210   Fortalleiza   Fortress

      Digna he de valor   Your steadfastness
      a vossa firmeiza   is worthy of value;
      con rezão vos couba   this fortress rightfully
      esta fortalleiza   suits you.

211   Ramalhete   Bouquet

      As razas e flores   Roots [branches?] and flowers
      vaisse por a mão   come from the hand [are passed from
      desta aquem o mundo   hand to hand?],
      rende a sugeição   from here the world
                                       surrenders itself.

---

89.   You cry in pain
      Pain without relief,
        (. . .) which cruelly
      Love ill-treats us.
            (Borges translation in Castel-Branco, "The Presence of Portuguese Baroque in the Poetic Works of the Sisters of Santa Monica in Goa," 256)

Entrada de Bonifrate para Festa dos Reis 113

212 Asafate

As flores mais bellas
as mais ricas rozas
vaise por as mãos
de outra m[ai]s fermoza

Wicker Basket

The most beautiful flowers and
the finest roses
come from the hands
of another [who is even] more beautiful.[90]

10 recto

213 Balança

Quando achai a balança
veio que os pezos te falta
pois não apezos que basta
apezar as esquivanças

Scales

When you find balance,
you will find yourself without worries,
for your troubles are not enough
despite your shirking [of your duty].

[When I found the scale,
I saw that the weights were missing,
for there are no weights enough
to counterbalance evasions.?]

214 Cadeado

Toda discrição
na prudençia a pura
estes ricas prendes
vos deu a ventura

Lock

All discretion
is refined in prudence;
fortune has given you
these fine gifts.

215 Burbaleita

Este rumo segue
tão bem os amantes
que a vida perde
por lux inconstante

Butterfly

Lovers [of the world]
follow this path so well
that [eternal] life is lost
for lack of light.[91]

---

90. the hands of another: a reference to God. He is responsible for the world's beauty, and regardless of how beautiful the world may appear, He is more beautiful.

91. The path of a butterfly is compared to a person stumbling in the dark. As a result of falling in the dark, lovers are damned to hell.

216	pavão	Peacock

        Quem no mundo emprega   Whomever in the world makes a show
        a sua afeição   of her affection
        tem os acidentes   has the qualities
        do mesmo pavão   of a peacock.

217	livro	Book[92]

        Se quereis senhoras   Ladies, if you want
        fizica saber   to know medicine,
        so para este livro   you can only learn it
        podeis aprender   from this book.

218	rozario	Rosary

        Em virgem podeis   You can always meditate
        sempre meditar   on the Virgin
        e com sua aiuda   and with her help
        os Çeos alcançar   reach the Heavens.

219	ancora	Anchor

        A sorta te ofereiçe   Fate offers you
        felix esperança   joyful hope;
        lograi as venturas   you shall attain good fortune
        sem temer as mudanças   without fearing change.

220	coração abrazado	Burning Heart

        Felix coração beaventurado   The joyful and blessed heart,
        que no amor divino   that which burns
        andais abrazado   with Divine Love.[93]

---

92. The Bible is clearly the book in question, and its words are the medicine for the soul.

93. This verse consisted of only three lines. We do not know why.

221   tigre

    La vos vai o tigre
    por seres raivoza
    vede não vos muda
    minha bella roza

Tiger

The roar of the tiger comes
when you are angry;
see to it that you don't fall silent,
my beautiful rose.

222   penna e tinteiro

    Dezabafar podeis
    roza nacarada
    ia tens o tinteiro
    e a penna aparada

Quill and Inkwell

You can say what you feel,
nacreous rose,
when you have an inkwell
and a trimmed quill.

223   pelicano

    Podeis contemplar
    neste pelicano
    fineizas que obra
    hum Deos Soberana

Pelican

By contemplating
this pelican
you can see the delicate work
wrought by the Sovereign God.

224   sin castigas

    Sois mui venturoza
    tereis fim ditoza
    pois vos sahio chagas
    de Deos amarozo

Without punishment

You are very fortunate;
you will come to a blessed end
because the Loving God
bled for you.

10 verso

225   espada rodella

    Boa esprevenção
    he para huma guerra
    sahi vos Senhora
    espada e rodella

Sword and Shield

For good protection
in a war
the Blessed Virgin gives you
a sword and shield.

226 dois A.A. — Two "A"s[94]

A sorte vos dá
o que linda data
Amor e auzençia
he o que vos mata

Luck gives you
that which is a beautiful thing,
Love and Loss
is that which kills you.

227 S — S

Saudades faz
a vida acabar
não há paçiençia
para a soportar

Longing makes
life end;
there is no patience
to bear it.

228 4 ssss — 4 Ss

Quem taos prendas logras
mereçe coroa
tributar ia pode
a vossa pessoa

Whoever achieves such gifts
deserves the crown;
your Person
is worthy of tribute.

229 burrafodor — Sprinkler

bem mereçeis minha roza
premio de muito valor
vos vai o burrafador
chea de agua cheiroza

You well deserve, my rose,
a prize of great value;
the sprinkler comes to you
full of fragrant water.[95]

230 Jarro baçio — Pitcher and basin

A não seres tão engraçada
forais muito mais fermoza
em fim levais por ditoza
jarro baçio de prata

If you were not so amusing
you would be much prettier,
[but] in the end you will happily carry
a silver pitcher and basin. [empty silver jar?]

---

94. This quatrain could be renamed "the two Ls" because, fortunately, both *amor* and *auzençia* translate into English using words that begin with the same letter, namely the letter l, *love* and *loss*.

95. Just as a sprinkler waters a rose, an aspergillum waters a nun.

231 aliabas

    Achaçe aqui muitas pennas
    nesta aliaba que ves
    com ella ferir podeis
    a quem tanta vos enagena

Quiver

    In this quiver here you will find
    many arrows;
    with them you can wound
    whoever so deceives you.

232 rato

    Quando querais recrear
    pode levar do barato
    este balhador rato
    que sabe muy bem dançar

Mouse

    When you seek entertainment,
    you can get this cheap
    dancing mouse
    that knows how to dance so well.

233 cuelho

    Eu dera serto hum olho
    se me sahiçe cueilho
    vosse tome a meu conçeilho
    fassa della loga molho

Rabbit

    If a rabbit got away from me,
    I would keep an eye out for it;
    take my advice
    and make a stew out of it soon.

234 Coração com rozas

    Alegres cuidados
    venturozo dita
    logreis em Jesus
    glorias infinita

Heart with Roses

    Be joyful, vigilant,
    blissful, and happy:
    you will find in Jesus
    infinite glories.

235 pucaro

    quem se não vos meu tezouro
    esta sorte teria
    pucaro de prata
    de vossos labios bizarria

Cup

    Who but you, my treasure,
    would have the good fortune
    to ennoble this silver cup
    with your lips.

236 Concha

    Este concha vai vazia
    porque a perola della
    sois vos aurora bella
    estremo de bizarria

Conch

    This shell will be emptied
    because of the pearl within;
    you are the beautiful dawn,
    the utmost of elegance.

237   Saco

Esta saco levais cheo
porque as vossas suadades

11 recto

são tão grandes na verdade
quais não ignoro eu

238   Roda de linha

De ociozidade vem
em caza muita ruina
com este roda de linha
passareis a vida bem

239   Sombreiro

Para hirdes ao teiro
e chegar the o Convento
para so[l] chuiva e vento
e grande guarda sombrero

240   Plumas

Vossa bizarria suma
muitos lauros mereiçe
porem a sorte the oferasse
em vitima estas plumas

241   Carro

Jurarão pois os amantes
canonizar vos prinçeiza
por constante afirmeiza
te poem em carro triunfanta

Sack

You fill this sack
with your longings,

which I do not ignore
and are truly great.

Spinning Wheel

From laziness [idleness?] comes
much ruin in the home;
with this threadwheel
you will spend your life well.

Hat

For coming up the hill
and arriving at the Convent,
for the sun, rain, and wind,
it is a fine thing to keep a hat with you.

Feathers

Your paramount elegance
deserves many laurels;
however fortune has gone so far as to offer up
these feathers as victims.

Chariot

Admirers swear
to canonize you, princess;
by your constancy and steadfastness,
they put you in the triumphant chariot.

242 Cofre

> Em este cofrinho formoso
> Cupido vos há guardado
> encerrado vossos cuidados
> estes suspiros penosos.

Coffer

> Cupid keeps you in
> this charming little coffer;
> your cares and heavy sighs
> are locked away.[96]

243 gurgaleita

> Coração lata pata
> esta fazei mana aqui
> ulha para vos ia vi
> hum gurgaleita de prata

Water jug

> This sister here makes
> the heart go pitter-patter;
> looking at you I see
> a silver gurgaleita.[97]

244 espeito

> Lianor vem sem respeito
> para os pes the quemar
> lorença mais devagar
> porem ambos com espeito

Stake

> Leonor remains defiant
> until the flames reach her feet;
> Lorença holds out longer,
> but both are burned at the stake.[98]

245 Sapato

> Quem dá tudo quanto pode
> não lhe fica mais que dar
> eu vos venho ofertar
> estes sapatos de frades

Shoe

> He who gives all he can
> has nothing left to give;
> I come to offer you
> these friars' shoes.

---

96. In this little charming box
    Cupid has locked you,
    Shut off your sorrows
    these painful sighs.
    (Borges translation in Castel-Branco, "The Presence of Portuguese Baroque in the Poetic Works of the Sisters of Santa Monica in Goa," 256)

97. *laṭa paṭa*: in Marathi and Kannada, it is the onomatopoeic sound imitating something beating, such as horses' hooves or a heart; see James T. Molesworth, *A Dictionary: Marathi and English* (Bombay: Bombay Education Society Press, 1857), 707, and the online *Alar Kannada-English* corpus at https://alar.ink/.

    gurgaleta: clay water pitcher with a spout that gurgles when poured. In this quatrain, the gurgling of water being poured from a *gurgaleta* is likened to the pitter-patter (*laṭa paṭa*) of an excitedly beating heart.

98. Leonor and Lourença are the mother and wife of Antonia da Silva. The Inquisition tortured them on suspicion that they were crypto-Jews. See introduction, pp. 20–21.

toca asubio emtra dois violens, canta malos malos	A whistle blows; enter two guitarists singing "malos malos"[99]
toca asubio entra escarramuça	A whistle blows; the "beloved"[100] enters

Mestre / Master

246 Meu querido escarramão
     meu bem minha alegria
     venho empregar em vos
     toda minha alegria

My dear beloved,
my dearest, my joy,
I put all my happiness
in you.

Malavar / Malavar

247 Se auzencia tanto mata
     como pode hum bem viver
     hum amor que desbarata
     esparança mal sofrer

If [your] absence is so deadly,
how can one live well?
One can hardly bear
A love that squanders hope.[101]

Caneri / Canarim

248 Se de mim a vais de crer
     quer auzente o prezente
     meu amore ****
     a teus pés mui contente

If you will trust in me,
whether [you are] absent or present,
my love [resides?]
at your feet, very happy.

Cafre / Cafre

249 Daime cá este anel
     prenda tão mã lograda
     pois vos fostes a c****
     de eu andar a restada

You give me this very ring
a gift so undeserving,
for you were the cause
of my capture.

---

99. *malos malos*: woe woe.

100. In this song, *escarramuça/escarramão* seems to be a term of endearment for Christ or God. See introduction, p. 38.

101. If absence kills so much
       how can one live well
       a love that shatters
       hope barely suffers.

   (Borges translation in Castel-Branco, "The Presence of Portuguese Baroque in the Poetic Works of the Sisters of Santa Monica in Goa," 256)

11 verso

    Mestre   Master

250 Muitas veizes este lenço   Many times this handkerchief
      em lagrimas se emsopava   is soaked in tears,
      ausente de vossa vista   [as I am] absent from your sight,
      toda chea de saudade   full of longing.

    Malavar   Malavar

251 Nunca vos amei desizo   If you were not perfect[102]
      para serdes vos mal maçado   I would not love you so firmly,
      nem empreguei em vos   nor would I put
      o meu cego cuidado   my blind trust in you.

    Caneri   Canarim

252 Sugeito a vosso querer   I subject myself to your will
      a vossa vista abastado   and to your bountiful sight,
      minha linda assuçeina   my beautiful açusena flower,
      minha rica esmeralda   my gorgeous emerald.

    Cafre   Cafre

253 Daime cá estes graças   Give me these very bounties,
      meu querido escarramão   my dear escarramão;
      vos sois minha lux   you are my light,
      prenda do meu coração   gift of my heart.

    toca asubio emtra dois renoas   A whistle blows, enter two Portuguese
    canta ~~ni*** ***** ****** anta~~   singing

      a tirei com hum pist**   "I removed it with a line"[103]

---

102. *mal maçado*: "poorly kneaded"? Perhaps *maçado* is derived from the word *massa*, meaning dough. Therefore, the expression could mean something like "poorly kneaded" or "poorly formed," signifying "not perfect." This is largely conjectural.

103. An editor removes the above phrase by drawing a line through it.

	toca asubio entra dois bugios	A whistle blows, enter two monkeys

Mestre / Master

254 Amor naçeu para nos / Love was born to us [God loves us
e não naçeu para vos / and not to you; and not you]
saltar queria / you wanted to jump,
cocarali temeria [?] / you were afraid [?].

Malavar / Malavar

255 Dos montes vie*** / We came from the mountains
correndo e saltando / running and jumping.
nos montes trapando / Climbing in the mountains
as frutas comemos / we ate the fruits.
amor naçeu[104] para nos / Love was born to us [God loves us
e não naçeu para vos / and not to you. and not you]

Caneri / Canarim

256 Dis qui amor laia[105] bugio / Some say love is like a monkey:
fazei cara para gente / You make [making] faces at people
raganhado sua dente / chattering your teeth,
fazei corpo quente frio / you run hot and cold.

Cafre / Cafre

257 Dis qui amor laia bugio / Some say love is like a monkey:
faz olhos sono sono / Eyes become [making eyes?] heavy with sleep,
no corpo mutios momos / you make ridiculous gestures
mostrando seus brios / revealing your vigor.

---

104. The phrase "amor naçeu" is illegible in the manuscript; however, we have supplied it here because it is a repetition of two lines from quatrain #254.

105. *á laia de*: in the manner of.

Entrada de Bonifrate para Festa dos Reis 123

	Mestre	Master
258	Dis qui amor laia bugio faz manhã como quem dorme quando lhe perta a fome trapa nos alvores sobrios	Some say love is like a monkey: You reach the morrow like someone who is sleeping, when you reach hunger, [when hunger strikes] you arise in the sober dawn.

toca asubio entra Mai marica / A whistle blows, enter Mother Marica
com seu caferinho / with her slave boy

toca asubio entra velha com seu / A whistle blows, enter an old woman
filho e Pai / with her son and father

Cantiga da Velha / The Old Woman's Song

	Mestre	Master
259	que me dis de hum velho honrado que queria hum carapuça esta velho e carapuceiro carapução sua velha balha dadão	I heard about an honorable old man who wanted a hood; the hood-maker made him a fancy hood, and his old wife danced, ding-dong.

	Malavar	Malavar
260	que me dis de hum velho honrado que queria huma camiza este velho e camizeiro camisão sua velha balha dandão	I heard about an honorable old man who wanted a shirt; the shirt-maker made him a fancy shirt, and his old wife danced, ding-dong.

	Caneri	Canarim
261	que me dis de hum velho honrado que queria hum caçaque este velho e caçaqueiro caçaquão sua velha balha dandão	I heard about an honorable old man who wanted a jacket; the jacket-maker made him a fancy jacket, and his old wife danced, ding-dong.

Cafre / Cafre

12 recto

262 que me dis de hum velho hon-   I heard about an honorable old man
     rado   who wanted some shorts [pants?];
     que queria hum calção   the shorts-maker made him some fancy
     este velho calcãozeiro calcaião   shorts,
     sua velha balha dandão   and his old wife danced, ding-dong.

Mestre / Master

263 que me dis de hum velho hon-   I heard about an honorable old man
     rado   who wanted some shoes;
     que queria hum sapato   the shoe-maker made him some fancy
     este velho sapateiro sapatão   shoes,
     sua velha balha dandão   and his old wife danced, ding-dong.

toca asubio emtra bai de supo   A whistle blows, enter a *bai de supo*

Cantiga / Song

264 chipeti   [a winnowing basket full of marigolds?]
     supa supa supa gonde fulali   beautiful, beautiful, beautiful marigolds
     ~~lambatati moga quei~~   flowering
     ~~supa guelem sonora~~   What [. . .] love/flower[106] is this
     ~~sai b*** che go** cor~~   sweet sound
     ~~supa moga la supa supa~~   [colors?]
                                       beautiful love there, beautiful, beautiful

toca asubio entra dois morisco   A whistle blows, two moriscos arrive
canta ** sai murisco   a morisco enters singing ***

---

106. *moga*: could mean "love," but it could also be another flower; see the entry on "mogarins" in Castro, *A Cinza dos Myrtos: Poemas*, 186.

Entrada de Bonifrate para Festa dos Reis

Espada de fogo

Mestre

265 ninguem tem na mundo
tal abelidade
diga vos senhora
em realidade

Malavar

266 E couza para admirar
ver esta invenção
**rder a espada
não quemar a mão

Caneri

267 O Senhoras Madres
dezei me verdade
vistas algum dia
esta abelidade

Mestre

268 Esta espada de fogo
sempre trago comigo
que he nova traça
para matar inimigo

toca asobio entra donna aldonça
de gala sai ella

entra emcamizade
 bolas de fogo[107]
Depois fas fogo na tigela com
isto acaba

Flaming sword

Master

Let me tell you, Senhora,
that, in truth,
no one in the world has
such skill.

Malavar

It is something to admire
to see this trick,
to hold this sword
that does not burn the hand.

Canarim

O my Senhoras Mothers,
tell me the truth,
have you ever seen
this kind of skill?

Master

I always bring this
flaming sword with me'
it's a new style
designed to kill the enemy.

A whistle blows; Donna Aldonça elegantly arrives; she leaves

[The Master] enters [again] cloaked,
then [the Master] puts the fireball in a
bowl [of water] and with this [action] it
goes out.

---

107. *bolas de fogo*: Written in a different hand. These words were added to clarify that the word *fogo* refers to the fireballs that have appeared throughout the show.

126 Entrada de Bonifrate para Festa dos Reis

	Mestre	Master
269	A deos minha Madres que eu me quero hir depois não digais que de vos não despedi	Goodbye, my Mothers, for I want to go, after I leave, don't say that I did not bid you all farewell.

Cartepaço da Muzica

1 verso

Este cartepaço he da muzica do treceiro ano da Madre Francisca do Sacramento Prioreza de Ano de 176[6]	This notebook contains the music of the Prioress Mother Francisca do Sacramento, written in her third year, in the year 176[6]

Cantiga para hir a horta — **Song to go to the garden**

1. Caminhemos para a horta
 com muita aflição
 pois asim emporta
 festeiar a São João

 Let's go out to the garden
 with great fervor,[1]
 as it is important
 to celebrate Saint John.

 Volta — Refrain

2. Venha sem dilação
 as flores mais eselente
 a festeiar reverente
 O Naçimente de São João

 Come without delay,
 most exquisite flowers,[2]
 to reverently celebrate
 the Nativity of Saint John.

3. Tudo he hoie alegria
 tudo neste dia he festa
 as flores desta floresta
 mostra sua bizarria

 Today everything is joyous,
 on this day everything is festive,
 the flowers of this flower garden
 show their elegance.

---

1. *aflição*: affliction, distress, trouble, woe. Bluteau explicitly links aflição with bodily pain, "pena do corpo," (*Vocabulario Portuguez*, 1:154). We have chosen the word "fervor" as it is connected to "fever," and this has both the older sense of a pathological heat of the body (one of its humors) but also a more contemporary sense of ardor, passion, or excitement.
2. The nuns are the flowers, and the garden is the convent.

4	As flores em união punhão algres neste dia fazer dança e fulia em louvor de São Jão	Flowers, in unison, make merry on this day, dancing and reveling in praise of St. John.

2 recto

Prioress Francisca do Sacramento[3]

5	A roza como rainha mostra sua belleza nossa amada Prioreza toda hermoza caminha	The rose,[4] like a queen, displays its beauty; [just like] our beloved Prioress in all her loveliness strolls.

Subprioress Joanna de Santa Rosa

6	O lirio flor honesto mostra que a todas agrada nossa segunda Prellada caminha com grande gesto	The honest Lily flower delights all with its display; [just like] our Subprioress who walks with such composure.

First Prelate Izabel de Aprezentação

7	A sulena flor sublimada asiste nesta festa real nossa Madre Izabel he digna de ser louvada	The sublime Sulena flower attends this royal festival; [Just like] our Mother Isabel so worthy of praise.

---

3. We have added the names of the verse's subjects in italics. These names and dates do not appear in the original manuscript.

4. The rose like a Queen
   Irradiating her beauty
   Our beloved Prioress
   Walks very beautifully.
   (Borges translation in M. Carmen d'Assa Castel-Branco, "The Presence of Portuguese Baroque in the Poetic Works of the Sisters of Santa Monica in Goa," 253)

The rose is a symbol of mature beauty, as seen in Matia Periera da Sylva's famous five-volume anthology of the best Portuguese poetry, *A Fenix Renascida: Ou Obras Poeticas dos Melhores Engenhos Portuguezes* (Lisboa: Na offic. dos Herd. de Antonio Pedrozo Galram., 1746). The Prioress, Madre Francisca do Sacramento, was forty-three years old at the time these *cantigas* were composed.

Second Prelate Britis de Trindade

8	Pois a nossa Madre Britis que hé tambem de Trinidade digo que hê huma lus que tem muita claridade	Then there is our Mother Britis, who is also called "of the Trinity"; I say that she is a light that shines brightly.
9	A flor que hé maravilla são aquellas que com veo[5] parese flor do çeo que entre outras mais brilha	The flower that is a marvel, among all those with a veil, is like the flower of heaven that shines more brightly than others.

Novices

10	A flor que chama misticas seja embora indiana emtudo são soberanos as nossas bellas noviças	The flower that is called *mestiças*, even though Indian, [is like] our lovely novices, who are in all things sovereign.

Postulants

11	As que são clovinas hê flor que pode agradar a ellas quer conparar as nossas lindas meninas	Those that are *clovinas* are flowers that can please; these can be compared to our beautiful little girls.

Lay Sisters

12	Angelica me leva a vista e tem muita suavidade nossas leigas na verdade são amante de Baptista	The Angelica flower, which captivates my gaze, has so much mildness; truly our lay sisters are lovers of the Baptist.

---

5. Emend *veo* → *véu*: veil.

Augustinian friars

13	Giraçol flor sublimado com mais bello arminho os filhos de Agostinho nos robo todo agrado	The sublime Sunflower with a most beautiful ermine coat,[6] [is like] the sons of Augustine [who] steal our attention.
14	Fuguetinho pello ar arebentão de quando em quando não anda as flores bricando não lhe suçede queimar	[Like] fireworks in the air, bursting forth from time to time, the flowers are not playing[7] and they do not burn.[8]
15	luminarias e fugeira na horta ja se começa hi de ver flor com preça cada qual seja primeira	Bonfires and fireworks are starting [to be lit] in the garden; Come quickly to see the flowers [because] each and every one is preeminent.

Convida a Reverendissima Madre Prioreza as religiosas para hir a horta

The Most Reverend Mother Prioress invites the nuns to go to the garden

2 verso

16	A todos sem exepção hoje quero convidar para vir afesteiar a dia de São João	Today, I want to invite everyone, without exception,[9] to come and celebrate Saint John's Day.

---

6. The sunflower, and in particular the "double sunflower," is known for its fuzzy, fluffy, soft texture. Here, the nuns compare the soft, almost fur-like texture of this flower to the weasel's ermine coat. This ermine coat, which is white and tipped with black at the end, is in turn compared to the white robes with a black cincture worn by some Augustinian friars residing in India. The phrase "robo todo agrado" is odd in this context, but the meaning seems to be that the friars demand the nuns' attention because they look so sharp in their white robes and black cincture. This is not the only time the nuns will suggest a physical attraction to the neighboring Augustinian friars; compare *Cantiga dos Padres*, pp. 146–48, vv. 89–102.

7. The flowers are not literally bursting like fireworks, so they do not burn.

8. vv. 13–14: dedicated to the Augustinian friars, these verses are meant to be taken together.

9. The Prioress is inviting not only the professed and lay nuns, but also the novices, popillas, and most likely the servants and staff who worked in the convent as well. In other words, the whole community

17	Venha todos este mosteiro com estremada alegria festeiar tão bella dia com afecto verdadero	Everyone in this monastery, come with utmost joy to celebrate such a beautiful day with true passion.
	a todos	to everyone [refrain]
18	He mui justo hè de rezão que com fogos repetidos tem hoje aplauze devidos ao nosso São João	It is right and just that today, with many fireworks, proper praise is given to our Saint John.
	a todos	to everyone [refrain]
19	Todas sem huma faltar para a horta agora venha pois quero eu lã tenha hoje huma dia singular	One and all come to the garden now, for I want to have you there on this special day.
	a todos	to everyone [refrain]

Cantigas a São João   **Songs to Saint John**

20	Os Astros se esmerão tanto hoje em seu luzimentes por tributar rendimentes aos pes de nosso Santo	Today, the celestial bodies increase in their brightness, in order to pay tribute at the feet of our Saint.
21	A lua mui dezeioza de mais lustrar neste dia para o curço que fazia por se mostrar estremoza	The eager moon shines even brighter on this day, to demonstrates great passion in the course that it takes.
	os Astros	the celestial bodies [refrain]

---

is invited.

22	Mi vulgar opininão segundo ousso afirmar que costuma o sol bailar no dia de São João		In my humble opinion, according to what I have heard, the Sun typically dances on St. John's day.
	os Astros		the celestial bodies [refrain]
23	Tambem ja ouvi dizer que as estrellas neste dia hum baile de a alegria costumão todos fazer		I have also heard That, on this day, all the stars typically perform a joyous dance.
	os Astros		the celestial bodies [refrain]
24	Mas se he no mundo interio São João tão desfiado mais se verá ezaltada hoje no nosso Mosteiro		But of all the places in the whole world [where] St. John is so honored, today, in our monastery, he will be most exalted.
	os Astros		the celestial bodies [refrain]
25	Será com muita rezão muito por nos aplaudido por cá na terra ter çido Erimitam São João		It is quite right and praised by us, that the hermit Saint John has been here on earth.
	os Astros		the celestial bodies [refrain]
26	oh meu eremitam amado oh meu Santo esclareçido		Oh my beloved hermit, Oh my brilliant Saint,

3 recto

	hoje sereis mais querido e por nos mais venerado		today you will be most loved and most venerated by us.
	os Astros		the celestial bodies [refrain]

	outra cantiga a Madre	**Another song to Mother [Francisca]**[10]
		Prioress Francisca do Sacramento
27	De Francisca la bizarria oy cantamos com primores qual roza entra las flores tiendo del prado alegria	Today we exquisitely sing about the elegance of Francisca, who is like a rose among flowers, bringing joy to the garden.
28	com regozijos las flores le tributa rendimiento com gallardos conplimientos dando mui fragante olores con reçiprocos amores aclama gala del dia	With joy, the flowers pay her tribute with generous compliments, giving off such fragrant scents with mutual love proclaiming the jubilation of the day.
	de Francisca	of Francisca [refrain]
29	que lleva la palma esplica entalle y hermozura com estremada cordura la fama llena publica thezoura y joya mais rico de **** y gallardia	Sculpted and beautiful describes she who carries the palm with so much prudence; her public fame is full of such rich treasures and jewels of **** and elegance.
	de Francisca	of Francisca [refrain]
30	Margarita y esmeralda zefiro robim flamante jaçinto y Diamante y la perola estremada tudo eres sublimada oriental pedraria	Margarite crystals and emeralds Shining sapphires and rubies, jacinths and diamonds, also the pure and perfect pearl: you are [like] these sublime gemstones of the orient.[11]
	de Francisca	of Francisca [refrain]

10. Note that the next three cantigas are in Spanish.

11. In his *História da Fundaçaõ do Real Convento de Santa Mónica da Cidade de Goa, Corte do Estado da Índia, e do Império Lusitano do Oriente* (Lisboa: António Pedrozo Galram, 1699), Frei Agostinho

	Cantiga a Madre Suprioreza	**Hymn to the Mother Subprioress**

Subprioress Joanna de Santa Rosa

31 Com vozes mui generoza   With such bountiful voices
    cantemos todos louvores   let us all sing the praises
    a las sublimes primores   to the sublime exquisiteness
    dela Suprioreza hermoza   of the beautiful Subprioress.

32 Asombro y admiracion   Dazzling and worthy of admiration
    es su rara hermozura   is her rare beauty;
    suma graçia y cordura   the utmost grace and prudence
    llena toda su acçion   suffuse all her actions;
    com tan alta elevaçion   due to your great stature
    la vista hace dichoza   the sight of you creates happiness.

    con vozes   with voices [refrain]

---

de Santa Maria compares the Mónicas to the gemstones of the Orient:
> The minerals of India not only produce resplendent pearls in their fisheries, fiery rubies, brilliant emeralds, and pure diamonds in their quarries; they also create, in their mines, rich sapphires, the figure and symbol of enduring souls which is not disproportionate to the state of the widowed castes, to celebrate with them new marriages to that loving Lord, who everyone seeks and none despise. The golden bonds of His love can well be fired with these graceful stones. The graceful and resplendent sapphire was, in the eyes of God, D. Filipa Ferreira, whose virtues and actions demand a large volume. (Livro IV, Capiltolo I, 486)

Daisy and emerald
Shining sapphire or ruby
Hyacinth and diamond
Also pure and perfect pearl
You are the sublime oriental
Precious stone of Francisca.
> (Borges translation in Castel-Branco, "The Presence of Portuguese Baroque in the Poetic Works of the Sisters of Santa Monica in Goa," 252)

33	Adornada da belleza supo vençer coraçones singular son sus blazones nuestra bella suprioreza pues fortuna con firmeza le rinde tan carinhoza	Adorned with beauty, knowing how to conquer hearts, her accolades[12] are special; Our lovely Subprioress, indeed, fortune resolutely yields such a caring person.
	con vozes	with voices [refrain]
34	Pues un hermozo protento una primavera de Abril	Indeed, April spring is a beautiful harbinger,

3 verso

	oy con glorias de mil e mil logro dichozo convento sin fim siglos de contento eternize su fama glorioza	today, with thousands of glories, this blessed convent earns endless centuries of contentment, its glorious reputation eternal.
	con voces	with voices [refrain]

Cantiga para o Santo — **Song for the Saint**

35	Con aplauzo y contento festeiem el mejor dia con regozijo y alegria del Baptista el naçimiento	With praise and joy we celebrate the best day with rejoicing and happiness for the birth of the Baptist.
36	de Izabel y Zacaria naçe oy este luzeiro a ser de Dios pregonero que su vos de melodia con tan sacra armonia que será mayor protento	Isabel and Zacharias[13] on this day gave birth to this light to be God's preacher. His melodious voice, with such sacred harmony, will be a great harbinger.

---

12. *blazones*: name of a literary piece composed of small verses with flat rhymes and containing the praise or the blame of what one wanted to "recognize," see Emile Littré, *Dictionnaire de la Langue Française, Supplément* (London: Hatchett, 1875–1876), 43.

13. Luke 1:1–80. Isabel and Zacharia are the parents of John the Baptist.

con aplauzo   with praise [refrain]

37 Ioan es nombre de primor
que toda graçia encierra
buenes dias y la tierra
a dar naçe por su Senhor
como sagrado precurçor
del Divino entendimiento

John is the first among names
in all grace; he encompasses
blessed days and the earth.
His Lord had him born
as a sacred precursor
of the Divine understanding.

con aplauzo   with praise [refrain]

38 La dicha deste infante
publique em el orbe con valor
pues oy naçe como un flor
dando olores fragrantes
a vozes con glorias cante
oy al Ioan neste Conviento

The joy of this infant
is bravely announced to the world.
For today, he is born like a flower
giving off fragrant scents.
Today, in this convent,
glorious voices sing to St. John

con aplauzo   with praise [refrain]

Cantiga a Madre Prioreza   **Song to the Mother Prioress**

39 que hoje hé o dia
em que festeiamos
a Baptista Jõao
que tanto estimamos

Today is the day
in which we will celebrate
John the Baptist,
whom we hold in such high esteem.

40 Demos pois as vivas
com muito luzimente
a Madre Francisca
chamada do Sacramento

So, let us
vigorously cheer
Mother Francisca
called "of the Sacrament."

41 Nossa Prioreza
fermoza na bizarria
quanto he dotado
de rara beleza

Our Prioress,
beautiful in her exquisiteness,
how great is her gift
of rare beauty.

42	Na prudençia he único hè em prendas tal que no mundo todo não hã outra igual	One of a kind in prudence, as well as in gifts; in the whole world she has no equal.
43	Chegão seus conçeitos quazi a competir	Her ideas spring forth as if competing

4 recto

	como rayos do sol no major luzir	with the rays of the sun to see which shines more brightly.
44	hè tão singular na sua eloquencia que a sinçero e humero thé faz conpitençia	Her eloquence is so excellent that she is in competition with Cicero and Homer.
45	hè notorio he patente e o vosso grande talento e muito claro no entendimente Senhora Francisca do Sacra- mento	Your great talent is well-known and obvious and your learning is clear, Senhora Francisca do Sacramento.
46	Por que a prudençia nos desse ouzadia só para diz ellos hera perde o dia	Your wisdom makes us bold enough to tell them that they have lost the day.

Cantiga para Madre Supriorezа **Hymn for the Mother Subprioress**

47	Só huma vos sublimada e não outra vos que quer louvores pode dizer a esta segunda Prellada	Only one voice,[14] and no other, needs be raised to be able to sing praises to this second Prelate.

---

14. Emend *vos* → *voz*.

48	Por muito que é subtilleza não poderá bem louvar hoie se queira empenhar a Madre Suprioreza	However subtle [that voice] is, it will not be able to give just praises if one wants to dedicate [itself], today, to the Mother Subprioress.
	só huma	only one [refrain]
49	Se o meu fraco entendimento a mais pudeçe chegar não secara de louvar tão alto mereçimento	If only my weak understanding could reach higher, then I would not run dry of praise for one so worthy.
	só huma	only one [refrain]
50	Posso dizer com serteza sem nenhuma afectação que digna de veneração hé a Madre Suprioreza	I can say with certainty without any affectation that [the one who] deserves veneration is the Mother Subprioress.
	só huma	only one [refrain]

Cantiga para as Madres Ofiçiaes — Hymn for the Mothers who hold Offices

Mother Izabel de Aprezentação

51	Hé a Madre Izabel abssoluta Prellada digna de ser louvada por ser flor deste vergel[15]	She is Mother Izabel, Absolute Prelate, worthy to be praised for being a flower in this garden.
52	Porteira fizerão quem logre prendas taes que ninguem mereçe mais este cargo que lhe devão	They made her Gatekeeper, she who possesses such gifts; No one deserves more this position that they have given her.

---

15. *vergel*: synonym for *horta, jardim, pomar*.

Mother Britis de Trindade

53	A segunda Abssoluta ninguem o pode igualar Madre Britis de Trindade por ser ella mais singular	The Second Absolute [Prelate] [is] Mother Britis de Trindade; no one can equal her as she is so extraordinary.

4 verso

54	toda hé muy perfeita toda hé muy bella de melhor agrado não hã outra como ella	Everything [about her] is perfect, everything [about her] is beautiful, she is most pleasing, there is no one like her.
55	Por Madre do Seleiro preziste neste lugar como flor mais singular deve louvar primero	As the Mother of the Granary, you have stayed in this place; like the most extraordinary flower, you deserve praise first.

Mother Senhorinha de Jesus

56	A Madre Senhorinha de Jesus tambem hé a conçelheira por ser ella primeria os brios nella relus	Mother Senhorinha de Jesus is also a councilor; being the foremost, her noble character shines forth.
57	A Mestra das Obras tem tambem outra ocupação que por sua boa condição a conselho leva tambem	The Mistress of Works also has another position: because she is so competent she is also on the Council.
58	Convem louvar a esta Madre Mestra das Obras venha colher desta festa nas abundâncias sobras	It is fitting to praise the Mother Mistress of Works, who has come to gather from this feast the abundant leftovers.

Mother Maria de Assumpção

59	A nossa Madre Maria que se chama de Assumpção trata a Sancristia con grande prefeição	Our Mother Mary, who is called "of the Assumption," takes care of the Sacristy with great perfection.
60	No lindo nomem que tem esta Madre Reverenda mostra ser huma tal prenda que lhe não chegue a ninguem	In that beautiful name that this Reverend Mother has, [she] reveals such a gift that no one else can come close to.

Mother Maria de São Joaquim

61	logo[16]	Then
	Em terçeiro lugar segue como serafim a nossa Madre Maria chamada de São Joaquim	In third place follows, like a seraphim, our Mother Mary called "of Saint Joaquim."
62	Digo em fim que hé Angelica Soberana hé deste Jardim a bella espadana	I say, in the end, that she is a Sovereign Angel; she is the beautiful cattail[17] in this garden.

Mother Jozepha de Santo Agostinho

63	Por ultimo deve lovar a Madre Jozefa por ser ella tambem a conselhera singular	Finally, one must praise Mother Jozefa because she is also a special councilor.

---

16. The word *logo* was added later. It is not clear if it is supposed to be part of v. 61 or not.

17. *espadana*: cattail.

64	Esta Madre hé a madresilva bella o rico jasmim digão louvores desta	This Mother is a beautiful honeysuckle,[18] a sweet smelling jasmine; they give praises to this [Mother].

Mother Roza de Assumpção

65	A Madre Roza tambem de Assumpção chamada deve ser mais ezaltada pello ocupação que tem	Mother Roza is also called "of Assumption"; she ought to be most exalted for the position that she holds.

5 recto

66	Tem tão divina incunbençia tambem Santo ocupaçoens que só cuida em confiçoens em bem de conçiençia	She has such divine charge, and also blessed tasks, that she only takes others into her confidence[19] in good conscience.
67	Vigario de coro ser não só essaz mereçia mas ainda mais podia esta Madre mereçer	She is worthy not only of being the vicar of the choir, but furthermore, this Mother is worthy of even more.

Mother Anna de São Joachim

68	A Madre Anna chamada de São Joaquim rege o coro como outra serafim	Mother Anna, called "of Saint Joaquim," rules the choir like another seraphim.

---

18. *madresilva*: honeysuckle.

19. *confiçoens*: this could be read as "confessions"; "she only cares about confessions / [made] in good conscience." However, it is doubtful that Madra Roza was hearing other nuns' confessions.

Mother Pascoa da Ressurreição

69	A Madre Pascoa chamada de Resurreição he nossa ropeira de grande estimação	Mother Pascoa, called "of the Resurrection," is our laundress held in high esteem.
70	Mas que avia dizer que os mainatos ter avia mestra que não mereçia nem podia ter +	But further one might say that the launderers[20] do not deserve such a good master.
71	Sempre no Noviçiado a religião se esmerou por esta cauza o fiou somente no seu cuidado	In the Novitiate religion is always honed;[21] for this reason, [the Novices] are left solely in her care.
72	huma Mestra de boa condição devia as novissas ter para bem ensinadas ser nos costumes da religião	The novices ought to have a skilled[22] Mistress so that they are well taught in religious practices.

Mother Ignaçia de Encarnação

73	A Madre muy singular Ignaçia de Emcarnação tem bella condição para as popillas tratar	The very special Mother Ignaçia of the Incarnation has such an ability to deal with the Popillas.

---

20. *mainata*: "Indivíduo responsável por lavar e engomar a roupa, na antiga Índia Portuguesa, em Angola e em Moçambique; lavador, lavandeiro [individual responsible for washing and ironing clothes, in the old Portuguese India, Angola, and Mozambique; washer, laundress]," see *Dicionário Priberam da Língua Portuguesa* [online], 2008–2021, https://dicionario.priberam.org/mainata.

21. *esmerar*: to do something with perfection, with extreme care.

22. *boa condição*: competent, accomplished, skilled, experienced.

74	foi aserto e discrição as popillas entregar quem só lhe sabe dar tão linda educação	With certainty and discretion, the Popillas were given over to the only one who knows how to give them such a beautiful education.

Mother Anna de Nazereth

75	A Madre Anna de Nazare chamada por ser ella muy bella em tudo estremada	Mother Anna, is called "of the Nazarene," for she is very beautiful and stands out in all things.
76	Na verdade hé digna de maior lugar por ser em tudo Provizora singular	In truth she is worthy of a greater position, for in all ways being an extraordinary Provisora.

Mother Violante do Coração de Jesus

77	A Madre Violante do Coração de Jesus para mestra das mossas muy singular se relus	Mother Violante of the Heart of Jesus, as the Mistress of the Girls, shines so extraordinarily.

5 verso

78	Tão bellamente os trata tão bem insino lhe da que mestra tão singular outra como ella não há	How beautifully she takes care of them, how good the instruction she gives; as such an extraordinary teacher there is no other like her.

Mother Britis de Santa Maria

79	A nossa Madre Britis chamada de Santa Maria acompanha os medicos com garbo e alegria	Our Mother Britis, called "of Blessed Mary," accompanies the doctors with elegance and joy.

80	Muito mais de vos diria minha linda roza em *tudo* muy brioza he huma rica pedraria	There is much more to be said about you, my pretty rose; you are always lively and a precious gem.
81	Aviza Mestra das novissas tenha o lugar com atenção pois com muita rezão louvar a ella todas venha	Know that the Mistress of the Novices takes her position seriously, so it is right that all come to praise her.

Mother Maria de Jesus

82	Grande novidade será Madre Maria de Jesus que essa galhofa se fas com os raios de sua lus	It will be a great novelty, Mother Maria de Jesus, that people could frolic with rays of her light.

Cantiga para Madre Escrivam **Song for the Mother Scribe**

Mother Caetana de Jesus Maria

83	A Madre Escrivam hé huma bizarria hé do mundo melhor prenda essa Senhora Reverenda Caetana de Jesus Maria	The Mother Scribe is an elegant one: this Reverend Senhora, Caetana de Jesus Maria, is the greatest gift to the world.
84	Como a penna de flores e roza dei lhe na mão para escrever tambem de ouro pode mereçer esta Senhora tão primoroza	With a rosy, flowery, pen in her hand in order to write; this Senhora of distinction also deserves a golden [pen].
	a Madre escrivam	Mother Scribe [refrain]

85	Só poderá hoje achar no depozito tal protento para honrrar ao convento no mesmo lugar deve estar	Only today will one find a wonder in the depository, in order to honor the convent she should stay right where she is.
	a Madre escrivam	Mother Scribe [refrain]
	as Madres Depozitarias	**Mother Treasurers**
	Mother Bibianna de São Miguel *Mother Barbora de Jesus Maria*	
86	As duas Angelicas cherozas que no depozito com bizarria eziste com alegria esses flores olorazas	There are two fragrant *angelicas* in the depository, these two fragrant flowers [are] joyful and elegant.
87	Bibianna por soberana se mostra muy brioza Barbora por airoza goza premaneçe ufana aplaudem todas **** por estas asuçenas preçiozas	Bibianna, so masterful, shows great vivacity. Barbora, dignified, enjoys long-lasting glory. Eveyone praises the **** of these precious azucena flowers.
	As duas	two [refrain]
88	Bibianna garbo dedia Barbora bonina engraçada ambas flores galharda	Bibianna, livley *dedia*,[23] Barbora, lovely daisy, both elegant flowers

6 recto

	de prado alegria pois todas as pedrarias aclama por Senhoras fermozas	in a meadow of joy, indeed, all the gemstones[24] declare them to be beautiful Senhoras.

---

23. *dedia*: an unknown type of flower.
24. *pedrarias*: gemstones that represent the nuns of the convent.

	Cantiga dos Padres	**Song of the [Augustinian] Fathers**
89	Não justo acabe a festa sem louvar aos graçianos nossos queridas Irmãos que sahe hoje mui ufanos	It is not right to end the feast without praising the Graçianos, our dear Brothers, who proudly come forth today.
90	Pretendo subir mui alto temo não poder chegar em lovar a huns sugeitos que hé em tudo singular	I wish [my song] to soar, but I fear I cannot [be so eloquent], when praising these men who are extraordinary in all things.
91	Com meu curto entender e com meu pouco alcançar dou prinçipio ao meu intento em vossas prendas publicar	Despite my limited understanding and [despite] my meager abilities, my utmost intention is[25] to proclaim your gifts.
92	A vossos Reverendissimos Padres a vos graçianos bellos a vos cofre de perfeiçoens dediço este obzequio	To you, Most Reverend Fathers, To you, most beautiful Graçianos, To you, storehouses of perfection, I dedicate this obsequy.[26]
93	Nesse abito que vestis en essas mangas que levais ser filho de aguia africano ao mundo pantenteais	In this habit that you wear, in these sleeves[27] that you bear, you present [yourself] to the world as a son of the African Eagle.[28]
94	Se por gentil e galhardo lovores todos mereçeis digo que sois anjos e serafins e muito mais nos paraçeis	Because you are genteel and elegant you deserve all praises; I declare that you are angels and seraphim, and to us you seem to be much more.

---

25. or: "I begin with the intention / to proclaim your gifts."

26. *obsequy*: here the meaning is clearly from the Latin *obsequium*, "ready compliance with the will or pleasure of another, esp. a superior," (*OED*) and does not mean a funeral rite or ceremony.

27. *mangas*: sleeves here are a metonym for the whole robe.

28. *aguia africano*: Saint Augustine.

95	Se de briozas vos chama não digo nada asertado pois vossos brios e primores deve ser realçado	When you are called lively, I am not saying anything inappropriate; indeed, your liveliness and splendor should be brought forth.
96	Amantes he estremozas e com tanta discrição com subtileza e traça sabeis robar coração	Passionate lovers with so much discretion, with subtlety and artifice, know how to steal the heart.[29]
97	Tão rendido nos dexais captiva sem liberdade que no altar do seu querer sacrifiçio de vontade	You leave us so vulnerable, captive, without liberty, that on the altar of your desire [we are] a willing sacrifice.
98	Se pretendeis ter riqueza não vades longe buscar hide ao convento de graça que tudo lã hai de achar	If you seek abundance you don't have to look far; [just] go to the Convento de Graça and there you will find everything.
99	Nelles tudo achareis e tendes tudo ao mão pois tem tudo de subeja e nada vos faltarai	Among them you will find [everything] and have everything at hand; indeed, you have everything in abundance and lack for nothing.

6 verso

100	cobranco de mor valia diamante de fino ouro perollas mais pedrarias emserrado neste thezouro	A collection of great worth, diamonds, fine gold, pearls, and other gemstones, are enclosed within this treasure.[30]

---

29. This felicitous translation comes from Anna Weerasinghe, "Sister Mariana's Spyglass: The Unreliable Ghost of Female Desire in a Convent Archive," April 6, 2021: https://nursingclio.org/2021/04/06/sister-marianas-spyglass-the-unreliable-ghost-of-female-desire-in-a-convent-archive/.

30. The "treasure" is the Convento da Graça itself.

101	Não tenho mais que dizer nem me fica que falar porem para dizer tudo seria nunca acabar	I have nothing more to say and I will not continue to speak, because to say everything would be to never stop.
102	Por fim digão todas viva vivão os nossos galhardos vivão os Padres Agostinhos de todas prendas dotado	Finally, everyone say "Long Live"! Long live our gallant ones, Long live the Augustinian Fathers, who are endowed with all gifts.

Cantiga de Cupido — **Song to Cupid**

103	Olha mana qui dizastre para Cupido ja suçedei dis qui ja endodecei sem mais tirti nem quarti tira la manda por acá	Look, O sister, what a disaster befalls you because of Cupid; they say that you are mad, you can't tell three from four. take her from there [and] send her over here
104	locuras qui amante fazei elle ia tomã paixão com raiva e com afliçar tudo juizo ja perdei	You also make your lover crazy; he is already impassioned, angry, and afflicted, you lose all good judgment.[31]
105	Elle tambem fazei locura tudo gente zonba mais ris despreza fala chi chi chama Cupido de burlla	He does crazy things: mocking and laughing at everyone, he contemptuously says "chi chi";[32] [That is why he is] called Cupid the Mocker.[33]

---

31. Foolishness you lovers do
    He is passionate already,
    Full of rage and afflicted
    I have lost all common sense.
    (Borges translation in Castel-Branco, "The Presence of Portuguese Baroque in the Poetic Works of the Sisters of Santa Monica in Goa," 254)

32. *chi chi*: (1) clicking of the tongue in disapproval, or (2) *xixi* is a common onomatopoeic sound imitating urination (English: pee pee).

33. *burla*: fraud, mockery.

106	Ora churã dezesperado ora está dã rizada tambem fazei matinada gritá correi enfadado	One minute they are weeping desperately,³⁴ the next they are laughing;³⁵ then they are singing, and then they run and scream with vexation.
107	Elle sizo nunca tinha mas agora está perdido totalmente andã despido quebra aza afinha azinha	He never has common sense, but now he is [completely] lost; he walks totally naked, his wings broken and stripped down.
108	Su arco frecha ja enterra num tem bom qui defendei zonbaria tudo está sofrei num pode para ninguem frecha	Already his bow and arrow are buried; no good person defends him, he suffers complete ridicule, and cannot shoot his arrows at anyone.³⁶
109	Tudo rua está paçia com grande dezesperação querei rança coração asim elle esta me*sa	He walks down every street, with great desperation; he wants to rip out³⁷ your heart thus, he is ****.
110	Para oespital ia levã cura laia laia esta fazei para Cupido num murrei macho no pé a lança	They bring [him] to the hospital, and you administer³⁸ the cure in this way: so that Cupid does not die, put shackles on his feet.³⁹

---

34. *dezesperar*: to become hopeless, to feel hopeless.

35. *enriçar*: to become confused, embarrassed.

36. Perhaps *para* here means "he stops," and then the verse would read, "he cannot stop anyone's arrow."

37. Emend *rança* → arrança.

38. *fazer laia laia*: perhaps from *à laia de*, "in the manner of," "by the way of," see ("à laia de" in *Dicionário Priberam da Língua Portuguesa* [em linha], 2008–2021). This phrase also occurs in the *Entrada*, v. 65.

39. *macho no pé a lança*: a similar phrase is found in the 1734 *Relação* when Archbishop Ignácio de Santa Teresa threatened the disobedient sisters with having "outras lançarlhes machos nos pès, e algumas nas mãos [some bound by their feet and others by their hands]" in order to punish them; see Daniel Michon and D. A. Smith, *To Serve God in Holy Freedom: The Brief Rebellion of the Nuns of the Royal Convent of Santa Mónica, Goa, India, 1731–1734* (London: Routledge, 2020), 40 and 43.

	Outro Cantiga	**Another Song**
111	Barbora por singular sahio hoie com amor aprefecoar con primor a esta festa prinçipal	Today, the extraordinary Barbora goes about with love to perfect, with excellence, this main feast.

7 recto

112	Huma jantar grandioza dais hoie nesta meza aplaudindo con firmeza a vossa Prellada amaroza	Today, you put on a grand dinner at this table, strongly praising your Beloved Prelate.
113	quiz estes neste dia mostrar vossa verdade que a mais na realidade a esta rica pedraria	On this day you want to demonstrate your truth, which is that you truly love this rich gemstone.[40]
114	com despendio ponposa aplaudis muy constante a vossa *hia amante esta Prioreza ditoza	You constantly praise, with lavish expenditure, your **** beloved: this blessed Prioress.

	Cantiga de Comunidade	**Song of the Community**

Mother Clara de Jesus: 1706–1768

115	Reverrendissima Madre Clara chamada de Jesus vossas partes e vertudes deste Convento relus	Most Reverend Mother Clara, called "of Jesus," your duties and virtues shine forth from this Convent.

---

40. The gemstone is the prelate, Prioress Francisca do Sacramento.

Mother Francisca de São José: 1715–1776

116 Madre Francisca de São Jozé
na discrição e primores
digna de muitos louvores
dotadas de parte hé

Mother Francisca de São José
in discretion and exquisiteness
you are worthy of many praises
and gifted with good sense.

Mother Joanna de Santa Teresa: 1741–1788

117 Madre Joanna de Santa Thereza
convem hoje neste dia
louvar com destreza
com muzica e armonia

Mother Joanna de Santa Teresa,
on this day it is appropriate
to skillfully praise [St. John]
with music and harmony.

Mother Anna de Jesus Maria: 1742–1808

118 Venha sem dilação
fazer huma fulia
na festa de São João
a esta Anna de Jesus Maria

Anna de Jesus Maria,
come without delay
to perform the fólia[41]
at the feast of St. John.

Mother Marianna de Assumpção: 1745–1786

119 que ezaltado se vem hoje
esta festa de São João
que muitos sem nellas juntas
vemos a Mariana de Assumpção

How ennobled [we will be], if she comes today
[to] this Festival of St. John,
where many, gathered together,
[will] see Marianna de Assumpção.[42]

---

41. *fólia*: a noisy Portuguese dance form. Dancers are accompanied by rattles and other instruments. See introduction, pp. 42–43.

42. This is a particularly difficult quatrain to translate. If we take these lines more literally as written:
    line 1: que ezaltado se vem hoje – how exalted we see today
    line 3: que muitos sem nellas juntas – where many without them together
    line 4: vemos a Mariana de Assumpção – we see Mariana de Assumpção
none of these options help us understand the meaning of the verse any better.

152 Cartepaço da Muzica

Mother Roza de Santa Anna: 1747–1787

120   Esta Madre Roza
        que tras o sobre nomem Santa Anna
        em tudo e mais singular
        como a flor espadana

This Mother Roza,
who bears the name "Santa Anna,"
is extraordinary in everything
just like the cattail flower.[43]

Mother Maria de São Joseph: 1748–1821

121   Maria de São Jozé
        hé muita emgraçada
        digna de ser louvada
        bizarra em tudo he

Maria de São Jozé
is so graceful;
she deserves to be praised
for all her elegance.

Mother Anna de Assumpção: 1749–1791

122   Madre Anna de Assumpção
        hé dos olhos bello agrado
        porque hé jardim das flores
        hé de bonino hum prado

Mother Anna de Assumpção
is the one with such pleasing and beautiful eyes
because she is like a flower garden,
like a daisy in a meadow.

Mother Pascoella de Ressurrieção: 1751–1781

123   A Madre Pascoella
        que hé de Ressureição

Mother Pascoella,
who is "of the Resurrection,"

7 verso

        ninguem tem que lhe diga
        hé fermoza sem senão

no one has to tell her
that she is a flawless beauty.

---

43. The cattail is commonly referred to as the plant with a thousand uses. Using the cattail as a metaphor to suggest that Madre Roza de Santa Anna is a polymath is much more apt than when it was used to describe Madre Madre Maria de São Joaquim's beauty (see p. 140, v. 62), as cattails are not especially beautiful (at least in our opinion).

Mother Archangella de Gloria: 1751–1794

124 Se com gloria festeia
São João o prezente dia
sõ a Madre Arcangella
nos faz a galenteria

If one "gloriously" celebrates
Saint John on this very day,
only Mother Archangella
wins us over.

Mother Anna do Sacramento: 1752–1784

125 A esta Madre Anna
chamada do Sacramento
hé dos astros que mais brilha
neste nosso firmamente

Mother Anna,
called "of the Sacrament,"
is the brightest star
in our firmament.

Mother Antonia de Santa Rosa: 1752–1776

126 A nossa Madre
Antonia de Santa Roza
hé de todas das flores
a florezinha mais vistoza

Our Mother,
Antonia of the Holy Rose,
is the showiest little flower
among all the flowers.

Mother Bernarda de Santo Agostinho: 1754–1811

127 Louvar a Madre Bernarda
de Santo Agostinho em verço
e querer fechar na mão
a grandeza de univerço

Praise Mother Bernarda
of Saint Augustine in verse;
she wants to hold the greatness
of the universe in her hand.

Mother Escolastica do Sacramento: 1755–1776

128 Não pode deixar de ser
hum conheçido protento
esta Madre que se chama
Escolastica do Sacramento

It cannot denied
that this Mother called
Escolastica "of the Sacrament"
is a recognized wonder.

154 Cartepaço da Muzica

Mother Joanna de Ave Maria: 1755–1797

129 Joanna de Ave Maria   Joanna de Ave Maria
     hé a flor perengrina   is a peregrina flower,[44]
     e por ser toda alegria   and because she is full of joy,
     e deste jardim bonina   she is a daisy in this garden.

Mother Elena de Santa Anna: 1756–1781

130 Venha hoie com alegria   Mother Elena de Santa Anna
     com gosto mais ufana   joyfully comes today
     aplaudir este dia   with zeal, as well as pride,
     Madre Elena de Santa Anna   to praise this day.

Mother Izabel de Madre de Deus: 1757–1820

131 Valhame Madre de Deos   Protect me "Mother of God,"
     São João me socorra   save me St. John,
     que veia Madre Izabel   may Mother Izabel come
     vir com muita pachorra   with great patience.

Mother Maria de Anunçiação: 1759–1798

132 Digo com muita atenção   I say with all due respect,
     com donaire e desdem   and with decorum and reserve,[45]
     que Maria de Anunçiação   that Maria de Anunçiação,
     nella muita graça tem   has so much grace inside her.

Mother Maria de São Miguel: 1759–1774

133 Maria de São Miguel   Maria de São Miguel
     hé bizarra quanta basta   is as elegant as can be,
     amais a Deos mui fiel   and what's more, so faithful to God,
     para que elle vos ****   that she **** you.

---

44. *peregrina: Jatropha integerrima*. An evergreen shrub with glossy leaves and clusters of star-shaped red, pink, and vermillion flowers. Its English names include Spicy Jatropha and Fire-Cracker.

45. *desdem*: although it has the meaning of scorn or disdain, clearly here it has a different meaning, perhaps "reserve" or "modesty."

Mother Luiza de São João: 1759–1772

134 A galhofa deste dia
      tão festiçeo como hi

The revelry of this day,
so festive as it is,

8 recto

      a ninguem melhor conpete
      que a Luiza de São Joze

nobody can compete
with Luiza de São Joze.[46]

Mother Paula de Anunçiação: 1759–1789

135 Paulla de Anunçiação
      hé asucena bizarra
      pois cauza afeição
      a sua linda e bella cara

Paulla de Anunçiação
is an elegant azucena flower,[47]
for her pretty and beautiful face
creates warm feelings.

Mother Eugenia de Santa Maria: 1760–1772

136 Eugenia de Santa Maria
      apluadi mui contente
      esta festa de alegria
      e a vos hé preteçente

I happily praise
Eugenia de Santa Maria;
this joyous festival
is dedicated to you.

Mother Thereza de Jesus: 1760–1777

137 Neste dia singular
      que a claridade relus
      hé bem que louvernos
      Madre Thereza de Jesus

On this extraordinary day
in which brightness shines,
it is fitting that we praise
Mother Thereza de Jesus.

---

46. This verse is an excellent summary party atmosphere at the festival. It is a day of revelry: dancing, singing, and "having a blast" (to keep with the theme of fireworks). Luiza appears to be the life of the party.

47. *açucena*: a type of lily, possibly the Madonna lily (*Lilium candidum*) or the St. Joseph's lily (*Hippeastrum johnsonii*).

Mother Luiza de Santa Alexandre: 1760-1779

138   Bem mereçia Madre
Luzia de Santo Alexandre ser
aquella religiosa que
capriçio faz desapareçer

Mother Luzia de Santa Alexandre
is worthy of being
the nun who
makes whims disappear.

Mother Francisca de Anunçiação: 1760-1773

139   Sõ Francisca de Anunçiação
tambem tem igual louver
mas digame por vida sua
se neste dia há outra flor

Francisca de Anunçiação
also deserves equal praise [as others]:
but swear to me on your life,
if on this day there [ever has been] another flower
    [like her].

Mother Mariana de Santo Christo: 1760-1773

140   Quem poderá Madre Mariana
de Santo Christo formar
nestes verços em louvor
que lhe pudeçe ajustar

Who else but Mother Mariana
de Santa Christo could write
these verses of praise
that are able to suit you [so well].[48]

Mother Joaquina de Anunçiação: 1761-1779

141   Venha sem dilação
na festa de São João[49]
fazer huma fulia
esta Joaquina de Anunçiação

Joaquina de Anunçiação,
come without delay
to the feast of St. John,
to perform the fólia.

---

48. Perhaps Madre Mariana de Santa Christo was one of the authors of these songs?
49. Venha sem dilação / na festa de São João: the same phrase is found in v. 118.

Mother Joaquina de Santa Ana: 1761–1831

142   Venha hoie com alegria
com garbo mui afana
aplaudir este dia
vos Joaquina de Santa Anna

You, Joaquina de Santa Ana,
joyfully come today
with elegance, as well as pride,
to praise this day.

Mother Maria do Coração de Jesus: 1761–1812

143   Madre Maria do Coração de Jesus
festeiai com rezão
assim a Madre Prioreza
como ao gloriozo São João

We should rightfully celebrate
Mother Maria do Coração de Jesus;
also the Mother Prioress
along with the glorious Saint John.

Mother Maria de Jerarchia: 1762–1796

144   De Jererquia seleste
venha a Madre Maria
festeiar esta festa
com prazer e alegria

From the "Divine Hierarchy"
let Mother Maria come
to celebrate this festival
with enjoyment and delight.

Mother Elena de Madre de Deus: 1762–1812

145   Elena de Madre de Deus
hé mui perfeita e bella
de melhor agrado
não há outra como ella

Elena de Madre de Deus
is very perfect and beautiful;
most agreeable,
there is no one like her.

8 verso

Mother Rita do Coração de Jesus: 1763–1772

146   logo sem demora
comecemos azinha
a dizer muitos louvores
desta Madre Ritinha

Immediately, without delay,
let's quickly begin
to proclaim the many glories
of this Mother Ritinha.

Mother Maria de Santa Rosa: 1763–1792

147	Se quizer Madre Maria de Santa Roza hum louvor hé nesseçario buscar outro melhor orador	If Mother Maria de Santa Rosa desires a verse of praise, it is necessary to seek for another, better orator.[50]

Mother Joanna do Nascimento: 1766–1723

148	Vos o Madre Jennona de Divino Naçimento hum confessor vos dou que tenhais boa proçedimente	O Mother Joanna of the Divine Birth, a confessor affirms that you have good conduct.

Mother Maria de Trindade: 1766–1808

149	Festeiais a vossa dita Maria de Trindade de ser des Espozo de Christo que hé grande feliçidade	Celebrate your good fortune Maria de Trindade, in being one of the Spouses of Christ, which is the greatest happiness.

Mother Anna de Madre de Deus: 1767–1809[51]

150	Anna de Madre de Deus digo vos toda verdade tocha para caminhar o çeo hé regra de nosso Padre	Anna de Madre de Deus, I truly proclaim to you [that] the law of our Father is the torch for the path to heaven.[52]

---

50. In other words, she is so exceptional that the authors cannot praise her adequately.

51. Madre Anna de Madre de Deus is the last of the nuns who had professed to the black veil by July 1767. The subsequent quatrains are dedicated to Novices (Noviças), Lay Sisters (Irmã Leigas), and Postulantas (Popillas).

52. *tocha para caminhar o çeo*: illuminates the way to heaven.

Noviça Roza de Santa Maria[53]

151	O mundo deixastes Roza de Santa Maria no religião amai a Deos com muito alegria	You left the world, Roza de Santa Maria; through religion you love God with much happiness.

Popilla Joaquina de Madre de Deus: 1768–[54]

152	de Madre de Deos sois menina Joaquina como a vosso Divino Espozo sede muita fina	You are "of the Mother of God," Joaquina, little girl; be very fine like your Divine Spouse.

Popilla Roza do Sacramento: 1770–1794

153	De flor tendes o nomem mais o apelido hé protento de chamar vos menina Roza do Sacramento	You have the name of a flower, and what's more your professed name is a wonderful thing to call you, little girl, Roza do Sacramento.

Popilla Thereza de Assumpção: 1771–1775

154	Thereza vos apelidaes tambem de Assumpção amai desta Senhora com amor de coração	Thereza, you are also named "of the Assumption"; your love for our Senhora is heartfelt.

---

53. Roza de Santa Maria does not appear in the *Book of Professions*; therefore, she chose not to pursue a life in the convent, chose to profess as a lay nun, or died before professing as a choir nun.

54. The *Book of Professions* does not supply a death date for Joaquina de Madre de Deus.

Popilla Lauriana de Jesus Nazareth[55]

155 Que rico nomem tendes
     menina Lauriana
     com Jesus Nazareno
     andai miuto afana

What a rich name you have,
Lauriana, little girl;
you proudly[56] walk
with Jesus of Nazareth.

Popilla Maria de Nazareth: 1773–1826

156 Maria de Nazare
     já que cria na religião
     caminhar a çeo
     com grande perfeição

Maria de Nazareth,
since she was raised with religion,
will walk the path to heaven
with great perfection.

Irmã Roza de Paraizo

157 Se no paraizo o***çe
     as flores que eu deziozo
     não faltar nesta festa
     huma roza de paraizo

If in paradise ****[57]
the flowers that I desire,
this festival will not lack
a Rose of Paradise.

9 recto

Irmã Ignes de Purificação

158 Bom sei eu Senhora
     Ignes de Purificação
     ninguem com mais primor
     festeiar pode a São João

I know well, Senhora,
that no one other than
Ignes de Purificação
can celebrate Saint John so deftly.

---

55. Laurianna de Nazareth, like Roza de Santa Maria, does not appear in the *Book of Professions*; therefore, she also chose not to pursue a life in the convent, chose to profess as lay nun, or died before professing as a choir nun.

56. *afana* → ufana, pride or honor.

57. *o***çe* → possibly *ofereçe*. If the flowers that I desire are offered in paradise...

Irmã Joanna de Baptista

159 Ninguem tem atenção
de Baptista estes primores
usar delle se não Joanna
por todos seres os seus amores

No one pays attention
to the perfections that the Baptist has
except for Joanna,
because of her love for all beings.

Irmã Izabel do Sacramento

160 Venha tambem Senhora Madre
Izabel do Sacramento
e neste dia não se perca
nem se quer hum so momento

Come also, Senhora Mother
Izabel do Sacramento,
on this day, and don't lose yourself
not even for a single moment.

Irmã Maria de Piedade

161 Venha festeiar a São João
com toda pontualidade
não fique de fora não
Maria de Piedade

Come celebrate Saint John
in a timely fashion;
no, no, Maria de Piedade,
don't remain outside.

Irmã Senhorinha de Purificação

162 Não se diminue tanto
de Purificação Senhorinha
por que este dia não permita
par[e]çe tanta na espinha

Don't diminish yourself too much,
Senhorinha de Purificação,
because this day it is not permitted
to seem so pitiful.[58]

Irmã Francisca de Assumpção

163 Se tanto *** empinhaçe
huma perolla com São João
mas outra couza eu diçera
de Francisca de Assumpção

If you were **** to pledge such
a pearl to Saint John,
but I would say otherwise
about Francisca de Assumpção.

---

58. *na espinha*: to look so thin, poor, or pitiful.

Irmã Mónica de Jesus Maria

164   E para que não pare
       direi com toda bizarria
       en a festa desta tarde
       Mónica de Jesus Maria

Mónica de Jesus Maria,
you speak with so much gusto
during this afternoon festival
so that it doesn't stop.

Irmã Jozefa de São Miguel

165   Entenda quanto quizer
       mas não diga que por fé
       Jozefa de São Miguel
       amante de São João hé

Believe as you will,
but don't say
[that] Jozefa de São Miguel
is the beloved of St. John because of her faith.[59]

Irmã Feliçoa de Jesus Maria

166   Hum astro mui brilhante
       por mais que me resta
       que hé Feliçia de Jesus Maria
       a mais rica desta festa

Felíçia de Jesus Maria,
is a brilliant star;
no matter how many remain,
she is the brightest at the festival.

Irmã Mariana de Madre de Deus

167   Mariana de Madre de Deos seja
       tão felis como brioza
       pois se neste hé eseciva
       no mais será estremoza

Mariana de Madre de Deus,
being as happy as she is full of brio,
for, if in this [world] she is effusive,
in the beyond she will be just as passionate.

---

59. This quatrain is quite confusing, and we would like to thank an anonymous reviewer for offering a few suggestions to make some sense of this. The *não* creates problems, and one solution is to break up line 2. Thus the verse suggests that faith *is not* the motivation behind Jozefa de São Miguel's devotion and rather that her devotion is due to some other reason.

Irmã Jozefa de Espírito Santo

168 A Jozefa aquella que
de Espirito Santo se chama
seu obrar por singular
anda nas azas de fama

Jozefa, the one
who is called "of the Holy Spirit,"
because her works are one of a kind,
she will soar on the wings of glory.

Irmã Antonia de Alleluja

169 Alleluja nossa Antonia
quem quer dizer alegria
porque muito grande o tem
quem ve esta galeteria

Hallelujah for our Antonia,
she who wishes to speak with joy,
because those who behold her fine words
will obtain greatness.

9 verso

Irmã Ritta de Santa Quiteria

170 Esta nossa Ritta
de Santa Quiteria se chama
se no amor de Jesus
todo abrazado se inflama

Our Ritta,
who is called "of Saint Quiteria,"[60]
if Jesus's love scorches everything,
then she is aflame.

Irmã Urçalla de Assumpção

171 A nossa Urçulla
de Assumpção com rezão
e outras muitos eçedem
sua boa condição

Our Urçulla
[is] rightly [called] "of the Assumption,"
[and] many others agree
with her righteousness.

Irmã Izabel de Jesus Maria

172 De Izabel de Jesus Maria
perdoe por caridade
que não cabe en poco verço
no seu louvor a meatade

[Speaking of] Izabel de Jesus Maria,
kindly forgive [us],
because we cannot fit in these few verses
half of the praise [you deserve].

---

60. Santa Quiteria was born in Braga, Portugal.

Irmã Magarida de Madre de Deos

173   Louvai verços meus / com muita atenção / a Margarida de Madre de Deos / hoie nesta ocazião

Today, on this occasion, / my verses very carefully / praise / Margarida de Madre de Deos.

Irmã Rozalia de Assumpção

174   Agora o Rozalia / de Assumpção tão emgraçada / de toda sois amiga / e iuntamente estimada

Now, Rozalia, / of the Assumption, so charming, / you are a friend to all / and by all held in high esteem.

Irmã Maria de Salvador

175   Vos Maria de Salvador / com muita propriedade / a mayor singularidade / conserve no seu primor

You, O Maria de Salvador, / with much propriety, / maintain your excellence / in your uniqueness.

Irmã Felíçia de Santa Anna

176   Aqui vem agora / com pasmo e admiraçoens / felíçia de Santa Anna / amiga destas funçoens

Now, here comes, / with astonishment and wonder, / Felíçia de Santa Anna, / friend of these festivities.

Irmã Maria de Santa Anna

177   Mayor que grande Baptista / the agora não naçeo / tambem Maria de Santa Anna / emtrar na festa mereçeo

None greater than the Baptist / has yet to be born; / Maria de Santa Anna has also / earned entry to the festival.

Irmã Anna de Anunçiação

178	De Anunçiação Anna não hé bem cá faltar por ser muita brioza a São João festeiar	It is not good for Anna de Anunçiação, who is very lively, to not be here to celebrate Saint John.

Irmã Francisca de Santo Agostinho

179	Francisca de Santo Agostinho convida para festa pedindo a São João que faça vosso Padrinho	Invite Francisca de Santo Agostinho to the festival, asking St. John to become her protector.[61]

Irmã Vitoria de Trindade

180	Não pode deixar de ser huma conheçida na verdade aquella que se chama Vitorina de Trindade	Truly, she who is called Vitoria de Trindade, cannot but be notable.

10 recto

Irmã Rozalia de Santa Rita

181	De Santa Rita Rozalia venha a festa esmaltar com rabo de gallo burrufar fazendo festa nesta dia	Rozalia de Santa Rita comes to enhance the festival, sprinkling merriment with a rooster tail[62] on this day.

---

61. *Padrinho*: protector or Godfather.
62. *borriçar* → borrifar: to lightly rain, to sprinkle. Here we are taking burrufar with fazendo festa; however, another way to translate this would be: "with the flourish of the rooster's tail, making festivities on this day." This translation would put the focus on Irmã Rozalia de Santa Rita's beauty rather than her good nature.

Irmã Lauriana do Coração de Jesus

182 Lauriana do Coração de Jesus Lauriana do Coração de Jesus
     vem com muita alegria joyfully comes
     festeiar esta festa to celebrate this festival
     com gala e fulia with jubilation and revelry.

Irmã Micaella dos Anjos

183 A Micaella dos Anjos Micaella dos Anjos
     deve ser estimada should be held in high esteem
     que por seus prestimos and for her services
     deve ser louvada ought to be praised.

Irmã Maria da Conçeição

184 Por sua conçeição Upon "Conception"[63]
     tomou a nossa Maria our Maria took
     hum sobrenomem que tira a surname that removes
     de peito a melencolia melancholy from the breast.

Irmã Joanna de Salvador

185 Joanna de Salvador Joanna de Salvador,
     sereis muita amada you will be much loved;
     servi a Deos desvellada serve God vigilantly
     e a relgião com amor and the Faith lovingly.

Irmã Anna de Salvador

186 Mas venha iuntamente But come as a group,
     em sua compania traga [and] in your company bring,
     de Salvador Anna que Anna de Salvador, who
     de São João será bem paga will be rewarded by Saint John.

---

63. "Conception" here refers to Irmã Maria da Conçeição's rebirth as a nun, so it is her birth as a nun.

Irmã Roza de Madre de Deos

187	Roza de Madre de Deos como estais lá no lugar descançada vinde cá dar quatro voltas antes de festa acabada	Roza de Madre de Deos, there at the place of rest, come here and turn around four times before this festival ends.

Irmã Maria de Santa Thereza

188	De Santa Thereza Maria tendes por obrigação deveis por miutos motivos festeiar a São João	Maria de Santa Thereza you are obliged to, and should for many reasons, celebrate Saint John.

+   +

189	A quem com tão grande gosto no que pode obedeçe bem iusto foi lhe desse a emfermeira o posto	It was quite just to give the post of nurse to she who, with such great enthusiasm, was as obedient as she could be.
190	hé acção tão meritoria das emfermas bem tratar quem nisso se ocupar serto pode ter a gloria	It is such a worthy deed to treat the sick well; whoever does it can certainly obtain glory.
191	O Madres vamos andã por que isto ia hé tarde	O Mothers, let's get going because it is already getting late;

10 verso

que eu sinto na verdade
desta galhofa acabã

indeed, I feel
this merriment is about to end.

192	Minha Senhora querida e excelente Prellada entendei que magoada himos com esta despedida	My dear Senhora and most excellent Prelate, know that we are upset to leave with this farewell.
193	Com grande gosto e alegria bem quizera Senhora estar a vossa prezenta lograr continuamente todo dia	I hope the Senhora is very pleased and happy; we will continue to enjoy your presence [even after] this day.
194	Fica empreza na memoria os aplauzos deste dia que com tanta bizarria lograõ todos desta gloria	The praise of this day will remain in our memory; may everyone enjoy this glory with such happiness.
195	Ficai com Deos Madres minhas a Deus o minhas fermozas hide descançar meus rozas hide com Deus o rainhas	Stay with God, my Mothers, goodbye, my Beauties, go rest, my Roses, go with God, O Queens.
196	Digo a todos por despedida podeis ia con Deus ficar elle nos deixe chegar para acabar con gosta e vida	I say to all as a Farewell, now you all may be with God; He let us reach the end with merriment and liveliness.

Cantiga de Amor **Hymn of Love**

197	Alerta amante coração a sofrer hum emgraditão que meu coração arufado não pode estar athe agora matei me antes embora e acabei vossa emfado	Beware, O Beloved, of the heart, which suffers from ingratitude, for my unruly[64] heart cannot remain so; kill me now and end your suffering.

---

64. *arrufado* → *arrufo*, a demonstration of annoyance (between friends, by keeping silent about the reason for it); also the word for a lover's quarrel.

198	se quereis dar a satisfação da culpas que tendes cometida que sempre em vossa vida ofendestes ao vosso coração sem cauza com tanta paixão andava tão agastada	If you want to make up for the faults you have committed throughout your life, [these faults] that have troubled your heart heedlessly and with so much passion, that have left you so afflicted,
199	Dizei minha vida meu bom em que vos tem ofendido este coração rendido que para afeição vos tem não com amor de vai e vam mas forte duro e pezado	Tell [me], my life, my sweetheart, how has this vulnerable heart, for which you have affection, and whose love does not come and go but rather is strong, firm, and weighty, offended you.
200	Ora seçai ia a peleja saberai toda a verdade	Now, give up the fight already and you will know the whole truth;

11 recto

	mal fogo que miuto arde brinco que ninguem de[seja] desde hoje tudo seja querer e ser adorado	a terrible fire that burns so, a sport that nobody wants, from this day forward may all be desired and adored.

Cantiga de Cupido   **Hymn of Cupid**

201	O mana currei vem ca vem ca ouvi hum pregão que amantes manda lança contra Cupido ladrão	O sister come here, come here and hear a proclamation that lovers [of God] read aloud against Cupid the thief.
202	Mandã que su pé su mão com corda filã marrado[65] que vergonha está passa aquelle triste restado	They command that his feet and hands be bound by a chord so that he may feel shame and he is left in sadness.

---

65. *amarrar*: to tie up (when talking about a dog).

203	Su olho mandã rancã por traidor atrevido que justiça estã passã eis coitado de Cupido	They command to pluck out his eye, for being an impudent traitor; that is the justice he faces, pitiful Cupid.
204	Su afã mandã corta elle estã desesperado para qui num pode fugi deste prizão dezastrado	They command to cut off his wings and leave him desperate, so that he cannot flee this disgraceful prison.
205	Su arco ia esta quebrado assim pregão esta fala tãobem esta manda [a]soite por tudo çidade chicotia	His bow is now broken and the proclamation has been spoken, and he is also commanded to be whipped throughout the city.
206	Com murrão groço esta dã ai Jesus que piedade mais mereçei na verdade tudo gente assim falã	Beat him with a heavy fist, "O Jesus have compassion"— Actually, everyone says you deserve more.
207	Tãobem manda rasteja por tudo rua coitado por hum falço mentirozo rapeçeiro e malvado	He is also commanded to crawl through all the streets, the wretch, for such a false liar is a swindler and wicked.
208	sentença ia publica delle morre enforcado com baraço ate passã este malaventurado	The sentence of death by hanging is proclaimed; this unfortunate one will die[66] with a noose around his neck.
209	Este estã bem mandado deixa paga su pecado agora este estã pagã com elle num querem nada	This having been so decreed, let him to pay for his sin; now that it has been paid, they want nothing to do with him.

---

66. *passa*: to leave [this world].

11 verso

210	Nos tarde ia conhece su ma condição babá que com penna e crueldade por nos tudo ia matā	We will soon learn your vile character, babá,[67] and we will painfully and cruelly extinguish all of it.
211	hum embargo ia sahi de tudo su vassallo que por rei conheçido num pode ser enforcado	The stay is given, as in the end a vassal close to the king cannot be hanged.[68]
212	Da morte ia escapā este rei de patarata sobre elle iustiça venha tenha vida mal lograda	Now, the king of lies escapes death; let justice be done, may his life be miserable.[69]

Cantiga da Madre Suprioreiza **Song of the Mother Subprioress**[70]

213	Publique a vozes sem seçar de Madre Suprioreiza os primores pois a mim me toca hoje darlhe a ella louvores	Proclaim with unceasing voices the excellence of the Mother Subprioress; it is up to me to give her praises today.

---

67. *babá*: an informal address of admonition.
68. The stay is given
    For such a vassal
    Known by the king
    Hanged cannot be.
    (Borges translation in Castel-Branco, "The Presence of Portuguese Baroque in the Poetic Works of the Sisters of Santa Monica in Goa," 255)
69. From death he escapes
    This fancy king,
    Let justice be done
    Let his life be a burden.
    (Borges translation in Castel-Branco, "The Presence of Portuguese Baroque in the Poetic Works of the Sisters of Santa Monica in Goa," 255)
70. This is the Prioress singing to the Subprioress.

214	Sahio hoje neste dia como magnanima generoza a entrar com dispendio para ostentar magestoza	She comes on this day, magnanimous and generous, sparing no expense to demonstrate her majesty.
215	O claustro quis armar com primor e admiração para me fazer aplauzo no noita de Sã João	She wanted to adorn[71] the cloister with exquisiteness and wonder in order to honor me on the night of San João.
216	Em fim Senhora minha Madre conpaneira amada quizestes mostrar fineizas para ostentar estremada	In the end, my Senhora, beloved Mother and companion, you wanted to show your sophistication to demonstrate your greatness.
217	Deus vos dei a vida saude dezejada para ser ardes a deus neste coro excaltada	God gave you life and good health to fervently serve Him in this exalted choir.
218	Não hera nessesario para vossas primores mostrar bem conheçido he de mim serdes com tudo singular	It was not necessary to show off your excellence, [as] it is well known to me that you are unique in every way.
219	Viva pois viva Joanna da Santa Roza Suprioreiza rica tem tudo estremoza	Long live Joanna de Santa Rosa, a wonderful subprioress, the greatest in all things.

Cantiga da Madre Ignaçia **Song to Mother Ignaçia**[72]

220	Lovar me convem a Ignaçia de Emcarnação não há duvida que ella hé nos primoures admiração	It is fitting for me to praise Ignaçia de Emcarnação; there is no doubt that she is admired for her excellence.

---

71. *armar*: to set up, or in this case, decorate with flowers and make beautiful.

72. Again, it seems the Prioress is singing these hymns of praise.

12 recto

221	Sois em fin Ignaçia minha diçipula amada que sempre vos estimei com ãfecto de desvelado	After all, Ignaçia, you are my beloved disciple; I always hold you in high esteem with unbridled affection.
222	quizestes nesta função mostrardes tão grandioza na festa de São João com desvelo afectuoza	You wanted, at this gathering, to demonstrate such grandiosity on the Feast of Saint John with unbridled care.
223	Sem reparar nos dispendios em tenpo de tanta pobre fiz estes hum recreijo mostrates vossa grandeiza	With no regard for expense in a time of such poverty, you have put on an event that demonstrates your greatness.
224	Com desvello e empenho por vossa muita vontade desvelastes com amor nesta festividade	With care and commitment, through your strong will, you lovingly unveiled these festivities.
225	Bem posso publicar a vozes vosso primor não fas duvida por vos cabe dar vos sempre louvar	I may well proclaim that you are the first among all these voices; [there is] no doubt that it suits you to always be praised.
226	E assim vos agradeiço que aplauzo tão simgular que hoje como magestoza em publico quizestes de mostrar	And so I thank you with such special praise, for wanting to show today how majestic you are.
227	E assim que agradeçida a mão vos bejo por favor que bem conheçido hé patente vosso amor	And so, with gratitude, please allow me to kiss your hand; It is well-known that your love is evident.

	Cantiga de Madre Bibianna	**Song to Mother Bibianna**
228	Cante neste dia muzica sem seçar a Madre Bibianna louvores sem seçar	Sing on this day unceasing music; [give] Mother Bibianna unceasing praise.[73]
229	Esta depozitaria por mostrasse generoza dei huma comssuada[74] muito grandioza	This keeper of the depository, in order to show her generosity, provided a dinner so very grand.
230	Em fim Senhora minha agradeço vos o favor com que quizestes manifestar os esseços do vosso primor	In the end, my Senhora, I thank you for your goodwill, which you wanted to demonstrate by the abundance of your greatness.
231	Em tempo de tanta penuria esta grandeza quizestes fazer sem repararinos gastos que nelle havia de ter	At a time of such penury you wanted to make this great [feast] happen taking no notice of the expense that would be incurred.

12 Verso

232	Bem mostrais Senhora que sois em tudo generoza pois destes huma conssuada rica e grandioza	You amply demonstrate, Senhora, that you are generous in all things, among these [you put on] a dinner so rich and grand.
233	Agradeço vos a fineiza com que quisestes honrar dando huma conssuada grandioza e singular	I appreciate the care with which you wanted to honor [us], by putting on a dinner so grand and special.

73. On this day, sing and play music unceasingly to Madre Bibianna.

74. *comssuada* → *consoada*: a specific term in Portuguese referring to the traditional Christmas Eve dinner or feast. However, here it cannot be the case, as the nuns are referring to the elaborate meal that has been prepared for St. John's Day.

234	Para mostrardes o afecto de vossa estimação estribastes em fazer este aplauzo a São João	In order to show the depths of your esteem, you undertook [the task] to give this praise to Saint John.
235	Em fim vos digo com todo fervor que sacrifíco mui rendida a vos servir com amor	Finally, I say to you, with all fervor, I happily made this sacrifice to serve you with love.

Cantiga de Madre Barbora **Song to Mother Barbora**

236	Madre Barbora he em fim huma rica pedraria por isso se apellida ella de Jesus Maria	Mother Barbora is indeed a splendid gem; for this reason, she is named "of Jesus Maria."
237	Empenhouçe neste dia com desvello de admiração fazer huma jantar na festa de São João	On this day, she undertook with admirable care to put on a dinner for the festival of Saint John.
238	Não ha quem possa dizer nem a vezes publicar os primores que nella mora hé Senhora sem igual	There is no one who can say, nor even proclaim, the perfections that live within her; she is a Senhora without equal.
239	Em tenso de tanta pobreza quis mostrar generoza dan ao hum jantar tão rica e grandioza	Under the stress of such poverty, she wanted to show generosity; she put on a dinner so bountiful and grandiose.
240	Justo he que vos dei Senhora mil louvores pois como grandioza magn- anima ezalça vossos primoures	It is right that you give this Senhora a thousand praises; indeed, with great magnanimity her greatness is exalted.

241   Barbora sois em fim
      huma pedra de valia
      por que sahistes liberal
      a honrarme neste dia

Ultimately, you are, Barbora,
a precious gemstone,
for you have been liberal
in honoring me this day.

242   A lingua me emmudeiçe
      para em vos falar
      que vossos brios e primores
      sempre deve publicar

My tongue has fallen silent
when [trying to speak] about you;
your dignity and greatness
always ought to be proclaimed.

13 recto

243   Sois rica depozitaria
      Barbora de Jesus Maria
      bem mostrais Senhora
      ser a joia de valia

You are a magnificent Mistress of the
Depository,
Barbora de Jesus Maria;
you well demonstrate, Senhora,
that you are a valuable jewel.

Cantiga a Madre Prioreiza   **Song to Mother Prioress**

244   Madre Francisca do Sacramento
      minha Madre querida amada
      nesta vida foi mayor gloria
      ver vos na cadeira da Prellada

Mother Francisca do Sacramento
my Mother, dear beloved,
in this life it was the greatest glory
to see you in the Prelate's seat.

245   Madre Francisca do Sacramento
      ben conheiço e veio
      que com vossas sombras Sen-
      hora
      tenho todos bems que dezeio

Mother Francisca do Sacramento,
so well I know and understand
that in your shadow,[75] Senhora,
I have all the blessings I desire.

246   Dezeio que tentiais muita vida
      por secullos dilatados
      no serviço do divino espouzo
      para serdes apremiada

I wish you to have a long life
of many centuries
and be rewarded
in your service of the Divine Spouse.

---

75. Literally, "in your shadow," but the meaning here is "under your protection." The Prioress is the mentor to whomever is singing this song; perhaps it is the Subprioress.

247	Este almoço vos ofereiço que a comunidade podeis dar Jannona e Clarinha desvelada e bem lhes podeis perdoar	I offer you this lunch that you can give to the community. Jannona and Clarinha unveiled, you can surely forgive them.
248	Caminhemos em gesolreut	Let us go in G
	a todas sem exepção em delasolret	With everyone in D
	Os Astros em gesolreut	The celestial bodies in G
	De Françisca em delasolreut	For Francisca in D
	Com vozes em gesolreut	With voices in G
	Com aplauzo em gesolreut	With praise in G
	que hoie he o dia em gesolreut	For today is the day in G
	Publique em gesolreut	Announced in G
	Madre Izabel em çesolfaut	Mother Izabel in C
	A Madre Escrivam em gesolreut	Mother Scribe in G
	as duas asucenas em gesolreut	The two azucenas in G
	Não hé iusto em çesolfaut	It is not fair in C
	Olha mana em çesolfaut	Look, sister in C
	de Comunidade em gesolreut	Of the Community in G
	Alerta amante em çesolfaut	Beware, O Beloved in C

Cupido em gesolreut	Cupid in G
louvar me em gesolreut	praise me in G
cante neste em gesolreut	sing on this in G
Madre Barbora em gesolreut	Mother Barbora in G
despedida em gesolreut	farewell in G
de Madre	of Mother

Appendix 1

Nuns Commemorated in Entrada de Bonifrate para Festa dos Reis

Name	Title or Nickname	Year Professed	Year Died	Verse #	Approx. Age in 1741[1]
Madre Emerençiana de Santa Maria	Mereciana	1689	1743	23–24, 37, 91	67
Madre Catharina do Sacramento		1689	1743	19–20, 35, 89	67
Madre Brites do Sacramento	Bitona	1690	1757	25–26, 38, 92	66
Madre Isabel de Madre de Deus		1691	1744	27–28, 39, 93	65
Madre Antonia de Encarnação	Antoca	1696	1756	44–45, 58, 94	60
Madre Anna de Jesus	Subprioress	1698	1750	21–22, 36, 90	58
Madre Ignaçia de Anunçiacão		1699	1752	46–47, 59, 95	57
Madre Anna da Virgem Maria	Aninha	1700	1762	50–51, 61, 97	56
Madre Paula de Espírito Santo	Paula	1700	1763	48–49, 60, 96	56
Madre Michaella da Conçeição		1702	1749	52–53, 62, 98	54
Madre Antonia do Sacramento		1703	1761	54–55, 63, 99	53
Madre Antonia de Santa Roza	Antica	1705	1742	56–57, 64, 100	51

Note: Table arranged by year of profession.

1. The Council of Trent (1545–1563) standardized various practices across the Catholic Church, including establishing a minimum age for profession as a choir nun. According to the council's decrees, sixteen was the minimum age for women to take solemn vows. Nevertheless, the age at which a woman might enter a convent would often vary. For example, some women may have chosen to enter the convent later in life, especially widows or women who had not married. Prior to profession, a potential nun would spend one to two years as a novitiate. Girls who entered at a very young age were called "postulants."

180 *Appendix 1*

Name	Title or Nickname	Year Professed	Year Died	Verse #	Approx. Age in 1741[1]
Madre Maria de Ressureição		1705	1744	101	51
Madre Clara de Jesus		1706	1768	102	50
Madre Antonia de Madre de Deos		1707	1755	103	49
Madre Holaya de Jesus Maria		1708	1743	104	48
Madre Antonia de Santo Agostinho		1710	1758	105	46
Madre Teresa do Sacramento		1710	1766	106	46
Madre Izabel de Aprezentação		1711	1767	107	45
Madre Senhorinha de Jesus		1712	1774	108	44
Madre Brites de Trindade		1713	1766	109	43
Madre Anna de Transfiguração		1714	1749	110	42
Madre Maria de Trindade		1715	1756	112	41
Madre Izabel da Virgem Maria		1715	1756	113	41
Madre Francisca de São José		1715	1776	111	41
Madre Lionarda de Trindade		1716	1742	114	40
Madre Anna de Trindade		1716	1746	115	40
Madre Luiza dos Querubins		1717	1747	116	39
Madre Mariana de Jesus		1717	1770	117	39
Madre Arcangela de Gloria		1717	1744	118	39

Nuns Commemorated in Entrada de Bonifrate para Festa dos Reis 181

Name	Title or Nickname	Year Professed	Year Died	Verse #	Approx. Age in 1741[1]
Madre Maria dos Gerarguias		1718	1745	119	38
Madre Luiza de Madre de Deus		1721	1764	120	35
Madre Francisca do Sacramento		1723	1776	121	33
Madre Luiza de Assumpção		1724	1742	122	32
Madre Anna Madre de Deos		1726	1764	123	30
Madre Eufrazia de Ressurreição		1727	1750	124	29
Madre Maria de Assumpção		1728	1788	125	28
Madre Brites de Santa Anna		1728	1762	126	28
Madre Joanna de Santa Rosa		1729	1773	127	27
Madre Maria de Annunciação		1729	1754	128	27
Madre Francisca de Annunciação		1730	1741	129	26
Madre Margarida de São Jozeph		1738	1750	130	18
Madre Caetana de Jesus Maria		1738	1766	131	18
Madre Anna de Ressurreição		1738	1747	132	18
Madre Maria de São Joachim		1738	1796	133	18
Madre Jozepha de Santo Agostinho		1739	1775	134	17
Madre Roza de Assumpção		1739	1781	135	17
Madre Maria de São Guillierme		1739	1763	136	17

Appendix 1

Name	Title or Nickname	Year Professed	Year Died	Verse #	Approx. Age in 1741[1]
Noviça Joanna de Santa Thereza		1741	1788	137	16
Noviça Bibiana de São Miguel		1742	1775	138	15
Noviça Anna de São Jochim		1742	1776	139	15
Popilla Juliana de Querobim				140	under 15
Irmã Luiza de Serafim				141	
Irmã Magdalena de Jesus				142	
Irmã Joanna de Jesus Maria				143	
Irmã Izabel de Santo Christo				144	
Irmã Roza do Paraizo				145	
Irmã Maria de Consolação				146	
Irmã Caetana de Jesus				147	
Irmã Maria de Jesus Nazareth				148	
Irmã Ignes de Purificação				149	
Irmã Joanna de Baptista				150	
Irmã Micaella de Anjo				151	
Irmã Izabel do Sacramento				152	
Irmã Rozalia de Madre de Deus				153	
Irmã Maria de Piedade				154	
Irmã Senhorinha de Purificação				155	

Nuns Commemorated *in* Entrada de Bonifrate para Festa dos Reis 183

Name	Title or Nickname	Year Professed	Year Died	Verse #	Approx. Age in 1741[1]
Irmã Maria de Christo				156	
Irmã Francisca de Assumpção				157	
Irmã Jozepha de São Miguel				158	
Irmã Mónica de Jesus Maria				159	
Irmã Aurea do Çeos				160	
Irmã Maria do Salvador				161	
Irmã Paschoa de Assumpção				162	
Irmã Anna de Santa Maria				163	
Irmã Filiça de Jesus Maria				164	
Irmã Rozalia de Santa Rita				165	

Augustinian Friars from Nossa Senhora de Graça

Padre Confessor	15–16, 33, 87
Padre Procurador	17–18, 34, 88

Appendix 2

Nuns Commemorated in Cartepaço da Muzica

Name	Office	Year Professed	Year Died	Verse # Cartepaço (Entrada)	Approx. Age in 1766
Madre Clara de Jesus		1706	1768	115 (102)	76
Madre Izabel de Aprezentação	Absolute Prelate Gatekeeper	1711	1767	7, 51–52 (107)	71
Madre Senhorinha de Jesus	Council Mistress of the Works	1712	1774	56–58 (108)	70
Madre Brites de Trindade	Second Prelate Mother of the Granary	1713	1766	8, 53–55 (109)	69
Madre Francisca de São José		1715	1776	116 (111)	67
Madre Mariana de Jesus Gloria*	Nurse?	1717	1770	189–90	65
Madre Francisca do Sacramento	Prioress	1723	1776	5, 27–30, 39–46 (121)	59
Madre Maria de Assumpção	Council Mother Sancristan	1728	1788	59–60 (125)	54
Madre Joanna de Santa Rosa	Subprioress	1729	1773	6, 31–34, 47–50 (127)	53
Madre Caetana de Jesus Maria	Mother Scribe	1738	1766	83–85, (131)	44
Madre Maria de São Joachim	Council Mother Gardener	1738	1796	61–62 (133)	44
Madre Jozepha de Santo Agostinho	Council	1739	1775	63–64 (134)	43

Note: Table arranged by year of profession.

Nuns Commemorated in Cartepaço da Muzica 185

Name	Office	Year Professed	Year Died	Verse # *Cartepaço* (*Entrada*)	Approx. Age in 1766
Madre Roza de Assumpção	Council Vicar of the Choir	1739	1781	65–67 (135)	43
Madre Joanna de Santa Thereza		1741	1788	117	41
Madre Bibiana de São Miguel	Mother of the Depositary	1742	1775	86–88 (138)	40
Madre Anna de São Joachim	Mistress of the Choir	1742	1776	68	40
Madre Anna de Jesus Maria		1742	1808	118	40
Madre Pascoa da Ressurreição	Council Laundress	1744	1770	69–70	38
Madre Ignacia de Encarnação	Mistress of the Postulants	1744	1790	71–74	38
Madre Ana de Nazareth	Provisora	1745	1774	75–76	37
Madre Mariana de Assumpção		1745	1786	119	37
Madre Barbora de Jesus Maria	Mother of the Depository	1746	1770	86–88	36
Madre Roza de Santa Anna		1747	1787	120	35
Madre Maria de São Joseph		1748	1821	121	34
Madre Anna de Assumpção		1749	1791	122	33
Madre Pascoella de Ressurreição		1751	1781	123	31
Madre Brites de Santa Maria	Mistress of Infirmary	1751	1793	79–80	31
Madre Archangella de Gloria		1751	1794	124	31
Madre Antonia de Santa Rosa		1752	1776	126	30

Name	Office	Year Professed	Year Died	Verse # *Cartepaço* (*Entrada*)	Approx. Age in 1766
Madre Anna do Sacramento		1752	1784	125	30
Madre Violante do Coração de Jesus	Mistress of the Girls	1753	1787	77–78	29
Madre Maria de Jesus	Mistress of Novices	1754	1790	81–82	28
Madre Bernarda de Santo Agostinho		1754	1811	127	28
Madre Escolastica do Sacramento		1755	1776	128	27
Madre Joanna de Ave Maria		1755	1797	129	27
Madre Elena de Santa Anna		1756	1781	130	26
Madre Izabel de Madre de Deus		1757	1820	131	25
Madre Luiza de San José		1759	1772	134	23
Madre Maria de São Miguel		1759	1774	133	23
Madre Paula de Anunçiação		1759	1789	135	23
Madre Maria de Anunçiação		1759	1798	132	23
Madre Eugenia de Santa Maria		1760	1772	136	22
Madre Francisca de Anunçiação		1760	1773	139	22
Madre Mariana de Santo Cristo		1760	1773	140	22
Madre Thereza de Jesus		1760	1777	137	22
Madre Luiza de Santa Alexandre		1760	1786	138	22
Madre Joaquina de Anunçiação		1761	1779	141	21

Nuns Commemorated in Cartepaço da Muzica 187

Name	Office	Year Professed	Year Died	Verse # Cartepaço (Entrada)	Approx. Age in 1766
Madre Maria do Coração de Jesus		1761	1812	143	21
Madre Joaquim de Santa Anna		1761	1831	142	21
Madre Maria de Jerarchia		1762	1796	144	20
Madre Elena de Madre de Deus		1762	1812	145	20
Madre Rita do Coração de Jesus		1763	1772	146	19
Madre Maria de Santa Rosa		1763	1792	147	19
Madre Joanna do Nascimento		1766	1823	148	16
Madre Maria de Trindade		1766	1808	149	16
Madre Anna de Madre de Deus		1767	1809	150	15
Noviça Roza de Santa Maria		—	—	151	
Popilla Joaqina de Madre de Deus		1768	—	152	13
Popilla Roza do Sacramento		1770	1794	153	11
Popilla Thereza de Assumpção		1771	1775	154	10
Popilla Laurina de Jesus Nazareth				155	9 [?]
Popilla Maria de Nazareth		1773	1826	156	8
Irmã Roza de Paraizo				157	
Irmã Ignes de Purificação				158	
Irmã Joanna de Baptista				159	
Irmã Izabel do Sacramento				160	
Irmã Maria de Piedade				161	

Name	Office	Year Professed	Year Died	Verse # *Cartepaço* (*Entrada*)	Approx. Age in 1766
Irmã Senhorinha de Purificação				162	
Irmã Francisca de Assumpção				163	
Irmã Mónica de Jesus Maria				164	
Irmã Jozefa de São Miguel				165	
Irmã Feliçia de Jesus Maria				166	
Irmã Mariana de Madre de Deus				167	
Irmã Jozefa de Espírito Santo				168	
Irmã Antonia de Alleluja				169	
Irmã Ritta de Santa Quiteria				170	
Irmã Urçalla de Assumpção				171	
Irmã Izabel de Jesus Maria				172	
Irmã Magarida de Madre de Deos				173	
Irmã Rozalia de Assumpção				174	
Irmã Maria de Salvador				175	
Irmã Feliçia de Santa Anna				176	
Irmã Maria de Santa Anna				177	
Irmã Anna de Anunçiaçãõ				178	
Irmã Francisca de Santo Agostinho				179	
Irmã Vitoria de Trindade				180	

Nuns Commemorated in Cartepaço da Muzica 189

Name	Office	Year Professed	Year Died	Verse # *Cartepaço* (*Entrada*)	Approx. Age in 1766
Irmã Rozalia de Santa Rita				181	
Irmã Lauriana do Coração de Jesus				182	
Irmã Micaella dos Anjos				183	
Irmã Maria da Conçeição				184	
Irmã Joanna de Salvador				185	
Irmã Anna de Salvador				186	
Irmã Rozae de Madre de Deos				187	
Irmã Maria de Santa Thereza				188	

Bibliography

Primary Sources

Works Translated in This Volume

Cartepaço de Muzica. Arquivo da Cúria Patriarcal de Goa, Panjim, 018 Livros de Conventos e Igrejas, 1766. Fourteen folios.

Entrada da Bonifrate para Festa dos Reis. Arquivo da Cúria Patriarcal de Goa, Panjim, 018 Livros de Conventos e Igrejas, 1740. Folios not numbered.

Archival Sources

Ave-Maria, Fr. Manuel de. "Manual Eremítico da Congregação da Índia Oriental dos Eremitas de Nosso Padre Santo Agostinho." Biblioteca Geral da Universidade de Coimbra, códex nº 1650, 837 folios; reprinted in *Documentação para a História da Missões do Padroado Portugués do Oriente*, edited by Antonio da Silva Rego, 11:95–832. Lisboa: Agéncia Geral do Ultramar, Divisão de Publicações e Biblioteca, 1954.

King João V. "Se perpetao silencio en tudo do que dizer respeito as Freiras da Santa Mónica," April 5, 1736. Historical Archives of Goa, Livro das Monções do Reino, no. 105 (codex 107), fl. 40r.

King Pedro II. "Carta de Rei Pedro II ao Câmara de Goa," March 3, 1703. Historical Archives of Goa, Livro das Monções do Reino, no. 67 (codex 76), fl. 63r.

"Lista das Fazendas que pessue O Convento de Santa Monica nesta Ilha de Goa, e nas Ilhas adjacentes," December 22, 1703. Historical Archives of Goa, Livro das Monções do Reino, no. 67 (codex 76), fls. 67r.–70v. and 79r.

Oliveira, Domingos Dourado de. "Parecer do Desembargador Domingos Dourado de Oliveira," January 18, 1703. Historical Archives of Goa (HAG), Livro das Monções do Reino, no. 68 (codex 77), fls. 239r.–247v.; reprinted in Cunha Rivara, *APO*-1: 161–72.

"Relação Sumaria e Verdadeira dos Proçidimentos que o Arçebispo de Goa Dom Ignaçio de Santa Thereza Teve com as Religiozas do Convento de Santa Mónica da Mesma Çidade no Anno de 1731 1732 e 1733," 1734. Archivum Romanum Societatis Iesu, Fondo Gesuitico 1433/9, no. 52 (Busta no. 74B).

Santa Anna, Diogo de. "Resposta por parte do insigne mosteiro de freira de Sancta Mónica de Goa," 1636, Arquivo National de Torre de Tombo (ANTT), Manuscritos da Livraria, no. 816.

———. "Regimento do Culto Divino é Observancias deste Insigne Mosteiro de Nossa Senhora Madre Santa Monica de Goa," 1627, Biblioteca Pública de

Évora, G. R. arm III e IV, No. 24; reprinted as "O Mosteiro de Santa Monica de Goa," in *O Chronista de Tissuary* 1, no. 8 (Agosto) (1866): 215–19.

Santa Teresa, Ignácio de. "Nomeação do Conservador, Mónicas." Arquivo National de Torre de Tombo, Conselho Geral do Santo Oficio, Liv. 284, 1731.

———. "Sentenças dadas contra algu[m]as Relig[ios]as na vizita de 1731," Archivio Apostolico Vaticano 367, Relationes Dioecesium Goan.

Contemporary Portuguese Dictionaries

Diccionario da Lingua Portugueza. Compiled by Rafael Bluteau, added to and enlarged by António de Morais Silva. Lisboa: Na Officina de Simão Thaddeo Ferreira, 1789.

Glossário Luso-Asiático. Compiled by Sebastião Rodolfo Dalgado. Coimbra: Imprensa da Universidade, 1921.

Novo Diccionario da Lingua Portugueza. Compiled by José da Fonseca. Paris: J. P. Aillaud, 1831.

Supplemento ao Vocabulario Portuguez e Latino. Compiled by Rafael Bluteau. Lisboa: Joseph Antonio da Sylva, Impressor da Academia Real, 1727–1728.

Vocabulario Portuguez e Latino. Compiled by Rafael Bluteau. Lisboa: Officina de Pascoal da Sylva, Impressor de Sua Magestade, 1712–1721.

Secondary Sources

Abreu, Miguel Vicente de. *Real Mosteiro de Santa Monica de Goa: Memoria Historica*. Nova-Goa: Imprensa-Nacional, 1882.

Alonso, Carlos. *Alejo de Meneses, O.S.A. (1559–1617), Arzobispo de Goa (1595–1612): Estudio Biográfico*. Valladolid: Estudio Agustiniano, 1992.

Alves, Ana Maria Mendes Ruas. "O Reyno de Deos e a Sua Justiça: Dom Frei Inácio de Santa Teresa (1682–1751)." PhD thesis, Universidade de Coimbra, 2012.

Anastácio, Vanda, ed. *Uma Antologia Improvável: A Escrita das Mulheres, Séculos XVI a XVIII*. Lisboa: Relógio D'Água Editores, 2013.

Asensio, José María. *Un Cervantista Portugués del Siglo XVII Quemado por El Santo Oficio de la Inquisición: Apuntes Biográficos*. Sevilla: E. Rasco, 1885.

Auge, Marguerite d', Renée Burlamacchi, and Jeanne du Laurens. *Sin and Salvation in Early Modern France: Three Women's Stories*. Edited by Colette H. Winn. Translated by Nicholas Van Handel and Colette H. Winn. Toronto and Tempe: Iter Press and Arizona Center for Medieval and Renaissance Studies, 2017.

Barata, José Oliveira. *História do Teatro Em Portugal (Séc. XVIII): António José da Silva (o Judeu) no Palco Joanino*. Algés: DIFEL, 1998.

Bethencourt, Francisco. "Os Conventos Femininos no Império Português: O Caso do Convento de Santa Monica em Goa." In *O Rosto Feminino Da Expansão Portuguesa Actas*, edited by Francisco Bethencourt, 631–52. Lisboa: Comissão para a Igualdade e para os Direitos das Mulheres, 1995.

Boxer, C. R. *Race Relations in the Portuguese Colonial Empire, 1415–1825*. Oxford: Clarendon Press, 1963.

Braga, Teófilo. *Cancioneiro e Romanceiro Geral Portuguez*. Vol. 1. Porto: Typografia Lusitana, 1867.

Castel-Branco, M. Carmen d'Assa. "The Presence of Portuguese Baroque in the Poetic Works of the Sisters of Santa Monica in Goa." In *Goa and Portugal: History and Development*, edited by Charles J. Borges, Óscar G. Pereira, and Hannes Stubbe, translated by Charles J. Borges, 248–57. New Delhi: Xavier Centre of Historical Research, 2000.

Castro, Alberto Osório de. *A Cinza dos Myrtos: Poemas*. Nova Goa: Imprensa Nacional, 1906.

Castro, Filipe Vieira de. *The Pepper Wreck: A Portuguese Indiaman at the Mouth of the Tagus River*. College Station: Texas A & M University Press, 2005.

Chartier, Roger. "Le Don Quichotte d'Antônio José Da Silva, Les Marionnettes Du Bairro Alto et Les Prisons de l'Inquisition." In *Jewish Culture in Early Modern Europe: Essays in Honor of David B. Ruderman*, edited by Richard I. Cohen, Natalie R. Dohrmann, Adam Shear, and Elchanan Reiner, 216–26. Pittsburgh: University of Pittsburgh Press, 2014.

Coelho, Victor. "Music in New Worlds." In *The Cambridge History of Seventeenth-Century Music*, edited by Tim Carter and John Butt, 88–110. Cambridge: Cambridge University Press, 2005.

Cole, Malcolm S. "Rondo." In *The New Grove Dictionary of Music and Musicians*, edited by Stanley Sadie and John Tyrrell, 2nd ed. New York: Grove, 2001.

Costa, Elisa Maria Lopes da. "A Jacobeia: Achegas para a História de um Movimento de Reforma Espiritual no Portugal Setecentista." *Arquipélago História, 2ª Série, XIV–XV*, 2010–2011, 31–48.

Cotarelo y Mori, Emilio. *Colección de Entremeses, Loas, Bailes, Jácaras y Mojigangas desde Fines del Siglo XVI á Mediados del XVIII*. Madrid: Casa Editorial Bailly-Bailliére, 1911.

Cotarelo y Valledor, Armando. *El Teatro de Cervantes: Estudio Crítico*. Madrid: Tip. de la "Revista de archivos, bibliotecas y museos," 1915.

Coulthard, Malcom. "Translation: Theory and Practice." In *Theoretical Issues and Practical Cases in Portuguese English Translations*, edited by Patricia Anne Odber de Baubeta and Malcom Coulthard, 1–16. Lewiston: Edwin Mellen Press, 1996.

Cruz, Duarte Ivo. *O Essencial Sobre o Tema da Índia no Teatro Português*. Lisboa: Imprensa Nacional-Casa da Moeda, 2011.

Fernandez, Esther. "Rebellious Silhouettes: Arabic Shadows to Optical Illusions in Iberia," nd.

Fréches, Claude-Henri. *António José da Silva et l'Inquisition*. Paris: Fundacao Calouste Gulbenkian, 1983.

Gomide, Ana Paula Sena. "Mestizajes y Las Mediaciones Culturales en los Espacios de la India Portuguesa (Siglos XVI y XVII)." In *Tratas, Esclavitudes y Mestizajes: Una Historia Conectada, Siglos XV–XVIII*, edited by Rafael M. Pérez García, Manuel F. Fernández Chaves, and Eduardo França Paiva, 369–82. Sevilla: Editorial Universidad de Sevilla, 2020.

Gonçalves, Margareth de Almeida. "A Edificação Da Cristandade No Oriente Português: Questões Em Torno Da Ordem Dos Eremitas de Santo Agostinho No Limiar Do Século XVII." *Revista de História (São Paulo)* 170 (2014): 107–41.

———. "'Despozorios Divinos' de Mulheres em Goa na Época Moderna: Eloquência e exemplaridade no Púlpito do Mosteiro de Santa Mônica (Frei Diogo de Santa Anna, 1627)." *Locus: Revista de História* 21, no. 2 (2015): 365–95.

———. "Doutrina Cristã, Práticas Corporais e Freiras na Índia Portuguesa: O Mosteiro de Santa Mônica de Goa na alta Idade Moderna." In *Corpo: Sujeito e Objeto*, edited by Marta Mega de Andrade, Lise Fernanda Sedrez, and William de Souza Martins, 115–38. Río de Janeiro: Pinteio, 2012.

———. "'Gloria de Deus, Ao Serviço Do Rei e Ao Bem Desta Republica': Freiras de Santa Mônica de Goa e a Cristandade No Oriente Pela Escrita Do Agostinho Frei Diogo de Santa Anna Na Década de 1630." *História (São Paulo)* 32, no. 1 (2013): 251–80.

———. *Império da Fé: Andarilhas da Alma na Época Barroca*. Rio de Janeiro: Rocco, 2005.

Harris, Max. *Sacred Folly: A New History of the Feast of Fools*. Ithaca: Cornell University Press, 2011.

Hudson, Richard. "The 'Folia' Dance and the 'Folia' Formula in 17th Century Guitar Music." *Musica Disciplina* 25 (1971): 199–221.

———. *The Folia, the Saraband, the Passacaglia, and the Chaconne: The Historical Evolution of Four Forms That Originated in Music for the Five-Course Spanish Guitar*. Rome: American Institute of Musicology, 1982.

Iyer, K. B. "Shadow Play in Malabar." *Marg: A Magazine of the Arts* 31, no. 3 (1968): 22–26.

James, Ben. "Convents in Lisbon: Practices against Seclusion." In *Gendering the Portuguese-Speaking World: From the Middle Ages to the Present*, edited by Francisco Bethencourt, 117–36. Leiden: Brill, 2021.

Klein, Herbert S. "The Portuguese Slave Trade from Angola in the Eighteenth Century." *Journal of Economic History* 32, no. 4 (1972): 894–918.

Littré, Emile. *Dictionnaire de la Langue Française, Supplément.* London: Hatchett, 1875–1876.
Martins, Mário, SJ. *Teatro Quinhentista nas Naus da Índia.* Lisboa: Brotéria, 1973.
Mellon, Joelle. *The Virgin Mary in the Perceptions of Women: Mother, Protector and Queen Since the Middle Ages.* Jefferson: McFarland, 2008.
Mendes, José Maria. "Inácio de Santa Teresa: Construindo a Biografia de um Arçebispo." PhD thesis, Universidade de Lisboa, 2012.
Mendes dos Remédios, J. *Vida Do Grande D. Quixote de La Mancha e Do Gordo Sancho Pança: Opera Jocosa.* Coimbra: França Amado, 1905.
Michon, Daniel, and D. A. Smith. *To Serve God in Holy Freedom: The Brief Rebellion of the Nuns of the Royal Convent of Santa Mónica, Goa, India, 1731–1734.* London: Routledge, 2020.
Molesworth, James T. *A Dictionary: Marathi and English.* Bombay: Bombay Education Society Press, 1857.
Montero, Hélder Julio Ferreira. *Os Bonifrates no Teatro Português do Século XVIII.* Salamanco: Luso-Española, 2009.
Norton, Caroline Sheridan. *Maraquita: A Portuguese Love Song.* London: Chappell & Co., 1840.
Panizza, Letizia, ed. *Paternal Tyranny.* Chicago: University of Chicago Press, 2004.
Pereira, A. B. de Bragança. *Etnografia da India Portuguesa.* Bastorá: Tipografia Rangel, 1940.
Perkins, Juliet. *A Critical Study and Translation of António José Da Silva's Cretan Labyrinth: A Puppet Opera.* Mellen Studies in Puppetry, v. 5. Lewiston, NY: Edwin Mellen Press, 2004.
———. "Translating António Da Silva's *O Judeu*." In *Theoretical Issues and Practical Cases in Portuguese English Translations*, edited by Malcom Coulthard and Patricia Anne Odber de Baubeta, 97–112. Lewiston: Edwin Mellen Press, 1996.
Pescatello, Ann M. "The African Presence in Portuguese India." *Journal of Asian History* 11, no. 1 (1977): 26–48.
Raggi, Giuseppina. "Rethinking the Artistic Policy of King John V of Portugal and Queen Maria Anna of Habsburg: Architecture and Opera Theatre." In *Politics and the Arts in Lisbon and Rome: The Roman Dream of John V of Portugal*, edited by Pilar Diez del Corral Corredoira, 187–225. Liverpool: Liverpool University Press, 2019.
———. "Trasformare la Cultura di Corte: La Regina Maria Anna d'Asburgo e l'Introduzione dell'Opera Italiana in Portogallo." *Revista Portuguesa de Musicologia* 5, no. 1 (2018): 18–38.
Rajagopalan, L. S., and Rustom Bharucha. "Sutradhara and Vidushaka." In *The Oxford Encyclopedia of Theatre & Performance*, by Dennis Kennedy. Oxford: Oxford University Press, 2003.

Rocha, Leopoldo da. "Uma Página Inédita do Real Mosteiro de Santa Mónica de Goa (1730–1734)." *Mare Liberum* 17 (1999): 240–66.

Román, María del Carmen Alarcón. "Convent Theater." In *The Routledge Research Companion to Early Modern Spanish Women Writers*, edited by Nieves Baranda and Anne J. Cruz, 103–14. London: Routledge, 2017.

Ruedas de la Serna, Jorge A. "Góngora in Spanish American Poetry, Góngora in Luso-Brazilian Poetry: Critical Parallels." In *Baroque New Worlds: Representation, Transculturation, Counterconquest*, translated by Patrick Blaine, 343–51. Durham, NC: Duke University Press, 2010.

Safeena, S. A., S. Priya Devi, and M. Thangam. *A Catalogue of Jasmine Accessions in Goa*. Technical Bulletin, no. 58. Old Goa: Horticulture Science Section, ICAR-Central Coastal Agricultural Research Institute, Indian Council of Agricultural Research, 2016.

Santa Anna, Diogo de. *Relaçam verdadeira do milagroso portento, & portentoso milagre, q[ue] aconteceo na India no Santo Crucifixo, q[ue] està no coro do observantissimo mosteiro das Freiras de S. Monica da cidade de Goa, em oito de Fevereiro de [1]636. & continuou por muitos dias, tirada de outra, que fez o Reverendo P. M. Fr. Diogo de S. Anna*, edited by Manuel da Silva. Lisboa: Manoel da Sylva, 1640.

Santa Maria, Frei Agostinho de. *História da Fundaçaõ do Real Convento de Santa Mónica da Cidade de Goa, Corte do Estado da Índia, e do Império Lusitano do Oriente*. Lisboa: António Pedrozo Galram, 1699.

Seltmann, Friedrich. "Schattenspiel in Kêrala." *Bijdragen Tot de Taal-, Land- En Volkenkunde* 128, no. 4 (1972): 458–90.

———. "Schattenspiel in Süd Tamiḷ-Nāḍu." *Bijdragen Tot de Taal-, Land- En Volkenkunde* 135, no. 4 (1979): 455–80.

Spies, Otto. "Das Indische Schattentheater." *Theater Der Welt* 2, no. 1 (1938): 1–3.

Sylva, Mathias Pereyra da. *A Fenix Renascida: Ou Obras Poeticas dos Melhores Engenhos Portuguzes*. Lisboa: Na offic. dos Herd. de Antonio Pedrozo Galram., 1746.

Tarabotti, Arcangela. *Convent Paradise*. Edited and translated by Meredith K. Ray and Lynn Lara Westwater. Toronto and Tempe: Iter Press and Arizona Center for Medieval and Renaissance Studies, 2020.

Vigas Oliveira, Rozely Menezes. "Cartas de Freiras: Os Dois Lados de uma Crise Conventual na Goa Setecentista." *Prajna: Revista de Culturas Orientais* 1, no. 1 (2020): 149–76.

———. "Em busca do 'Bem Comum do Convento': O Conflito entre o Convento de Santa Mônica de Goa e o Poder Episcopal na Primeira Metade do Século XVIII." *Revista Feminismos* 9, no. 1 (2021): 27–47.

———. *Nas Clausuras de Goa: A Comunidade das Mónicas no Monte Santo e Sua Economia Espiritual (1606–1721)*. Porto: Editora Cravo, 2023.

Wachtel, Nathan. *The Faith of Remembrance: Marrano Labyrinths*. Philadelphia: University of Pennsylvania Press, 2013.

Weaver, Elissa B. *Convent Theatre in Early Modern Italy: Spiritual Fun and Learning for Women*. Cambridge: Cambridge University Press, 2002.

Weerasinghe, Anna. "Sister Mariana's Spyglass: The Unreliable Ghost of Female Desire in a Convent Archive," April 6, 2021. https://nursingclio.org/2021/04/06/sister-marianas-spyglass-the-unreliable-ghost-of-female-desire-in-a-convent-archive/.

Wessels, Cornelius. *Early Jesuit Travellers in Central Asia, 1603–1721*. The Hague: Nijhoff, 1924.

Wicki, Josef, SJ. *Documenta Indica: Missiones Orientales*. Rome: Institum Historicum Societatis Iesu, 1948–1988.

Index

Alleluja, Antonia de, 163
Angola, 22
Anjo, Micaella de, 98
Anjos, Micaella dos, 166
Annunciação, Francisca de, 93
Annunciação, Maria de, 92
"Another Song," 46, 150
Antonia do Sacramento, 72–73, 75, 85
Anunçiação, Anna de, 165
Anunçiação, Francisca de, 156
Anunçiação, Ignaçia de, 30, 70–71, 74, 84
Anunçiação, Joaquina de, 156
Anunçiação, Maria de, 154
Anunçiação, Paula de, 155
Aprezentação, Izabel de, 87, 128, 138
Arquivo da Cúria Patriarcal de Goa, 2
Assumpção, Anna de, 152
Assumpção, Francisca de, 100, 161
Assumpção, Luiza de, 91
Assumpção, Maria de, 92, 140
Assumpção, Marianna de, 151
Assumpção, Pachoa de, 101
Assumpção, Roza de, 94, 141
Assumpção, Rozalia de, 164
Assumpção, Thereza de, 159
Assumpção, Urçalla de, 163
Augustine, Saint, 66, 146n28
Ave Maria, Joanna de, 154
azucena flower, 63–64, 145

Baptista, Joanna de, 98, 161
Bethencourt, Francisco, 4n11, 6
black-veiled nuns, 5, 12, 40, 158n51
blazones (accolades), 135n12

bonifrates (puppets), 12. See also *Entrada de Bonifrates para Festa dos Reis*
Book of Elections, 14n38, 50n101
Book of Professions, 11n37, 14n38, 29n75, 95n65, 159n53
Borges, Charles J., 61n17
Boxer, Charles, 21–22

cafre (African slave), 13–14, 22, 33, 57n2
canarim (Goan native), 13–14, 21–22, 57n2
caninha (astrologer), 29
"Cantiga of the [Augustinian] Fathers," 45, 130n6, 146–48
"Cantiga of the Mother Subprioress," 171–72
"Cantiga to Mother Barbora," 150, 175–76
"Cantiga to Mother Ignaçia," 48, 172–73
"Cantiga to Mother Prioressa," 176–78
Cartepaço da Muzica, 2–3, 15n39, 39–49, 50, 127–78, 184–89
Carvalho, Leonor Maria de, 20
Castel-Branco, M. Carmen d'Assa, 42
cattail, 152
Çeos, Aurea de, 101
Cervantes, Miguel de, 23, 25n69
Céu, Maria do, 43n95
chacotas (satirical songs), 59n9
Christo, Maria de, 100
"Community Hymns," 14n38
Conçeição, Maria da, 166
Conçeição, Michaella da, 31, 32, 72, 75, 85

confiçoens (confessions), 141n19
Consolação, Maria de, 97
Convento de Nossa Senhora da Graça (Goa), 2, 8
Convento de Santa Mónica (Goa). *See* Real Convento de Santa Mónica
Convento de Santo Agostinho (Goa), xiv, 2, 5
Coração de Jesus, Lauriana do, 166
Coração de Jesus, Maria do, 157
Coração de Jesus, Rita do, 157
Coração de Jesus, Violante, 143
Cotarelo y Mori, Emilio, 23n64, 25n69
Coutinho, Lourença, 20
cremation ritual, 26, 33, 79n48
Cruz, Duarte Ivo, 18
crypto-Jews, 20, 119n98

da Silva, António José, 19n53, 20, 66n27, 119n98
da Sylva, Matia Periera, 128n4
Dance of the Kite, 80–81
de la Torre, Julio, 25n69
Dourado de Oliveria, Domingos, 7

Encarnação, Antonia de, 30, 44, 84
Encarnação, Ignaçia de, 142–43, 172–73
Entrada de Bonifrates para Festa dos Reis (shadow-puppet show), 11–39, 179–83; composition of, 14–15; Indian traditions of, 16–18, 21, 26, 33, 79n48; manuscript of, 49–50; performance of, 1, 11–14
entremés (comic interlude), 23–26
"Espeito" (Stake), 20–21, 119
Espírito Santo, Jozefa de, 163
Espírito Santo, Paula de, 30.32, 71, 84
Estado da India, xvi, 3n7, 4, 7

Feast of Fools, 34n80
Felipe II of Portugal, 4, 5
Ferreira, Philippa, 4–5, 24–25, 134n11
Figueroa y Córdoba, Diego de, 25n69
fireballs, 14, 16–17, 28, 32, 76, 125
Fire-Bird, 16, 29, 68–69
fireworks, 43, 130
flaming sword, 39, 125
fólia (dance), 42–43, 151, 156

Gama, João de Saldanha da, 9
Gerarguias, Maria dos, 35, 90
Gloria, Arcangela de, 90, 153
Gonçalves, Margareth de Almeida, 6n18
Góngora, Luis de, 42
Gouva, Antonio de, 5n13

Hindu cremation ritual, 26, 33, 79n48
honeysuckle, 141
Hospital Real de Todos os Santos (All Saints' Royal Hospital), 20
"Hymn for the Mother Subprioress," 45, 134–35, 137–38
"Hymn for the Mothers who hold Offices," 45, 138–44
"Hymn of Cupid," 3, 47, 169–71
"Hymn of Love," 3, 47, 168–69
"Hymn to the Beloved," 38, 120–21

Inquisition, 20–21, 119
interludes (*entremeses*), 23–26

Jacobeia (Coimbra reformists), 8
jasmine flower, 96n68, 141
jatropha flower, 154n44
Jeffries, Lynn, 36n81
Jerarchia, Maria de, 157
jesters, 21
Jesus, Anna de, 27, 62–63, 83, 151
Jesus, Caetana de, 97

Jesus, Clara de, 35, 86, 150
Jesus, Magdalena de, 96
Jesus, Maria de, 144
Jesus, Mariana de, 37, 46–47, 90
Jesus, Senhorinha de, 36, 87, 139
Jesus, Thereza de, 155
Jesus de Nazareth, Maria de, 98
Jesus Maria, Anna de, 14n38
Jesus Maria, Barbora de, 48, 145, 150, 175–76
Jesus Maria, Caetana de, 93, 144–45
Jesus Maria, Feliçoa de, 162
Jesus Maria, Filiçia de, 101
Jesus Maria, Holaya de, 86
Jesus Maria, Izabel de, 163
Jesus Maria, Joanna de, 96
Jesus Maria, Mónica de, 100, 162
Jesus Nazareth, Lauriana de, 160
Jewish converts, 20, 119n98
João V of Portugal, 8, 10, 19
John the Baptist, Saint, 2, 98n69, 127–32, 135–36; feast day celebrations of, 155n46; parents of, 135n13

lily flower, 40, 155n47
Louzade de Sá, Gaspar de, 4n13
love song (*marquita*), 24
Luanda (Angola), 22

Macau, 3
Madre de Deos, Anna de, 91
Madre de Deos, Izabel de, 28
Madre de Deos, Margarida de, 164
Madre de Deos, Roza de, 167
Madre de Deus, Anna de, 158
Madre de Deus, Antonia de, 86
Madre de Deus, Elena de, 157
Madre de Deus, Izabel de, 64, 68, 83, 154
Madre de Deus, Joaquina de, 49, 159
Madre de Deus, Luiza de, 90

Madre de Deus, Mariana de, 162
Madre de Deus, Rozalia de, 99
Malavar, 13–14, 21
maraquita (love song), 24
Maria II of Portugal, 2
Maria Anna of Austria, 19
Maria Anne of Portugal, 109n87
marigold, 39
Mascarenhas, Pedro de (Count of Sandomil), 10
Meneses, Aleixo de, 3–6
Mexico City convents, 3
Mombasa (Kenya), 22
Monasterio de Santa Clara (Manila), 3
Monkeys' Song, 38, 122–23
Montero, Hélder Julio Ferreira, 19n52
Moreira, Tomé Gomes, 9
Mosteiro de Santa Clara (Macau), 3
Mother Treasurers, 45, 145

Nascimento, Joanna do, 49, 158
Nazareth, Anna de, 143
Nazareth, Maria de, 160
New Christians, 20

"Old Woman's Song," 38, 123–24
Oliveria, Domingos Dourado de, 7
opera, 19–21
Osóreio de Castro, Alberto, 2n4

palm groves, 106n81
Paraizo, Roza de, 97, 160
Pedro II of Portugal, 7–8
Perkins, Juliet, 19n53, 20n56
Pescatello, Ann M., 22n62
Philippines, 3
Piedade, Maria de, 99, 161
puppet shows, 12–19
Purificação, Ignes de, 98, 160
Purificação, Senhorinha de, 99, 161

Querobim, Juliana de, 96

202 Index

Querubins, Luiza dos, 89

Rāmāyana, 17, 21
Real Convento de Santa Mónica (Goa), 3–11; founding of, 3–5; map of, xiv; miracle at, 6–7; rebellion of, 8–11, 29, 149n39
Recolhimento de Nossa Senhora de Serra, 4
Recolhimento de Santa Maria Madalena, 4
Ressureição, Maria de, 85
Ressureyção, Anna de, 93
Ressurreição, Eufrazia de, 91
Ressurrieção, Pascoella de, 152
Resurreiçnão, Pascoa da, 142
rose, 40, 128n4, 168
Ruedas de las Serna, Jorge, 42

Sá, Gaspar de Louzade de, 4n13
Sá, Maria de, 5
Sacramento, Anna do, 153
Sacramento, Antonia do, 31
Sacramento, Brites do, 10–11, 27–29, 63–64, 67, 83
Sacramento, Catharina do, 2n4, 10–11, 13, 62, 82
Sacramento, Escolastica do, 153
Sacramento, Francisca de, 137
Sacramento, Francisca do, 34, 44–45, 91, 101n1, 133, 176; songbook of, 2, 127–78
Sacramento, Izabel do, 99, 161
Sacramento, Roza do, 159
Sacramento, Teresa do, 87
Saldanha da Gama, João de, 9
Salvador, Anna de, 166
Salvador, Joanna de, 166
Salvador, Maria de, 164
Salvador, Maria do, 101
Sandomil, Count of (Pedro de Macarenhas), 10

Sanskrit drama, 17, 21, 22
Santa Alexandre, Luiza de, 156
Santa Ana, Joaquina de, 157
Santa Anna, Brites de, 36, 92
Santa Anna, Diogo de, 6–7, 43n96
Santa Anna, Elena de, 154
Santa Anna, Feliçia de, 164
Santa Anna, Maria de, 164
Santa Anna, Roza de, 152
Santa Maria, Agostinho de, 7
Santa Maria, Anna de, 101
Santa Maria, Britis de, 143–44
Santa Maria, Emerençiana de, 27, 29, 63, 67, 83
Santa Maria, Eugenia de, 155
Santa Maria, Roza de, 159
Santa Quiteria, Ritta de, 163
Santa Rita, Rozalia de, 101, 165
Santa Rosa, Antonia de, 153
Santa Rosa, Joanna de, 44, 48, 92, 128, 134–35
Santa Rosa, Maria de, 158
Santa Roza, Antonia de, 31, 85
Santa Teresa, Ignácio de, 2, 8–9, 11, 29, 149n39
Santa Teresa, Joanna de, 151
Santa Thereza, Juana de, 11
Santa Thereza, Maria de, 167
Santo Agostinho, Antonia de, 86
Santo Agostinho, Bernarda de, 153
Santo Agostinho, Francisca de, 165
Santo Agostinho, Jozepha de, 94, 140–41
Santo Agostinho, Magdalena de, 9, 11
Santo Christo, Izabel de, 97
Santo Christo, Mariana de, 156
São Guilherme, Jozé de, 101n1
São Guillierme, Maria de, 94
São Joachim, Anna de, 95, 141
São Joachim, Bibiana de, 95
São Joachim, Maria de, 35, 94
São João, Luiza de, 155

São Joaquim, Maria de, 140
São José, Francisca de, 35, 88, 151
São Joseph, Maria de, 152
São Jozeph, Margarida de, 93
São Miguel, Bibiana de, 48, 95, 145, 174–75
São Miguel, Jozefa de, 162
São Miguel, Jozepha de, 100
São Miguel, Maria de, 154
Seltmann, Friedrich, 17n46, 18
Serafim, Luiza de, 96
shadow puppetry, 12–19, 21, 22
slavery, 13–14, 22, 33, 57n2
"Song for the Mother Scribe," 45, 144–45
"Song for the Saint," 135–36
"Song of the Community," 46–47, 150–68
"Song to Cupid," 3, 46, 148–49
"Song to go to the garden," 43–44, 127–30
"Song to Mother Bibianna," 174–75
"Song to Mother Francisca," 133
"Song to the Mother Prioress," 136–37
"Song to the Nurse," 47, 167
"Songs to Saint John," 44, 131–32
Spies, Otto, 17
sulena flower, 40
sunflower, 130
surangam flower, 30, 31, 70
sūtradhāra (stage-manager), 21

Transfiguração, Anna de, 88
Trent, Council of, 1, 179n1
Trindade, Anna de, 89
Trindade, Britis de, 88, 129, 139
Trindade, Lionarda da, 35, 89
Trindade, Maria da, 88
Trindade, Maria de, 158
Trindade, Philippa de, 4–5, 24–25, 134n11

Trindade, Vitoria de, 165
"Two Monkeys' Song," 38, 122–23

Virgem Maria, Anna da, 30, 32, 71–72, 84
Virgem Maria, Izabel da, 89

Wachtel, Nathan, 20n57
Weaver, Elissa B., 15n40
Weerasinghe, Anna, 37, 104n78
white-veiled nuns, 5, 12, 40

Zignoni, Giuseppe, 19n53

The Other Voice in Early Modern Europe:
The Toronto Series

Series Titles

MADRE MARÍA ROSA
Journey of Five Capuchin Nuns
Edited and translated by Sarah E. Owens
Volume 1, 2009

GIOVAN BATTISTA ANDREINI
Love in the Mirror: *A Bilingual Edition*
Edited and translated by Jon R. Snyder
Volume 2, 2009

RAYMOND DE SABANAC AND SIMONE ZANACCHI
Two Women of the Great Schism: The Revelations *of Constance de Rabastens by Raymond de Sabanac and* Life of the Blessed Ursulina of Parma *by Simone Zanacchi*
Edited and translated by Renate Blumenfeld-Kosinski and Bruce L. Venarde
Volume 3, 2010

OLIVA SABUCO DE NANTES BARRERA
The True Medicine
Edited and translated by Gianna Pomata
Volume 4, 2010

LOUISE-GENEVIÈVE GILLOT DE SAINCTONGE
Dramatizing Dido, Circe, and Griselda
Edited and translated by Janet Levarie Smarr
Volume 5, 2010

PERNETTE DU GUILLET
Complete Poems: A Bilingual Edition
Edited with introduction and notes by Karen Simroth James
Poems translated by Marta Rijn Finch
Volume 6, 2010

ANTONIA PULCI
Saints' Lives and Bible Stories for the Stage: A Bilingual Edition
Edited by Elissa B. Weaver
Translated by James Wyatt Cook
Volume 7, 2010

VALERIA MIANI
Celinda, A Tragedy: *A Bilingual Edition*
Edited with an introduction by Valeria Finucci
Translated by Julia Kisacky
Annotated by Valeria Finucci and Julia Kisacky
Volume 8, 2010

Enchanted Eloquence: Fairy Tales by Seventeenth-Century French Women Writers
Edited and translated by Lewis C. Seifert and Domna C. Stanton
Volume 9, 2010

GOTTFRIED WILHELM LEIBNIZ, SOPHIE, ELECTRESS OF HANOVER AND QUEEN SOPHIE CHARLOTTE OF PRUSSIA
Leibniz and the Two Sophies: The Philosophical Correspondence
Edited and translated by Lloyd Strickland
Volume 10, 2011

In Dialogue with the Other Voice in Sixteenth-Century Italy: Literary and Social Contexts for Women's Writing
Edited by Julie D. Campbell and Maria Galli Stampino
Volume 11, 2011

SISTER GIUSTINA NICCOLINI
The Chronicle of Le Murate
Edited and translated by Saundra Weddle
Volume 12, 2011

LIUBOV KRICHEVSKAYA
No Good without Reward: Selected Writings: A Bilingual Edition
Edited and translated by Brian James Baer
Volume 13, 2011

ELIZABETH COOKE HOBY RUSSELL
The Writings of an English Sappho
Edited by Patricia Phillippy
With translations from Greek and Latin by Jaime Goodrich
Volume 14, 2011

LUCREZIA MARINELLA
Exhortations to Women and to Others If They Please
Edited and translated by Laura Benedetti
Volume 15, 2012

MARGHERITA DATINI
Letters to Francesco Datini
Translated by Carolyn James and Antonio Pagliaro
Volume 16, 2012

DELARIVIER MANLEY AND MARY PIX
English Women Staging Islam, 1696–1707
Edited and introduced by Bernadette Andrea
Volume 17, 2012

CECILIA DEL NACIMIENTO
Journeys of a Mystic Soul in Poetry and Prose
Introduction and prose translations by Kevin Donnelly
Poetry translations by Sandra Sider
Volume 18, 2012

LADY MARGARET DOUGLAS AND OTHERS
The Devonshire Manuscript: A Women's Book of Courtly Poetry
Edited and introduced by Elizabeth Heale
Volume 19, 2012

ARCANGELA TARABOTTI
Letters Familiar and Formal
Edited and translated by Meredith K. Ray and Lynn Lara Westwater
Volume 20, 2012

PERE TORRELLAS AND JUAN DE FLORES
Three Spanish Querelle *Texts:* Grisel and Mirabella, The Slander against Women, *and* The Defense of Ladies against Slanderers*: A Bilingual Edition and Study*
Edited and translated by Emily C. Francomano
Volume 21, 2013

BARBARA TORELLI BENEDETTI
Partenia, a Pastoral Play: *A Bilingual Edition*
Edited and translated by Lisa Sampson and Barbara Burgess-Van Aken
Volume 22, 2013

FRANÇOIS ROUSSET, JEAN LIEBAULT, JACQUES GUILLEMEAU, JACQUES DUVAL AND LOUIS DE SERRES
Pregnancy and Birth in Early Modern France: Treatises by Caring Physicians and Surgeons (1581–1625)
Edited and translated by Valerie Worth-Stylianou
Volume 23, 2013

MARY ASTELL
The Christian Religion, as Professed by a Daughter of the Church of England
Edited by Jacqueline Broad
Volume 24, 2013

SOPHIA OF HANOVER
Memoirs (1630–1680)
Edited and translated by Sean Ward
Volume 25, 2013

KATHERINE AUSTEN
Book M: *A London Widow's Life Writings*
Edited by Pamela S. Hammons
Volume 26, 2013

ANNE KILLIGREW
"My Rare Wit Killing Sin": Poems of a Restoration Courtier
Edited by Margaret J. M. Ezell
Volume 27, 2013

TULLIA D'ARAGONA AND OTHERS
The Poems and Letters of Tullia d'Aragona and Others: A Bilingual Edition
Edited and translated by Julia L. Hairston
Volume 28, 2014

LUISA DE CARVAJAL Y MENDOZA
The Life and Writings of Luisa de Carvajal y Mendoza
Edited and translated by Anne J. Cruz
Volume 29, 2014

Russian Women Poets of the Eighteenth and Early Nineteenth Centuries: A Bilingual Edition
Edited and translated by Amanda Ewington
Volume 30, 2014

JACQUES DU BOSC
L'Honnête Femme: *The Respectable Woman in Society and the* New Collection of Letters and Responses by Contemporary Women
Edited and translated by Sharon Diane Nell and Aurora Wolfgang
Volume 31, 2014

LADY HESTER PULTER
Poems, Emblems, *and* The Unfortunate Florinda
Edited by Alice Eardley
Volume 32, 2014

JEANNE FLORE
Tales and Trials of Love, Concerning Venus's Punishment of Those Who Scorn True Love and Denounce Cupid's Sovereignity: *A Bilingual Edition and Study*
Edited and translated by Kelly Digby Peebles
Poems translated by Marta Rijn Finch
Volume 33, 2014

VERONICA GAMBARA
Complete Poems: A Bilingual Edition
Critical introduction by Molly M. Martin
Edited and translated by Molly M. Martin and Paola Ugolini
Volume 34, 2014

CATHERINE DE MÉDICIS AND OTHERS
Portraits of the Queen Mother: Polemics, Panegyrics, Letters
Translation and study by Leah L. Chang and Katherine Kong
Volume 35, 2014

Françoise Pascal, Marie-Catherine Desjardins, Antoinette Deshoulières, and Catherine Durand
Challenges to Traditional Authority: Plays by French Women Authors, 1650–1700
Edited and translated by Perry Gethner
Volume 36, 2015

Franciszka Urszula Radziwiłłowa
Selected Drama and Verse
Edited by Patrick John Corness and Barbara Judkowiak
Translated by Patrick John Corness
Translation Editor Aldona Zwierzyńska-Coldicott
Introduction by Barbara Judkowiak
Volume 37, 2015

Diodata Malvasia
Writings on the Sisters of San Luca and Their Miraculous Madonna
Edited and translated by Danielle Callegari and Shannon McHugh
Volume 38, 2015

Margaret Van Noort
Spiritual Writings of Sister Margaret of the Mother of God (1635–1643)
Edited by Cordula van Wyhe
Translated by Susan M. Smith
Volume 39, 2015

Giovan Francesco Straparola
The Pleasant Nights
Edited and translated by Suzanne Magnanini
Volume 40, 2015

Angélique de Saint-Jean Arnauld d'Andilly
Writings of Resistance
Edited and translated by John J. Conley, S.J.
Volume 41, 2015

Francesco Barbaro
The Wealth of Wives: A Fifteenth-Century Marriage Manual
Edited and translated by Margaret L. King
Volume 42, 2015

Jeanne d'Albret
Letters from the Queen of Navarre with an Ample Declaration
Edited and translated by Kathleen M. Llewellyn, Emily E. Thompson, and Colette H. Winn
Volume 43, 2016

Bathsua Makin and Mary More with a reply to More by Robert Whitehall
Educating English Daughters: Late Seventeenth-Century Debates
Edited by Frances Teague and Margaret J. M. Ezell
Associate Editor Jessica Walker
Volume 44, 2016

Anna Stanisławska
Orphan Girl: A Transaction, or an Account of the Entire Life of an Orphan Girl by way of Plaintful Threnodies in the Year 1685: *The Aesop Episode*
Verse translation, introduction, and commentary by Barry Keane
Volume 45, 2016

Alessandra Macinghi Strozzi
Letters to Her Sons, 1447–1470
Edited and translated by Judith Bryce
Volume 46, 2016

MOTHER JUANA DE LA CRUZ
Mother Juana de la Cruz, 1481–1534: Visionary Sermons
Edited by Jessica A. Boon and Ronald E. Surtz
Introductory material and notes by Jessica A. Boon
Translated by Ronald E. Surtz and Nora Weinerth
Volume 47, 2016

CLAUDINE-ALEXANDRINE GUÉRIN DE TENCIN
Memoirs of the Count of Comminge and The Misfortunes of Love
Edited and translated by Jonathan Walsh
Foreword by Michel Delon
Volume 48, 2016

FELICIANA ENRÍQUEZ DE GUZMÁN, ANA CARO MALLÉN, AND SOR MARCELA DE SAN FÉLIX
Women Playwrights of Early Modern Spain
Edited by Nieves Romero-Díaz and Lisa Vollendorf
Translated and annotated by Harley Erdman
Volume 49, 2016

ANNA TRAPNEL
Anna Trapnel's Report and Plea; or, A Narrative of Her Journey from London into Cornwall
Edited by Hilary Hinds
Volume 50, 2016

MARÍA VELA Y CUETO
Autobiography and Letters of a Spanish Nun
Edited by Susan Diane Laningham
Translated by Jane Tar
Volume 51, 2016

CHRISTINE DE PIZAN
The Book of the Mutability of Fortune
Edited and translated by Geri L. Smith
Volume 52, 2017

MARGUERITE D'AUGE, RENÉE BURLAMACCHI, AND JEANNE DU LAURENS
Sin and Salvation in Early Modern France: Three Women's Stories
Edited, and with an introduction by Colette H. Winn
Translated by Nicholas Van Handel and Colette H. Winn
Volume 53, 2017

ISABELLA D'ESTE
Selected Letters
Edited and translated by Deanna Shemek
Volume 54, 2017

IPPOLITA MARIA SFORZA
Duchess and Hostage in Renaissance Naples: Letters and Orations
Edited and translated by Diana Robin and Lynn Lara Westwater
Volume 55, 2017

LOUISE BOURGEOIS
Midwife to the Queen of France: Diverse Observations
Translated by Stephanie O'Hara
Edited by Alison Klairmont Lingo
Volume 56, 2017

CHRISTINE DE PIZAN
Othea's Letter to Hector
Edited and translated by Renate Blumenfeld-Kosinski and Earl Jeffrey Richards
Volume 57, 2017

Marie-Geneviève-Charlotte Thiroux d'Arconville
Selected Philosophical, Scientific, and Autobiographical Writings
Edited and translated by Julie Candler Hayes
Volume 58, 2018

Lady Mary Wroth
Pamphilia to Amphilanthus *in Manuscript and Print*
Edited by Ilona Bell
Texts by Steven W. May and Ilona Bell
Volume 59, 2017

Witness, Warning, and Prophecy: Quaker Women's Writing, 1655–1700
Edited by Teresa Feroli and Margaret Olofson Thickstun
Volume 60, 2018

Symphorien Champier
The Ship of Virtuous Ladies
Edited and translated by Todd W. Reeser
Volume 61, 2018

Isabella Andreini
Mirtilla, A Pastoral: *A Bilingual Edition*
Edited by Valeria Finucci
Translated by Julia Kisacky
Volume 62, 2018

Margherita Costa
The Buffoons, A Ridiculous Comedy: *A Bilingual Edition*
Edited and translated by Sara E. Díaz and Jessica Goethals
Volume 63, 2018

Margaret Cavendish, Duchess of Newcastle
Poems and Fancies *with* The Animal Parliament
Edited by Brandie R. Siegfried
Volume 64, 2018

Margaret Fell
Women's Speaking Justified *and Other Pamphlets*
Edited by Jane Donawerth and Rebecca M. Lush
Volume 65, 2018

Mary Wroth, Jane Cavendish, and Elizabeth Brackley
Women's Household Drama:
Loves Victorie, A Pastorall, *and* The concealed Fansyes
Edited by Marta Straznicky and Sara Mueller
Volume 66, 2018

Eleonora Fonseca Pimentel
From Arcadia to Revolution: The Neapolitan Monitor *and Other Writings*
Edited and translated by Verina R. Jones
Volume 67, 2019

Charlotte Arbaleste Duplessis-Mornay, Anne de Chaufepié, and Anne Marguerite Petit Du Noyer
The Huguenot Experience of Persecution and Exile: Three Women's Stories
Edited by Colette H. Winn
Translated by Lauren King and Colette H. Winn
Volume 68, 2019

Anne Bradstreet
Poems and Meditations
Edited by Margaret Olofson Thickstun
Volume 69, 2019

Arcangela Tarabotti
Antisatire: *In Defense of Women, against Francesco Buoninsegni*
Edited and translated by Elissa B. Weaver
Volume 70, 2020

MARY FRANKLIN AND HANNAH BURTON
She Being Dead Yet Speaketh: The Franklin Family Papers
Edited by Vera J. Camden
Volume 71, 2020

LUCREZIA MARINELLA
Love Enamored and Driven Mad
Edited and translated by Janet E. Gomez and Maria Galli Stampino
Volume 72, 2020

ARCANGELA TARABOTTI
Convent Paradise
Edited and translated by Meredith K. Ray and Lynn Lara Westwater
Volume 73, 2020

GABRIELLE-SUZANNE BARBOT DE VILLENEUVE
Beauty and the Beast: *The Original Story*
Edited and translated by Aurora Wolfgang
Volume 74, 2020

FLAMINIO SCALA
The Fake Husband, A Comedy
Edited and translated by Rosalind Kerr
Volume 75, 2020

ANNE VAUGHAN LOCK
Selected Poetry, Prose, and Translations, with Contextual Materials
Edited by Susan M. Felch
Volume 76, 2021

CAMILLA ERCULIANI
Letters on Natural Philosophy: *The Scientific Correspondence of a Sixteenth-Century Pharmacist, with Related Texts*
Edited by Eleonora Carinci
Translated by Hannah Marcus
Foreword by Paula Findlen
Volume 77, 2021

REGINA SALOMEA PILSZTYNOWA
My Life's Travels and Adventures: *An Eighteenth-Century Oculist in the Ottoman Empire and the European Hinterland*
Edited and translated by Władysław Roczniak
Volume 78, 2021

CHRISTINE DE PIZAN
The God of Love's Letter *and* The Tale of the Rose: *A Bilingual Edition*
Edited and translated by Thelma S. Fenster and Christine Reno
With Jean Gerson, "A Poem on Man and Woman." Translated from the Latin by Thomas O'Donnell
Foreword by Jocelyn Wogan-Browne
Volume 79, 2021

MARIE GIGAULT DE BELLEFONDS, MARQUISE DE VILLARS
Letters from Spain: A Seventeenth-Century French Noblewoman at the Spanish Royal Court
Edited and translated by Nathalie Hester
Volume 80, 2021

ANNA MARIA VAN SCHURMAN
Letters and Poems to and from Her Mentor and Other Members of Her Circle
Edited and translated by Anne R. Larsen and Steve Maiullo
Volume 81, 2021

VITTORIA COLONNA
Poems of Widowhood: A Bilingual Edition of the 1538 Rime
Translation and introduction by Ramie Targoff
Edited by Ramie Targoff and Troy Tower
Volume 82, 2021

VALERIA MIANI
Amorous Hope, A Pastoral Play: A Bilingual Edition
Edited and translated by Alexandra Coller
Volume 83, 2020

MADELEINE DE SCUDÉRY
Lucrece and Brutus: Glory in the Land of Tender
Edited and translated by Sharon Diane Nell
Volume 84, 2021

ANNA STANISŁAWSKA
One Body with Two Souls Entwined: An Epic Tale of Married Love in Seventeenth-Century Poland
Orphan Girl: The Oleśnicki Episode
Verse translation, introduction, and commentary by Barry Keane
Volume 85, 2021

CHRISTINE DE PIZAN
Book of the Body Politic
Edited and translated by Angus J. Kennedy
Volume 86, 2021

ANNE, LADY HALKETT
A True Account of My Life and *Selected Meditations*
Edited by Suzanne Trill
Volume 87, 2022

VITTORIA COLONNA
Selected Letters, 1523–1546: A Bilingual Edition
Edited and annotated by Veronica Copello
Translated by Abigail Brundin
Introduction by Abigail Brundin and Veronica Copello
Volume 88, 2022

MICHELE SAVONAROLA
A Mother's Manual for the Women of Ferrara: A Fifteenth-Century Guide to Pregnancy and Pediatrics
Edited, with introduction and notes, by Gabriella Zuccolin
Translated by Martin Marafioti
Volume 89, 2022

MARIA SALVIATI DE' MEDICI
Selected Letters, 1514–1543
Edited and translated by Natalie R. Tomas
Volume 90, 2022

ISABELLA ANDREINI
Lovers' Debates for the Stage: A Bilingual Edition
Edited and translated by Pamela Allen Brown, Julie D. Campbell, and Eric Nicholson
Volume 91, 2022

MARIE GUYART DE L'INCARNATION, ANNE-MARIE FIQUET DU BOCCAGE, AND HENRIETTE-LUCIE DILLON DE LA TOUR DU PIN
Far from Home in Early Modern France: Three Women's Stories
Edited and with an introduction by Colette H. Winn
Translated by Lauren King, Elizabeth Hagstrom, and Colette H. Winn
Volume 92, 2022

MARIE-CATHERINE LE JUMEL DE BARNEVILLE, BARONNE D'AULNOY
Travels into Spain
Edited and translated by Gabrielle M. Verdier
Volume 93, 2022

PIERRE DE VAUX AND SISTER PERRINE DE BAUME
Two Lives of Saint Colette. *With a Selection of Letters by, to, and about Colette*
Edited and translated by Renate Blumenfeld-Kosinski
Volume 94, 2022

DOROTHY CALTHORPE
News from the Midell Regions *and* Calthorpe's Chapel
Edited by Julie A. Eckerle
Volume 95, 2022

ELIZABETH POOLE
The Prophetess and the Patriarch: The Visions of an Anti-Regicide in Seventeenth-Century England
Edited by Katharine Gillespie
Volume 96, 2024

MARY CARLETON AND OTHERS
The Carleton Bigamy Trial
Edited by Megan Matchinske
Volume 97, 2023

MARIE BAUDOIN
The Art of Childbirth: A Seventeenth-Century Midwife's Epistolary Treatise to Doctor Vallant A Bilingual Edition
Edited and translated by Cathy McClive
Volume 98, 2022

MARGUERITE BUFFET
New Observations on the French Language, *with* Praises of Illustrious Learned Women
Edited and translated by Lynn S. Meskill
Volume 99, 2023

ISABELLA ANDREINI
Letters
Edited and translated by Paola De Santo and Caterina Mongiat Farina
Volume 100, 2023

MARY CAREY
A Mother's Spiritual Dialogue, Meditations, and Elegies
Edited by Pamela S. Hammons
Volume 101, 2023

ISABELLA WHITNEY
Poems by a Sixteenth-Century Gentlewoman, Maid, and Servant
Edited by Shannon Miller
Volume 102, 2024

CAMILLA BATTISTA DA VARANO
The Spiritual Life *and Other Writings*
Edited and translated by William V. Hudon
Volume 103, 2023

E. POLWHELE
The Faithful Virgins
Edited by Ann Hollinshead Hurley
Volume 104, 2023

HENRIETTE-JULIE DE CASTELNAU, COUNTESS DE MURAT
The Sprites of Kernosy Castle
Edited and translated by Perry Gethner and Allison Stedman
Volume 105, 2024

TULLIA D'ARAGONA
The Wretch, Otherwise Known as Guerrino. *A Bilingual Edition*
Translation by John C. McLucas
Edited by Julia L. Hairston
Annotated by Julia L. Hairston and John C. McLucas
Introduction by Julia L. Hairston
Volume 106, 2025

Pompeo Colonna
In Defense of Women. A Bilingual Edition
Introduction and critical edition of Latin text by Franco Minonzio
Translated and with Foreword and Postscript by Margaret L. King
Volume 107, 2024

Christine de Pizan
The Boke of the Cyte of Ladyes: *Brian Anslay's Translation of 1521 in Modernized English*
Edited by Christine Reno and Karen Robertson
Volume 108, 2025

Margaret More Roper
Writings of a Well-Learnd Gentlewoman
Edited by Elizabeth McCutcheon with Jaime Goodrich and William Gentrup
Volume 109, 2024